SELLING SEX

IN THE 21st CENTURY

Empowerment? Escorts In Their Own Words

SELLING SEX
IN THE 21st CENTURY

Empowerment? Escorts In Their Own Words

Written By
James Tugend

Commentary By
Dr. Christine Peterson, Ph.D.

Tugend Media
Los Angeles, CA

Selling Sex in the 21st Century: Empowerment? Escorts In Their Own Words

Original copyright 2003 by James Tugend

First edition copyright 2017 by James Tugend

With contributions by Christine Peterson, Ph.D. and anonymous contributors.

Published by Tugend Media, February, 2017

Tugendmedia.com

ISBN #978-1539104780

First Edition

*"What we think is a gesture of freedom
is a symptom of our cage."*

From "Ghost Birds" by Nicolas Pizzolatto
The Atlantic Monthly, October, 2003

*"My conflict is not shame, it's just
that I've sold myself short. I'm not
giving myself a chance. I've taken the
easy way out."*

Mary, sensual masseuse

*"There have been two major
transitions in heterosexual mating in
the last four million years. The first
was around 10,000 to 15,000 years
ago, in the agricultural revolution,
when we became less migratory and
more settled... The second major
transition is with the rise of the
Internet."*

*Justin Garcia, research scientist at Indiana
University's Kinsey Institute*

TABLE OF CONTENTS

PREFACE

In 2005, I wrote a book about how the Internet had radically changed the sex business and the lives of sex workers. It contained numerous interviews with sex workers, commonly called 'providers', and their clients, called 'hobbyists'. (Definitions of these terms vary.)

My original intention was to reduce prejudice towards sex workers and dispel the myth that they are all helpless victims of abuse, or cold, heartless lowlifes. I did years of research by interviewing them by phone or exchanging emails. I found that their lives and attitudes were far more diverse than I had thought and my intentions changed as I learned more. I didn't publish it at that time, but went back to it in 2016.

In 2017, most sex workers still say that nothing they have read reflects their reality. Mainstream media such as movies, television shows, television news, and documentaries still portray sex workers in old stereotypes, usually with well-developed bodies and attractive but blank-faced women who don't seem to care about anything. Well known feminists, women's charities and politicians have attitudes formed decades ago, which have little relationship to current realities, and routinely put out false information about sex slavery in the first world.

The sex world and the sex businesses have changed even further since I wrote the original book and I've updated accordingly. Most of the interviews and prices are from the early book. The prices for top-ranked independent providers seem to have doubled in many cases. The early book included running commentary by Dr. Christine Peterson, Ph.D. who was Chairperson of the Ph.D. Clinical Psychotherapy program at the Pacifica Graduate Institute at the time, as well as a professor and practicing psychotherapist. In the book she included the major psychological works on prostitution, commented on individual interviews and trends I was finding, and she compared the interactions of sex workers and their clients with that of psychotherapists and their clients. This led to a new theory, which she applied to human nature in general. She has subsequently expanded that theory, without reference to the sex business. Her original material remains in the book, with her approval.

Most previous books about sex workers have been dry academic books, heavy on laws and statistics, melodramatic stories designed to titillate and arouse readers, or designed to promote a narrow agenda.

My style of journalism has been to be as accurate as possible, while willing to insert myself into the story, even if it affects the outcome, along with a dash of, often self-deprecating, humor. It's a form of 'new journalism' but there are no combined characters or fiction, except for the names and locations, which I changed to protect identities.

It's the right time for a realistic and compassionate book on consensual sex for money, one of the few large-demand, high-paying professions in the U.S.A. that can't be shipped overseas.

DR. PETERSON'S PREFACE

Working with James Tugend on this material has opened up a whole other dimension for me to consider in terms of loving, giving, taking, and people using others in relationships. No rose-colored glasses included.

In exploring the experiences of adult female prostitutes, James Tugend seeks to understand and describe these individuals' perceptions of themselves, as well as their relationships to others and the greater whole of life.

This book held me tightly – I eagerly awaited the end of my workday so that I could delve into the world Tugend wrote about. I literally could not put it down. As a psychologist with 25 years of experience dealing with the many different kinds of relationships – from mother and child, friend and friend, lover and lover, to psychotherapist and patient – the relationship between the adult female escorts and their "hobbyists" [Tugend's term] have much in common with the others. Tugend invites these women to elaborate on their formative experiences – the traumas they have lived through and what they have done to survive their own personal hells. The stories told by Tugend's interviewees are filled with sexual, physical, and developmental trauma.

The men who pay for their services give brutally vivid accounts of what their own needs and longings are, and how they too are doing what they feel is needed to survive. The book elicited in me a fascination with the incredible power of relationships – a need that must be attended to in one way or another.

While there is a voluminous body of writing in the field of psychology regarding sexuality, this book focuses on sexuality as a commodity and attempts to address the lived experience of the adult female escort.

For centuries, prostitution has held the fascination of historians, sociologists, economists, political scientists, theologians, and philosophers. This 'oldest profession' has captured the imagination of writers of fiction, moviemakers, and others in popular culture. It has been presented as a crime, as psychopathology, as immorality, and as sexual perversion.

Radical feminists see prostitution as furthering the objectification and subjugation of all women. In this view, it is an act of sexual violence propagated by the dominant class (men) against the oppressed class (women), diminishing the worth and dignity of women throughout the culture.

In contrast, liberal feminist perspectives see all sex work, including prostitution, as a positive avenue for self-determination and increased economic power for women. They believe prostitution is a choice entered into freely. These persons claim prostitution is a much-needed arena for sexual exploration in a culture that restricts sexual expression through oppressive sexual norms, aligning them with other marginalized sexual groups such as fetishists, sado-masochists, transgendered and bisexual individuals.

As so well illustrated in this book, the reality of prostitution is more complex than one would think.

My interest in the general relationship between sexuality and relationships comes largely from my twenty-five years of practicing psychotherapy with persons who are 'looking for love in all the wrong places'; many of them reclaiming wholeness after conquering addictions. These professional experiences have led me to ponder the general relationship between addictions and sexuality.

In regard to prostitution specifically, my work with adult women who have been employed in the sex industry has been particularly intriguing. The complexity of these women's' relationships with their bodies, identities, self-images, sexual encounters, and relationships with others is consistently difficult and fascinating.

As a mother, I have been constantly awed by the power of my relationship with my children. I can experience exquisite joy by their physical touch and I have no doubt that they need my touch and my words to feel held and loved.

As a lover, I am keenly aware of this primitive and powerful merging with another, so that an adult experience can be momentarily transformed into pure infantile nakedness.

All of these relationships can be healing, or damaging. All rely on an element of Eros, an erotic component that cannot be denied. The escort does not attempt to camouflage the erotic, rather she capitalizes on it, she promotes it, and she advertises it.

James Tugend has perceived a level of despair and existential emptiness in many individuals involved in sex work. Abandonment, abuse, and betrayals have often led these persons not just to human loneliness, but also to a profound spiritual vacuum, and at times, deep-seated bitterness.

These feelings, however, are not limited to the escort's customer or to the escort. The need for intimacy in relationships is universal.

INTRODUCTION

Try to set aside your assumptions about the sex business.

It is interesting to see how the formerly marginalized groups Dr. Peterson refers to have been increasingly accepted by mainstream groups since the early draft of this book.

She wasn't stating a personal bias against them. When Chris wrote this Preface, I thought she was over-stating the anger I had uncovered, but now I think she was correct. Like many writers, I shared a skeptical attitude towards the establishment, and perhaps had been unusually accepting of anti-social attitudes. I've seen nothing to alter that viewpoint, except to be more tolerant of those who don't share it. Maybe more resigned.

The Internet first gained prominence from sex and pornography, which accounted for about sixty-five percent of its early public usage.

In the 21st century, the Internet has empowered independent escorts to select clients according to their own tastes. For them it can be like *Sex In The City* with financial benefits. Independent providers took power away from pimps, madams and escort agencies and, in many cases, the clients. This varies according to the provider's strengths and circumstances.

Opinions on prostitution are wildly diverse. There is no consensus on why someone becomes a sex worker, and how it affects their clients and themselves. Dr. Peterson and I agreed that our viewpoints might differ.

Feminists are now divided into three schools instead of two. The 'sex worker' branch believes sex work should be legalized and treated like other professions, but subject to governmental rules and possibly unions.

The 'abolitionists' believe it should be decriminalized but eliminated. They consider it a demeaning sign of male dominance and that prostitutes are helpless victims, controlled and sold by men, 'prostituted', as if they have no agency to make their own decisions.

The 'outlaw' branch of feminism thinks it is admirable. They see sex workers as proud, independent professional women taking charge of their lives and using entrepreneurship and female power to achieve high pay, freedom to choose when and with whom they work, and enhanced self-esteem. The attitudes of these groups towards those who disagree are often summed up in heated four-letter words, and they engage in righteous demonstrations. The Sex Workers Outreach Program (SWOP) exists internationally, and at the local and national levels. Self-described "Hoes" proudly stand up for themselves and each other to overcome discrimination and promote safety. The more I studied this field, the more I realized that each of these views is sometimes correct. All of them claim they favor decriminalization of sex work, except that the abolitionists call for police shutting down sex workers they claim are slaves, when they are not.

Public sexuality flaunted by famous entertainers has become routine. If you took the vocals out of some singing acts you'd have a strip tease. Nowadays it seems hypocritical to praise popular singers' acts and shame exotic dancers. A wider acceptance of sex outside of marriage, economic pressures on young people, a willingness of women to discuss sex acts with pride instead of shame, and easy contact through the Internet have changed young people's attitudes towards sex, and the sex business is much more prominent and profitable for many providers.

In their Internet ads, many providers claim to adore their work. In candid interviews opinions vary widely, and are sometimes contradictory within the same person.

I originally interviewed over sixty escorts and an equal number of exotic dancers. They demanded to know why I was writing the book before they would give interviews. Sometimes, if we really knew why we were writing something, we wouldn't need to write it. I never interviewed a woman who fit the stereotype of the 'whore'. My assumptions were challenged and I was forced to confront my own fascination with this subject.

I haven't covered sex slavery, except glancingly. It is a complex subject, which has been treated simplistically by mainstream media. On the one hand you have girls kidnapped in Africa and Eastern Europe, beaten, raped, and sold as genuine sex slaves. Sometimes they're forced into marriage, despite huge age discrepancies, as playthings to people in power, or to increase the population and earn money for the kidnappers.

On the other hand, a lot of Asian girls deliberately come to the United States to work in massage parlors and support their families back home. Some of them may have been forced, but the number of real slaves appears to be wildly exaggerated. I haven't interviewed any real sex slaves but I've spoken with women who the media might call sex slaves, and the book describes a glaring instance of misrepresentation on public television.

Some providers were manipulated into the business, have low self-esteem, use drugs and become jaded. Providers who would have difficulty sustaining a regular job because of medical conditions are able to make good money, but some pay a price for it.

Other providers find their work empowering, glamorous, lucrative, and say it elevates their self-esteem. They can use it as a foundation to provide for the rest of their lives. Independent escorts can cancel appointments or take considerable time off if they need a break or it interferes with higher priorities. A code of conduct has been established which has made interactions with hobbyists more friendly.

The providers and hobbyists spoke very well for themselves and I am passing on their biases, opinions and gossip. As one escort said, "More people lie about sex than lie about their age." Nevertheless, I often followed up and asked more probing questions, to see if they did what they had planned, and using what other providers had told me.

It's not my place to judge or homogenize their attitudes and behavior. I often found their experiences and opinions remarkable and moving.

CHAPTER I: FIRST CONTACTS WITH PROVIDERS

I tried to get my first interview by phoning **Marissa**, a twenty-one year old Italian who was listed at a website under "Massage."

Her face was blurred on her main page but she had a perfect figure, if you don't mind a woman being buxom. She was sitting on a fluffy bed, wearing only a bikini bottom. Like many providers under thirty-five, her website claimed she was a college student. It said she's "all natural", meaning no boob job. Her ad included a short video in which she applied lotion to herself, especially between her upper thighs. I gave her a ring.

Marissa immediately told me that she did 'rub-downs' but was not a licensed masseuse. She seemed more worried about giving an unlicensed massage than an unlicensed hand job. I said something about my book and I was listening to a dial tone. She'd hung up on me.

Lesson one. Providers put a phone number on the Internet to generate business. They get calls day and night from men who get a thrill out of just talking to them. If I were to pay them for their time they would tell me whatever they thought I wanted to hear, not to mention the cost.

I decided to email each of them first, stating that I was not a potential customer, but was writing a book that could affect the general perception of their work. I could word my intentions carefully. They could read it at a time of their own choosing and either discard it or reply.

I composed a standard query letter, individualized it to reflect their ads, and emailed versions of it to about a thousand providers. I emphasized that I wasn't interested in B.S. I also prepared a list of questions for those who chose to follow up, which I kept in front of me if we spoke on the phone.

The interviews took at least eighteen months. A lot of the time consisted of them interviewing me, just as they screened potential appointments. Once, after many emails back and forth, a woman said, "Okay, I believe you, but I don't have time. "

MY FIRST (PARTIAL) INTERVIEW

The first response came from **Mary**, a gorgeous young blonde who did sensual massage. Her ad clarified that there was no 'FS' (full service) or actual intercourse.

She described herself as a 'girl next door' type, but that was modest. Her face was obscured on her ads but her breasts were bulging out of her top. I have a personal theory that women tend to choose hairstyles that match their physical beauty, and she had the blonde hairdo that would go with a beautiful face. You can make an educated guess about a woman's face from behind, though some feminist women are tired of being stared at by strangers so they play it down. (Wonder if I'll get some shrieks for saying that.) I also believe there's a tendency for men who look like specific movie stars to enhance that similarity with their hairstyles. Mary's clients described her face as gorgeous. She wrote back:

> *Hello there,*
>
> *Thank you for your email. The "underworld" had been a strong source of fascination long before I got involved in it.... I have read many books on the subject and would love to help you out. I got involved in a rather strange way and am in the process of writing a memoir on my experiences... I have a BA in Creative writing and minor in women's studies and am a licensed/certified massage therapist but feel drawn to this industry for a variety of reasons...*
>
> *1. Power and control, 2. Adrenaline rush of going against the rules of society, and of course money...I look forward to helping you with your story and would like to help you via email or in person.*
>
> *Out of curiosity, how did you decide to write a book on this subject and what angle do you plan on approaching a topic that has been discussed since the beginning of time?*

Sincerely yours, Mary

She was intelligent and turned the questions back on me – as many of the providers did. I was particularly intrigued that one of her motivations was to challenge society's rules, which seems to be an essential quality for being a writer with depth. In the 50s I asked Professor Baum at Pomona College if it was necessary for a great writer to be kind of crazy, because so many of them have had problems such as substance abuse, anti-establishment views that got them in trouble, etc. He replied, "No. Only since the industrial revolution, when society went insane. "

I mentioned to Mary that I had been a writing teacher and might help her with her memoir. She kept putting off giving me an interview, but when she finally did we both learned a lot about ourselves.

Dr. Peterson wrote: "Power, control, and adrenaline rush typify what are commonly considered aspects of an arousal addiction. These are non-substance-related addictions that rely on the rush of adrenaline common to many high-risk behaviors (e.g. gambling.) Mary describes this to a tee."

Leslie is a twenty-five year-old slender brunette. Her ads emphasize her education, elegance, and numerous hobbies. She insisted on answering questions in writing. She was the first provider I interviewed and my questions were not as probing as my later ones. At that time I said I was writing a book or movie.

She replied,

> *Dear Jim:*
>
> *Nice to hear from you, and thanks for your interest! While I am not interested in being the subject of a film, I appreciate your consideration and trust that you will find someone who suits you with relative ease (many choices in this town). :)*
>
> *It can be a fascinating, yet at times painfully lonely lifestyle. It allows great freedom and enjoyment, but also requires some sacrifices that make one question one's choices. I truly believe it*

was a choice I could not avoid — those of us who enjoy it, and therefore excel, are really "meant" to provide this service in many ways. It suits me completely, and I only wish this type of employment didn't prevent me from having the other components of a full life that one seeks. Luckily, this is a fleeting thing one usually does for only a few years (akin to being a professional athlete or model), and therefore the "other" lifestyle is also attainable afterwards, with some careful choices and preservation of future plans.

If you have questions about anything, I'd be happy to help you out within the limits of my discretionary requirements. I do not seek pay or recognition, and therefore perhaps I cannot devote the time you seek to this project. But if I can assist in some way, please feel free to let me know.

Best regards,

Leslie Madison

I sent her some questions. Her reply:

Dear Jim:

Hi there again! You asked me to describe one or two wonderful experiences;

I will do so:

The first was a person with whom I spend one week each month here in San Diego, living at one of the region's finest hotels, and attending classes from there. He lives on the East Coast, but does not have to work — so he enjoys playing out here. We travel, dine, and enjoy town together, but I am able to keep my "real" life in check while he is here. We also spend time on the East Coast, when possible, and in Canada doing helicopter skiing (which we both enjoy.) He is a 39 year-old gentleman who has attended the world's finest schools, and is an all-around great guy. Divorced with two small children, he is not seeking a girlfriend who will trap him, as many women after his assets do, but rather an honest and stress-free companion to enjoy life with. This is what I provide.

We fly first class or private jet, and we dine at the best restaurants (although we can be found at a deli now and then — we love the pickles and salads!) We have done some yachting, out to Catalina (we both have sailing licenses), and we have spent time on the California Coast, Northern California, and other countries. We had a yacht on the Med once, for a week, touring the Greek islands; we have also skipped around in the Pacific a bit.

Another experience has been a gentlemen with whom I travel to other cities — I spend a week with him in his hotel suites, and generally am able to live life from there as normal — we meet in the evenings, as he must work all day. He is young, incredibly good-looking, impeccably dressed, very muscular, and a ton of fun. He is married, however, and I often wish that this weren't so...that can be hard. He has a beautiful, albeit distant and unaffectionate, wife, and two beautiful children. I feel lucky that he has chosen me, as he could clearly date anyone he wished. We have been to movies, shopping, dining out, playing sports, barhopping, dancing, and all the things people in their late 20s and early 30s do, and I legitimately LOVE hanging out with him and his best friends. We all go to Vegas on a private jet now and then, and his friends are hilarious! They treat me as they would any other friend, without judgment, and we all get on very well. It's a blast. We have been to Hawaii together, which was another lovely time — played lots of golf, did the day-spa thing, toured around the island, and trotted about in a 4-bedroom hotel suite which was one of the nicest I have seen thus far.

You asked about problems or conflicts that need to be overcome – I'm not too sure what you mean?

How one becomes an escort: I was in deep debt for grad school, single, someone told me about the 'Net'. I looked around and figured I could get all of that handled...so got a photographer, set up some ads, and the rest is history....

How the decision was made: I never questioned it. I enjoy meeting new people, and always screened heavily enough to know exactly with whom I was meeting.

Do I have friends in this business? No.

(I had asked her if she was a victim of the 'beauty trap', that is, do people treat her differently. I had never seen her face.)

The "beauty trap" is not really an accurate description of my experience, as I am not so beautiful that I am not taken seriously in my other endeavors in life. Unlike a model, I appear like an attractive lawyer or other professional... I have no plastic surgery, dying of hair, or other alterations that would make people assume I am of the "entertainment" community. Hope that helps!

Leslie

Her writing seems carefully elegant. She gets a lot of email, which she screens before giving out her phone number. A couple of years after this interview, she appeared to have had a breast enhancement, her photos became more erotic, and she revealed her face.

Dr. Peterson wrote: "The responses she provided speak to the issues of denial and rationalization as defenses against something. Her descriptions of wonderful experiences with two of her hobbyists sound quite glamorous on one hand but are filled with a desperate kind of neediness aimed at convincing herself of her own worth. The breast enhancement hints at her investment in maintaining her own objectification. However she may truly offer the men she sees more intimate contact than they have in any of their other relationships – free of the clinging dependency traps that terrify so many men."

EMAIL FROM DIANE

hi jim, Showing escorting as a wonderful adventure would be false. most of the girls that I know suffer from extreme self-esteem problems, alcohol and drug problems, even some of the most successful ones. it is impossible to maintain a healthy personal life because it is besieged with lies and half-truths and by the very nature of the beast most ladies cannot have the happy lives that our female counterparts enjoy. it would be a huge mistake to only portray one facet of this lifestyle since what you are talking about is the smallest part of this profession. for most the dark and evil side is the norm. I also have a journalism degree and have written two books, i have thought about writing this story myself but the truth is not about the success that i have enjoyed, but more about the sadness and despair that the majority experience. good luck,

hugs,

Diane

Dr. Peterson wrote, "Regarding Diane's comments on 'the happy lives that our female counterparts enjoy' – I questioned this notion as some sort of delusion because how many people – married or not – run around in a state of unending happiness? It seems the escort and the non-escort can share the same delusion – that the grass is always greener on the other side of the fence. Indeed, there may be escorts leading more fulfilled and happy lives than married women, and vice-versa. In other words, the message she so clearly stated is an important wake-up call to those who might want to romanticize the life of an escort. In bold comparison with Leslie, she offers profound reality-testing. But I think it would be good to challenge the notion that the female counterparts enjoy 'the happy lives'. This suggests that women who are not escorts have a perfect life – which is in itself a delusion."

After this, I revised my query letters to try to include more providers who had serious problems with this life.

FIRST PHONE INTERVIEW

My first telephone interview was with **Kelly Flynn**, an escort.

> *I'm interested, but I would need to confirm that you're for real and not some pervert just getting off by hearing stories.*

She wanted to know all about my background. I told her about my parents being successful in show business, and how, when I was six years old they took me to Billy Rose's Diamond Horseshow, a fancy striptease club and restaurant in New York. Billy Rose was the husband of Fanny Bryce, Barbra Streisand's character in *Funny Girl,* and my mother's roommate. Billy Rose was my mother's boss but she did almost all the producing, all before I was born. I can still visualize the topless dancers backstage and it probably set the tone for the rest of my life.

Dr. Peterson wrote, "Regarding your early exposure to strip clubs, six years of age was quite young to absorb and metabolize exposure to such adult sexuality. While parents might see themselves as 'open' or 'free thinkers', they do have to keep in mind what young children are able to understand and the tone they might be setting for the rest of their child's life."

Maybe Dr. Peterson is right, but I don't feel that way, even though I can recall the scene precisely. Maybe I threw her off by saying the backstage view of topless dancers set the tone for the rest of my life, but I meant that as a joke. My parents were nudists anyway. I underwent a lot of trauma at home. My parents sent me to a psychologist as a child. He said my complaints of abuse were accurate and I didn't need psychotherapy.

Kelly was intelligent and into various kinds of self-improvement. She granted the interview because she 'wants people to know how great it is'.

Kelly's main experience of being an escort was that it felt powerful, both the experience itself, and the financial freedom.

Before she was an escort she was insecure, shy, and self-conscious. Being an escort enabled her to completely get over her shyness, becoming very self-assured.

She had worked in a brothel in Australia. She said prostitution is not considered shameful there and people talk about it openly. Then she came to the United States and got married. When she was twenty-nine, she decided to just do it, become a sex worker. She was divorced when I spoke with her. At first she only did sensual massage, but after a few months she thought: why limit herself? She started working as an escort and felt that it brought more freedom than just doing massage. The word 'freedom' came up a lot in the interview.

At first she hooked up with an agency that took half her money. Then she saw one client exclusively for five months for $10,000. She met him through the agency and he took her off the market. He was very busy and didn't take up a lot of her time, but she finally realized that $10,000, though it seemed good at the time, was not great money for five months.

She learned that it was easy to do it all on your own. She took out advertisements and built a first-rate website that reflected her love of horses. Being independent allowed her much more freedom, twice the money per client, and her own choice of clients.

At first she worked all the time, for the money, but then she learned to relax, take her time, and live more of a personal life. She stressed that it's important to take time off when you feel the need to.

She said,

> Using agents is less work because they line up the clients, but you can only hope they'll screen well. They sometimes set the girls up with troublesome clients.

Her mom knew what she did but she couldn't tell her dad yet. All of her friends knew. She found it liberating to tell people the truth. Other people's PERCEPTION was the main problem.

Despite her own good feelings about her work, she believed that perhaps half of the escorts were badly affected by the perception of them and there was a lot of self-loathing. Some people felt that if society thinks they are bad, they must be.

She had three friends who were escorts. One of them had the same feelings as Kelly, but was still afraid to tell people what she did. The other two hated the work and hated men because of it.

She said,

> *No matter how independent you think you are, you're still affected by the attitudes of the world.*

I asked her about the negatives she had experienced.

Anonymity is difficult and there are some people, hobbyists and others, who knew her real identity. There was lots of gossip surrounding her and her work. But overall, there were no problems.

I asked if she was afraid of running into clients in an inappropriate situation. She had no fear of that because she lives outside of town in a remote community.

She said,

> *Sometimes pathetic losers have to pay for it. Some guys end up being almost like stalkers. They won't leave you alone and want extra time without paying for it. Some demand more and more affection and ask me to tell them that I love them. One client keeps wanting to see me without paying. I told him not to call, but he calls anyway, using another name.*

She quit escorting for six months and he kept calling.

Kelly stopped seeing clients if they obsessed over her. She didn't get as many two-hour minimum appointments as some providers. She said she "gets to see good hobbyists" and particularly liked to see her regulars. Sometimes she met clients in Las Vegas or Mexico. (Some providers put their names on an out-of-town website, or join a chat session for another town. When they travel to that town, they have already scheduled a series of customers.)

She loved having sex with a large number of men, so she lowered her price. It's not hard to understand why Kelly was very popular with the hobbyists.

Kelly said,

> *The Christmas holidays are sometimes a bit lonely in this business because it's family time and that's something we generally don't have.*

That's the end of Kelly's first interview. I wonder if her strong personality and self-confidence had something to do with men obsessing over her. Maybe it was the kind of men she chose to see. Whatever it was, it wasn't a major problem for her.

I had a surprising discussion with Kelly a few months later. I read on a chat room that she was retiring, so I called on her last day of work to wish her well.

She said she wanted a normal life, a boyfriend, and her parents to be able to talk about what she did. Having a regular man in her life was her chief motivation for retiring. She wanted to get into shape, because she planned on becoming a swimsuit model. She was thirty-one and had worked as an escort for two years.

Recently I noticed her advertising again so I wrote her. She replied,

> *Well since I last spoke with you, I took a break, then went back for 8 months and now I am currently going to school taking engineering. I've bought two houses and am very content. I'm not giving up working, just not while I am in school.*
>
> *Hope your book turns out the way you intend it to be!*
>
> *Kelly*

Dr. Peterson wrote: "Kelly's claims that she was shy and is now self-assured, and she credits this change to her work as an escort, yet along with the feelings of power, independence and freedom she describes she has been ripped off by agencies, has had to camouflage her work from her father, deal with clients who become obsessed and stalked her, probably desperately seeking a stable relationship, and she spends Christmas holidays alone.

"Regarding your comment that, 'Being an escort enabled her to completely get over her shyness' – she may have developed a harder and more self-assured exterior to defend against the vulnerability she likely still feels.

"She loves having sex with a large number of men, so she lowered her price. This rings false and makes me wonder what is going on under the false bravado."

Yuki, a Japanese woman, never signed up for a paid website. She listed herself in a free Yahoo group where singles meet, posted a photograph of her body, and listed her profession as "Escort." (A mainstream website such as Yahoo would probably not allow that today.)

She immediately received more offers than she could handle. She was in her mid-thirties and had previously done some X-rated modeling without revealing her face.

When I first spoke with her, Yuki had only been working as an escort for a month. She went into it because she couldn't pay her bills. She was filled with trepidation before she saw her first customer. He was very sweet and she was surprised to find that she had no problem with the sex. She limited herself to two clients per day and didn't understand how some women could see several more.

She was raised in a very conservative family in Japan, and told me she never would have imagined that she would be doing this. When she came to America she was not promiscuous, but over the years she became more so, and was particularly attracted to black men.

When she began escorting, she immediately started paying off her debts and found the life very easy. With refreshing honesty she said, "My body is my most marketable asset." When I asked about her feelings, she blurted out that being an escort was "sweet revenge."

I asked, "Revenge against who?"

She couldn't or wouldn't tell me, and claimed she didn't know what she meant when she said that. She only worked a few months before a gentleman "took care of her" exclusively.

Dr. Peterson wrote: "The statement that she wasn't promiscuous but became more so is a provocative comment. Perhaps it led her into the escort business. I am curious about the cultural aspect Yuki brings into the interview. That she was raised in a 'very conservative family' might have many meanings, but to consider what degree of shame and self-loathing she might have to contend with would be important.

"I also would be curious about her attraction to black men – is that an added 'insult' against her family of origin? What does it mean? She didn't change from "not promiscuous" to promiscuous overnight. What really happened to her?

We'll never know. I couldn't get her to tell me more and she's not on the Internet anymore. I also wonder about the "sweet revenge." Was it revenge against her mother's strictness? Against men? The whole world?

Native Japanese traditionally were more open about sexuality than Americans, as their religious tradition does not consider sex a sin. Without giving an opinion, some have said that the Bible doesn't say very much about sex because Jews and early Christians apparently thought it was natural, and Jesus defended a prostitute, but I'm straying far from my expertise. Japanese also don't have the American tradition of fear and loathing towards homosexuality, but native Japanese have told me there is a history of racial prejudice.

CHAPTER II: THE INTERNET REVOLUTIONS

I'm going to use the word 'he' for hobbyists and 'she' for providers for convenience. The Internet revolutionized the sex business in overlapping stages. Sex workers used to be limited to a few means of obtaining customers. There were brothels, pulp magazine give-a-ways with photos and phone numbers, streetwalkers, bar girls, and call girls, the latter usually working through a pimp or madam. These categories still exist, but the Internet has created a massive exposure for sex providers and their customers. Now there is the CAM girl, sitting on a bed in Russia, with a computer and camera sending live video to viewers who type instructions. Celebrities have nationwide clubs where, for an online fee, they tell their fans daily what they're doing or thinking, sell calendars of themselves, or attend large parties where they simply greet their paying fans. Dominants advertise that they treat clients like worms and demand money without even meeting, and many pages full of pictures of women offering sex services such as dances, massages, and sexual or social specialties

"We are in uncharted territory [when it comes to Tinder et al,]" wrote Justin Garcia, a research scientist at Indiana University's Kinsey Institute for Research in Sex, Gender, and Reproduction. He wasn't talking about prostitution, but the scope of the change seems equally large in the sex businesses.

He wrote, "There have been two major transitions in heterosexual mating in the last four million years. The first was around 10,000 to 15,000 years ago, in the agricultural revolution, when we became less migratory and more settled, leading to the establishment of marriage as a cultural contract. The second major transition is with the rise of the Internet." The Internet was said to be a major factor in a majority of divorces, because of websites with sections called 'personals' that facilitate meeting potential mates.

Some anthropologists believe that prostitution was also behind the formation of villages, and thus, civilization itself.

WEBSITES SERVICING THE SEX BUSINESS:
ESCORT MALLS

These online sites display ads for numerous providers classified under different categories of service, such as: 'Escort', 'Massage' (Therapeutic, Sensual, or Tantric)', 'Blonde', 'Asian', 'Brunette', 'S&M' (sado-masochistic), 'Dominatrix', 'Submissive', 'In-call', 'Out-call', 'Couples', 'TS' (transsexual) and sometimes 'Gay'. 'In-call' means the provider has the place for the rendezvous. 'Out-call' means the provider goes out to meet the client.

Providers can offer only one or the other, or a choice, at different prices. If the provider works out of a pad with several other girls, she might not offer out-call, or charge more for it. You can't tell from their photographs which are trans sexual, but they indicate 'TS'. There are categories for 'Elite' escorts, meaning very expensive and often require a lengthier engagement, and there are some inexpensive escort sites. The same provider can appear under several categories, such as, 'Massage', 'Escort.' 'FS' means full service, full sex.

Each listing has a photo of the provider and name. Selecting a listing leads to more photos and information about her, including how to reach her: email, an unlocked phone, or her website. These pictures are sometimes not the actual provider one will meet, and they might link to an agency, even if the ad implies she is an independent provider. Agencies often put photos on these malls, not indicating that the person pictured works for them. Some malls only represent one city or area, but the largest companies have different sites for many locations.

Their faces are blurred or out of frame on most of these sites. Other sites show graphic nudity and some show faces. The photos look real, though they may be years old or digitally enhanced. Most profiles link to personal websites.

Providers put a lot of effort into their websites because the sites help determine the type of hobbyists they attract. They change them frequently. Unless a hobbyist is going to see someone he has hired before or relies on a particular agency, the hobbyist will search the Internet, see a provider who strikes his interest, then follow online instructions on how to contact her, talk or exchange emails, and if they agree to meet there are instructions on exactly what to do.

They generally insist that the hobbyists show the cash in an open envelope right away, without comment, placing it where the website instructed them. It's planned so the hobbyist doesn't see the provider pick up the money, which could be used against her if he is in law enforcement (LE.) If it was explained on her website, any questions about what they will get for the cash will end the session.

Some providers describe themselves as ladylike and able to blend in socially at any occasion, while others are blunt, humorous, or claim to be sexually insatiable. Many will only see respectful men over a certain age. Most will not see anyone who is not immaculately clean, and some insist he be gentlemanly, polite and respectful.

These websites are effective for the agencies because a regular client might request a specific provider, and if that escort is unavailable, the agency can recommend another provider and clients can look her up online.

PRIVATE WEBSITES

Escorts' websites usually look professional and sexy or elegant. They can be extensive and well written. Many of the women look as attractive as professional models and there are usually several photos, often on or near a bed.

Home page. A photo or two and comments such as how much she loves giving pleasure, how horny she is, something about her personality, or the variety of roles she can portray. There may be a an agreement page or announcement indicating you must be over eighteen, not offended by nudity, allowed to view this site in your state, and are not law enforcement. An individual may exclude certain races, nationalities, or men under a certain age. Sub-menus on the front page include categories such as:

- **Bio.** What she wants you to know or believe about her background.

- **Gallery.** Different photos, possibly touched up by photo editing tools, usually blurring the face. Or pictures of someone else.

- **Availability.** She may be on vacation or only work certain days or hours.

- **Services.** They are discreet about what they will do, and some-times say they will not do certain things.

- **Rates.** Price lists for time and activities. Could be one hour for 'An Introduction', Two Hours – 'A Taste of Heaven'. Overnight, or Two Days. Usually price breaks are offered for more time. Many providers refuse to quote prices online. The ones that do may not allow any discussion of payment in person, because the police may need that to make an arrest.

- **Travel Arrangements.** Special conditions and two-way, first class tickets are spelled out.

- **Contact.** Phone, email, or both. They won't accept a call from a phone that is blocked and doesn't show your number. Some accept texts only.

- **Travel schedule**. Some providers tour around the country or even the world, and make appointments in advance. Some providers post a calendar with available times indicated.

- **Booking.** In some cases a provider publishes her calendar online. A hobbyist can contact her and try to fill an open spot. The first step is to fill out a questionnaire.

- **Gifts.** They list their favorite wines, jewelry or clothes by brand, or gift certificates for fashionable clothing brands. Some providers request exotic vacations.

REVIEW BOARDS

Review boards are websites where hobbyists post personal reviews of their sessions with providers. Online review boards brought a new level of enticement and reliability, transforming the interaction between providers and hobbyists.

They are broken down like the malls, starting with location, names, photos and services they provide. Usually providers have been reviewed by numerous hobbyists. The review board averages out the basic details and then each review is independently published.

Many hobbyists will only see women whose reviews appeal to them. By writing detailed accounts of their sessions, hobbyists say they are able to relive their experiences.

Some hobbyists say they are on a mission to seek out the services of the highest-rated providers on the Internet.

THE EROTIC REVIEW

The Erotic Review (TER) is the most prominent review board and covers most of the free world. Other review boards are often less graphic. There are local sections of TER, and sometimes review boards for specific towns or states.

TER is open to the public for free. Each provider's review is in two parts, the General Section for Basic members, and the 'Juicy Details' for VIP members. It costs $20 a month or two published reviews to be a VIP member.

They used to claim eighty million members, but under new management, in 2017, they declined to give me their membership numbers. As I write this, there are about 67,000 people and 1.5 million reviews on TER. There are local and general discussion boards and a magazine in the works in England. They do not allow advertising by providers, so they are not representing or acting as an agent for them, and are presumably unbiased

BASIC MEMBERS

With some restrictions pertaining to laws and personal sensitivity, anyone who is over 18 can become a Basic member. If a Basic member wants to read general reviews, he or she fills in the location, selects general categories, and sees a list of providers, followed by a list of reviews of each. If he is looking for a particular provider he can just put in her name and hope she hasn't changed it.

The Basic member part of TER contains a form covering all a provider's physical attributes as well as personality, dimensions, body type, age range, if and how she is shaved, nationality, hair color, types of service, links to her websites or mall postings, personal contacts, how well she speaks different languages, whether or not she smokes in or out of the session, whether or not it is the girl advertised, how easy she is to reach, does she deliver as promised, show up on time, and whether her breasts are 'enhanced', and if so, how well done.

(Enhanced breasts are usually not a turn off if they were well done.) There is a choice of one-word descriptions of their breasts, like 'perky' or 'saggy'. The photo might be the same person ten or fifteen years or twenty pounds earlier. The reviewer rates the provider overall from one to ten. These reviews have more details than the malls and are more believable, because they show the responses of hobbyists who have seen that particular provider.

There is also a category for new reviews. As to the actual sessions, the Basic members can only describe the stages in getting together and a vague description of how he liked the session. If he was robbed or ripped off there will be a red sign prominently displayed and the letters 'ROB', which stand for Rip-Off Bitch.

VIP MEMBERS

Only VIP members can read the "'Juicy Details', A VIP membership costs $20 per month, or you can write two reviews that are accepted. This is the ultimate kiss-and-tell, a "touch-by-touch" account of exactly what (or who) went down in a session. What they did and how well they did it. They give ratings from one to ten. To rate higher than seven on performance, a provider has to perform certain sex acts. Theoretically, sensual massage stops at seven or eight. Girls know what they have to do to get top ratings and can decide for themselves. Unless she was rude or indifferent, the graphic details can enhance the provider's popularity. Some providers rely on them to entice clients.

The Juicy Details are pornographic, very detailed, and obviously subjective. Since they use fake names, hobbyists can be surprisingly honest if, for example, they had a premature ejaculation. A review may be poor if the hobbyist didn't like the session, but very enticing if they did. They won't be published if they aren't detailed enough, and are only posted long after the sessions so the providers won't know who wrote them. A VIP member can read all these sex acts and imagine doing them with the girls in the photographs.

TER's website contains a glossary of terms that are common in the sex business and abbreviations for those terms.

The hobbyists often try to have sex in as many positions as possible, have multiple orgasms, and use these abbreviations in their reviews. A disclaimer states that the reviews are fictional and for entertainment purposes only. There's a legal distinction between a reviewer claiming an escort performed sex acts and the provider advertising that she will do them, but I've heard of some courts using reviews as supporting evidence against a provider.

TER doesn't take any advertising from providers, so it is not involved in any transaction and the reviews seem fairer. They won't print a review if it is suspect.

Without reviews it's impossible to tell what the provider will do. Providers' ads have to be oblique to avoid arrest for solicitation, so reviews give hobbyists some idea of what to expect. Once a client is with a woman it's awkward for him to back out. It's not like a customer can take a complaint to court if she was not attractive as advertised, didn't do anything or robbed him. A girl might advertise under 'massage' but her reviews indicate she provides full sex.

Review boards are a double-edged sword for the providers. Good reviews provide a flood of potential customers, but the reviews can be embarrassing for the providers to read, even if they are favorable. Some providers never look at them. Other providers and agencies ask potential clients not to write a review on the grounds that their intimacies should be private. TER goes along with that. They will also remove a fake negative review if the provider can prove he never saw her.

The first review **Taylor** read about herself on TER was a poor one and was painful for her to read. She tried to get TER to remove it, but they wouldn't do that just because it was negative. She learned to try harder to please the clients, and it worked.

Taylor told me,

> *In the nineties you could basically advertise anything on the Internet and the phone would ring off the hook. Then in year 2000 suddenly there was a four-month period when everything changed. Unless you were reviewed on TER and got good reviews, you were out of business.*

She might be exaggerating but her point is clear.

TER offers advice on the proper protocol for seeing providers. Providers who've been in the business a long time told me that clients today are more considerate than they used to be, and they attribute that largely to peer pressure on the review boards to treat the providers well. Mary didn't provide sex but her reviewers felt that she genuinely cared about them and that she loved to tease them and prolong their pleasure.

Maxx99, a hobbyist, wrote me,

> *I find the reviews to be very erotic and when I'm 'on the fence' about seeing a provider, reading an erotic tale about an experience with her is sometimes all that's needed for me...*

Becca's childhood was good and her parents were still married. **Becca** went to church regularly and was leading a double life. She was also a receptionist for a business. Before she was an escort, Becca was a counselor for troubled teenagers in Colorado. She took a break from counseling but she plans to go back to it some day. Money had a lot to do with her decision.

She said,

> *When you date, most men just want sex.*

This was frustrating because she wanted a man who was really interested in her. She still wanted a long-term relationship, though she had been interested in escorting since her early twenties. Reading books like *Mayflower Madame* made it sound glamorous.

She started with an escort agency that told her nothing. They just threw her in a room with a twenty year-old who was a nasty person. She never got good advice from the agency on how to handle difficult situations. She became an independent escort and started doing much better after that.

> *If you are self-motivated you become independent. With an agency, you just sit around and wait for calls. An independent has to monitor calls, do advertising, and make the appointments.*

She told me that being an escort helped her overall because she used to be quiet and now she can be more assertive, but it has lowered her self-esteem. Before she became an escort she used to feel very attractive, but now she felt more self-conscious because she has no breast implants. After we exchanged a few emails and phone conversations, I discovered that her lowered self-esteem was based on a review which said that she, "appears much older than she says" and had "saggy boobs." She still knew she was pretty, but not compared to the other providers her clients might be seeing. She was a compulsive shopper but it didn't make her feel better. Maybe there was a correlation between compulsive shopping and her self-esteem concerning her appearance. This illustrates the danger of advertising with a picture that's not an accurate depiction. She was not taking into account that other providers on the Internet also enhance their looks by photographic magic. Becca's feeling less attractive because of her review was unusual, but I don't recall any providers who enjoyed reading reviews of their sexual escapades.

I sent her encouraging emails, but couldn't get it out of my mind, so I wrote, "Dear Becca: Thanks again for the interview. I am still thinking about your reaction to the rude review. You might want to stop reading reviews. And remember, this was just one guy. I feel like sending him a letter, not blasting him, but reminding him he is writing about human beings with feelings, and his review had a negative impact on an otherwise nice person. However I won't do it without your permission.

> *Dear Jim,*
>
> *I just wanted to take a quick minute to let you know I received your emails, and I just want to thank you for being so very nice, caring, and for trying to make me feel good. I truly do appreciate your sincerity! You are a very nice man and I'm glad we have met.*
>
> *I am sending you a couple other pics of me so you get a better idea of who you are talking to, okay? Also, you mentioned you would like to write that bad reviewer guy a letter...I would love it if you did! :-) I have a screen name on TER that people wouldn't suspect is a woman, and I have thought of writing him myself to tell him pretty much what you would like to tell him. But, I just*

*haven't done it yet. So, Jim, I would really like it
if you wrote him.*

*I will write more tonight or tomorrow. I would
like to give you more of my inner feelings of how
I feel, but as I mentioned, I do write better. I
think it just allows me to get my thoughts
together and express them well. I will be doing
that for you, okay?*

Take care!

Ruth (my real name)

I sent her reviewer a letter and forwarded her a copy:

"I'm a writer and filmmaker in Los Angeles, and I'm writing a book about the real world of escorts. Most providers say that being an escort has raised their self-esteem. The one exception is Becca, who had her self-esteem rather shattered by your review on TER. She was always confident of her good looks until then. You know how women are. This is very damaging. I know it was not deliberate. You qualify your review by pointing out you have a particular preference for thin women.

"In show business, we have a policy to NEVER publicly criticize the way a woman looks. You are dealing with the self-respect of feeling human beings. It's not a private conversation between guys. Other clients thought Becca was beautiful. It's not as if she's a mean, evil person.

"TER is useful and exciting, but it can have a dark side too. It breaks two pretty good rules: one about kissing and telling, the other about criticizing women's looks. Most reviewers are pretty generous in giving high points to the appearances of providers. I suggest you be a little discreet. Maybe tell the provider more about your taste before the meeting. You sound like an intelligent, decent person and I'm sure you don't want to actually hurt someone who never meant you any harm."

Actually, the photos she sent me privately show her looking considerably older than the photos she shows online.

I realized I was breaking an old journalistic rule about the writer staying out of the story, however new journalism allows it.

Dr. Peterson wrote: "If Becca has to lead a double life then she is likely too guarded/defended to have any authentic intimacy in either life. She wanted someone 'really interested in her', but is in a lifestyle that would make that unlikely – is a man interested in her because of her church-going / counselor side, or for her escort side?

"While her self-esteem might have been re-injured by the cruel review, it was more than likely fundamentally fragile. Compulsive shopping can be an attempt to soothe many wounds – but it so often seems to be an attempt to fill up a bottomless pit. There is momentary pleasure, but nothing of substance stays and the gnawing hunger quickly reasserts itself. This seems to be the core dynamic of most addictive and/or compulsive behaviors."

REVIEWS REVEAL VARIETY

Backdoormn wrote a review of **Hunny**, a full-figured African American woman in her early 20's. He went to see her because over the phone she offered "Greek" (anal sex), which was his favorite.

She was listed under "massage" but she didn't actually give him a massage. Even though he had sex with her in several positions, he gave her low marks because he could tell she was faking her orgasms and was too mechanical for the price.

Carni was listed under 'Blonde/Massage' in Miami. She was around twenty-six but looked younger. One reviewer described what a thrill it was to have her rub her breasts on his private parts while he was looking at her pretty face. He later touched her breasts while she gave him "a nice hand job." Another hobbyist paid more and received unprotected oral sex.

Celine, originally from the Mediterranean, had only been in the business a short while, yet she was one of the highest-rated escorts in Los Angeles. She told me that she got great reviews because she was extremely active and enthusiastic in bed.

She met potential clients for coffee to decide if she wanted to date them. I didn't understand that until after I met her for an interview over coffee. She chose the Beverly Hills Hotel and ordered champagne and shrimp cocktails.

Celine was the only escort I met who got into the business inadvertently. She didn't know any men in Los Angeles, so her girlfriend set them up on a double date. Celine eagerly went all the way, and her girlfriend later handed her fifteen hundred dollars. Celine was surprised, but her girlfriend explained, "You don't think we do this for free do you?"

Celine had a sparkling personality and often accompanied a gentleman to dinner and the theater without having sex. No matter how much they love sex, which varies widely among escorts, they all seem delighted when they're paid just for companionship.

Because of her glowing reviews on TER she had so many regulars that she didn't need any new customers, so she didn't have to worry about undercover police. She said she never worried about them anyway because she felt her intuition could ferret them out. It could also be a false sense of confidence, since she'd only been in the business a short time. She said, "I feel like I have a lot of husbands."

She said that her girlfriend was actually prettier than she, but she just lay there during sex and was jealous when Celine became so popular.

Celine had a sleeping disorder that made it difficult for her to get up in the morning, so this profession could be a saving grace for her financially.

As an aside, some prominent filmmakers who have dated some of the most beautiful women in the world have privately said that the great beauties are often not the best lovers. They seem to feel that they're so good-looking, it's enough to just let you do it. I'm not going to reveal my sources, for fear of sullying your image of your most revered stars. I'm sorry to say that I can't verify this personally.

Speaking of beauties, TER ran a series of contests in which members voted on which providers had the best lips, boobs, face, buns, or 'coochie' (vagina.) Contestants submitted photos from anywhere in the English-speaking world and TER showed the photos, with links to the women's ads. Political correctness has no place in this environment.

The winners were all in their thirties and looked natural. In my opinion, they all looked good. Seattle had two of the five winners, one of whom only charged $250 an hour, which would probably be $700 in 2017. With TER's vast reach, I'm sure she had more business than she could handle after the contest.

AUTHENTICITY OF REVIEWS

TER goes to great lengths to get honest reviews. The hobbyists use pseudonyms, called 'handles', and TER delays publishing reviews so the providers won't know who wrote what. I asked **Sabrina** if the reviews of her were true or if the guys exaggerated.

She said her reviews were true, except when they say that she swallows. She added,

> *Nobody swallows. That's a lie. You only swallow*
> *if you're in love. That's the difference between*
> *like and love, spitting versus swallowing.*

Her reviews say she is sweet, eager, and imaginative, usually going beyond what the client would expect. She treats each client like he was her lover. In one case he barely got in the door before she dropped to her knees, pulled his pants down, and went down on him. She will serve fine wine, gourmet food, or whatever strikes her fancy.

At first she totally resented the reviews. She said, "It's one thing to be there, another to read about it." Then she realized it's a great marketing tool, since her reviews are so favorable. Business is great for the first week after a new review comes out.

Amanda, a Hispanic escort said,

> *Sometimes they lie. They lie down and cum in*
> *five seconds and I try hard to bring them back*
> *again. Because, okay, if you cum in five seconds*
> *that's not fun. It's like if you go to Las Vegas and*
> *you throw all your money in a slot machine, and*
> *then you have three days. What do you do all that*
> *time with no money?*

It's like a competitive sport. But some hobbyists admit their shortcomings. **Martian** said he was nervous because he had been talking with **Erica** for so long his anticipation was immense. Besides, it was the first time he had seen an escort without bringing his wife for three-way sex. He couldn't last.

At one point Taylor managed a "house" – a group of sensual masseuses. She decided to kick-start the operation by pretending online to be various hobbyists and eventually reviewing her girls herself. Taylor made up twelve 'handles' which are names one goes by to be anonymous, and provided each of them with his own personality, writing style, sexual preferences, and fetishes. She wrote it out in a notebook. TER would catch her if she used the same computer address so she posted reviews from different Kinkos for each handle. She started by posting reviews of girls she was not managing. She looked at what legitimate hobbyists had written about them, came up with something original, but not too different, and included enough racy details to make it interesting. She even went into chat rooms disguised as her fictitious men.

One of her fictional characters would write that he had gone to see a girl another character had recommended, and they would thank each other or sometimes slam each other. Gradually she established a believable group of hobbyists, and then transferred their attention to her own girls. First one; then another. When a hobbyist goes to a house or 'pad' and sees one girl, he often runs into another girl and subsequently returns to have a session with her.

Taylor's girls were becoming popular, but suddenly TER caught on to her and shut down all reviews of her girls. She doesn't know how they found out but it shows the lengths to which TER goes to keep the reviews honest. She had to make up all new names for her girls and gave up trying to trick TER. Taylor says some other review boards aren't as thorough.

I questioned her further about the hobbyists and their reviews.

She wrote back,

> *The men who write reviews usually give around the same numerical ratings for performance, appearance, and so on. If they don't feel they can fall in line with what other hobbyists wrote in their reviews, or if the girl just lay there, they will tend to not write a review rather than stand up and write something different. There's*

> *camaraderie amongst hobbyists. And girls can't*
> *be consistent, like all sevens and eights or all*
> *nines. I'm surprised I don't get more sixes in*
> *appearance. I'm thirty-eight, and I'm being*
> *compared with twenty-six year olds. If I were a*
> *nasty person I would get a five or six in*
> *appearance.*

There are some escorts who get all nines and tens. The reviewers usually describe multiple sex acts in a variety of positions, lasting anywhere from half an hour to many hours.

Taylor wrote,

> *The guys exaggerate. The girls lie, the guys just*
> *exaggerate. The girls talk badly about the other*
> *girl who does more.*

It's impossible for TER to have honest reviews all the time. One escort insists on knowing the hobbyist's handle before she books an appointment so she can read his previous reviews. She also wants to approve what he writes about her. A provider and the hobbyist might make a deal: in exchange for a great review the client will buy one session, get one free.

Karri tells clients it's okay to review her on TBD [The Big Doggie], because they don't go into graphic details, but asks them not to post reviews of their sessions on TER. She feels it jeopardizes both parties' safety.

Occasionally a review might be unfair or even written by a rival provider. The girl can appeal and have it removed if she can prove it was fake.

Some hobbyists resist reviewing a girl so they can "keep her to themselves" for a while.

Providers with high ratings have more potential customers than they can possibly see, so they can be more selective and charge more. Some escorts put a link from their private websites to the review boards, even if their reviews are poor. They didn't realize their reviews were poor. Any time a person visits a provider's website, follows a link from there to TER, and signs up, TER pays the provider 38% of any VIP membership income due to that introduction, in perpetuity.

Dr. Peterson wrote: "This chapter is powerful in how it describes how the women are objectified – reducing the relationship to a commodity. The image that came to my mind is the judging panels at the gymnastic Olympics – rating each athlete on a scale of 1-10. Somehow it doesn't seem as harsh there, but probably feels that way to the athletes who receive a 6 or 7, just like the escorts do."

WHOSE PICTURE IS IT?

TER occasionally polls its members, and today a poll on what makes hobbyists decide which provider to see shows that the provider's photographs are the biggest deciding factor, which is ironic, since the photograph may be inaccurate. It is common for escorts to use another person's photographs and one of the typical questions reviewers answer is whether the provider was the girl in the photographs.

SCREENING HOBBYISTS ONLINE

Screening is not new, but in 2017 it's virtually universal. It can be a chore, and frightening to hobbyists, who are giving sex workers personal information that could get them in trouble. Now screening can be done by websites such as Preferred 411 (P411.com.) The hobbyist pays P411 a modest annual fee to check him out. The provider only has to check with the company. The escort still can't tell anything about the hobbyist's personality but it's like getting pre-cleared for a commercial flight. Some providers check with a couple of other providers the client has seen.

CHAPTER III: ASPECTS OF THIS LIFE

ACCEPTANCE

More women seem willing to enter the sex business today. Sexual mores are a lot looser than they used to be. Perhaps they're influenced by pop stars performing nearly nude and dancing erotically. Television and cable shows regularly depict nude actors having sex. There are other factors, such as young people having money problems. Many women support themselves, are often responsible for raising children, and marry later in life. Many women don't want to be dependent on a man.

SEXUAL PROWESS

Professional sex workers usually develop greater sexual prowess than the average woman. Certainly this is true of the providers who get top reviews by hobbyists. If they were inexperienced when they started, the hobbyists helped them along.

Sabrina says that when she has a boyfriend she has to dumb down her sexuality or it's a tip off. Some escorts can move from one sex position to another without separating, keeping their clients on the brink, and reviving them after they climax. I wish they taught that when I was a kid.

Dr. Peterson wrote: "Your comment, 'I wish they taught that when I was a kid,' while amusing, is also confusing. Do you wish a woman could have done that to you as a kid, or do you wish you had learned to do this with your sex partners as a kid?"

My sex partners as a kid? I'm afraid there's not much for me to talk about, but guys would boast, and I don't think they had even invented all those positions yet. I never heard of "Reverse Cowgirl" until I started research for this book.

Back to the providers. Taylor said,

> *Put me in a bikini next to a twenty-one year old model and I'm not going to come out on top. I'm easily ten pounds overweight, but you put the*

> *twenty one year old next to me doing a blow job, and if they closed their eyes they'd know the difference.*

While some of them actually climax with their clients, others don't but are good at faking it. Comparing reviews with what providers told me privately, it is clear that hobbyists really can't tell the difference. It seemed that the women who faked climaxes tended to get higher ratings by hobbyists for really enjoying it.

Brooke gets great reviews, because all her reviewers say she loves sex so much. But she told me that she just, "makes the best of it."

Dr. Peterson wrote: "Taylor has become very good at giving her clients what they want and acting as if she is enjoying it. In the psychological world, that ability is often discussed in terms of one's false self (polite, caring, sexual, etc.) trumping one's true self (angry, rude, bitter, etc.) with the underlying purpose to not expose the true self because she could get (authentically) abandoned, rejected, or simply not survive. If the false self is rejected this sting is less."

Sounds like acting. One escort quit the business, but her enhanced sexual prowess is one thing she has no regrets about.

DONATIONS

The prices in this book were from the years 2000 to 2002. It seems they have more than doubled since then, far above the rate of inflation They're called 'donations' so it's less blatant that clients are paying for sex. The websites state that any money or other consideration is for their time only. Anything else that occurs is purely voluntary.

In one case, the same website that advertised escorts for $250 per hour in 2004 now charges $1,000. They may be representing a different level of sex workers. Other providers don't seem to have changed their prices that much. I suspect this is influenced by what's happening in the world and how it affects attitudes. In theater, producers have been famously unable to determine why they will be sold out one day and half-empty the next. It doesn't match up with any type of event but is more like a mood in the air.

Leslie's minimum was four hours, so she avoided clients who just wanted quick sex, and ended up spending less.

Diva, a five-foot tall porn star, charged a thousand an hour for a private session, but the fourth hour was free. That was a lot then, but porn stars charge much more because hobbyists have seen them on videos and are paying to fulfill their fantasies. Clients' fantasies can include the smallest minutiae, and their satisfaction is often geared to fulfilling these details.

Porn stars can headline at strip clubs that advertise when they will appear. They make most of their money that way and by sending out a special series of photos, or seeing hobbyists privately, because porn producers usually don't pay them much. A black porn star named **Lovely** charges fifteen hundred per hour, and forty-five hundred for anal.

Sensuous massage usually costs more in big cities like Los Angeles and New York. Once the hobbyist is on the table and aroused, the provider will often ask for more money to provide additional services.

On the higher end of providers, **Cheryl** charged up to fifteen thousand for an evening. I asked her if she got many customers at that price. She wrote,

> Jim,
>
> I have been on vacation and just got back to over 800 emails!!! Quickly I will address your question :)
>
> It's two things.....Many of the girls at that rate have major titles and credits and feel they meet incredible men so to make it worthwhile to them it has to be a lot of money.
>
> Others it's a self worth thing and they feel like this, they only want to do this if they can meet someone very wealthy in hopes of meeting someone to have an affair, arrangement, or find their Prince. and these girls do not want to see many men, one now & then which is all that can afford this rate.
>
> No there are not many $15k bookings

There are several $10k bookings

Xoxox

Despite the high hourly rates charged by the high-end escorts, many providers are not able to save money. Their overhead expenses include advertising, lingerie, hair salons, phone, and nice pads to work in. Customers book time but don't show up. A provider may have to go through a hundred phone conversations or emails for every session. Escorts might end up seeing two to five clients a week. They often lie about how busy they are to appear highly ranked. In order to keep their spirits up they might buy expensive clothes, food, or drugs. Either because they earned it so quickly, or they feel it's dirty money, many providers spend it as rapidly as they earn it.

Dr. Peterson wrote: "The life of 'pretending' is not limited to escorts. I cannot think of many professions in which people do not attempt to present their success in exaggerated ways. I know a number of psychologists who lie about how busy they are, how long their waiting list is, and how much they can charge for an hour of psychotherapy. These other professionals may use diversions (such as buying clothes, food, or drugs) to give them a sense of their own self-importance."

There are 'serial callers' who make numerous phone calls to providers but are really not going to book a session.

Taylor said,

> *They just want to play with you. One guy calls a hundred girls a day. There's one man who gets an appointment, shows up, looks them up and down, sneers and says, "You're not the girl in the ad", and walks away, to make the girl feel hurt.*

CASH AND DASH

One of the most valuable aspects of a review board is that it alerts clients to rip-off artists. Women sometimes advertise that they'll show you the time of your life, but when they show up they do a little dance and demand more money. There's also what's called 'cash and dash'. The woman gets the client to take off his clothes, grabs the money and runs out.

When a hobbyist has been ripped off, he was often careless and failed to check out the provider with TER or another review board. Many hobbyists feel a sense of kinship. If a hobbyist is cheated, he typically writes about the incident, giving the provider's name and description, and says, "I took one for the team."

Here's a rip-off described on TER. An Internet ad showed a voluptuous blonde, around twenty-two years old. One hobbyist said it was late at night, he was horny, the escort he usually saw was unavailable, and he didn't bother to check out the new girl's reviews with TER. She sounded really sexy over the phone, insisted she was the girl in the picture, and said that she came alone. He rented a hotel room. Two people showed up: a skinny, middle-aged Asian woman, and a six-foot five-inch Hispanic man who looked like a gangster. The 'driver' demanded and took the money, then waited outside the door while the Asian woman insisted on more money or she would have her 'driver' beat him up. He managed to get her out the door without paying more. Two other clients had different experiences with this team but no one got any sex.

Another reviewer on TER wrote that he got burned when an escort agreed to see him without her doing any screening. He said, "I've since learned that getting an appointment with a good provider is like getting an appointment set up with the royal family."

Since prostitution is usually illegal, the customers can't call the police when they get ripped off.

Reviews of sex are not necessarily fair. One escort got consistently high reviews except for one, in which he gave her a six out of ten for performance, saying she was not very enthusiastic.

I read the review and noticed that the guy said, "I was in a hurry, and I just wanted to bang her and get out of there."

No wonder she wasn't very responsive. I spoke to the provider, who said,

> *What does he expect! He just wanted to rush in, bang me doggie-style and run out. I'm not a machine.*

WHAT YOU SEE AND WHAT YOU GET

I wasn't shocked to discover a fair amount of duplicity in the sex business. Many of the providers' online ads look like they could model for Victoria's Secret or Playboy. Even if it is the same girl, she might not look as great in person. As mentioned earlier, the person you actually meet might be neither the person you talked to on the phone nor the one in the pictures.

It appears to me that a single ad sometimes includes photographs of different people or body parts. Sometimes the reviewer will say it wasn't the same girl as in the picture, but they didn't mind because the girl looked even better than the one on the website. TER has a box for reviewers to click 'Yes' or 'No' if it was the girl in the picture. Yet almost all advertising is slanted, so what do you expect?

SHAME OR SATISFACTION

Most of the women I interviewed had positive feelings about their work, but some of them were strongly affected by the public's negative perception of it. It is usually difficult for a provider to maintain personal relationships outside the business. Some avoided seeing their families so they wouldn't have to lie to them. They can be lonely during the holidays.

My original query letter mentioned improving the public perception of providers.

Ginger, a college student in New Orleans who works as an escort on the side, wrote: "*Please, show that in other parts of the world the adult entertainment industry does not have the horrible stigma attached to it as it does in this country that was founded by Puritans.*"

When I first contacted **Sabrina**, she said,

> *Asking whether or not I can elevate the image of escorts and working girls would assume that I approve of the lifestyle. I can't say it hasn't been good to me. But I still believe that anything that one cannot discuss in public without fear of retribution is probably not an admirable thing to be doing. The ball is in your court.*

She later said,

> *I try to not feel ashamed. I'm not proud of being an escort at all. I imagine what my grandmother would think.*

Sabrina said she had a very high IQ but she had an attention deficit disorder (ADD), which made it difficult for her to keep an office job. Our discussions were a means to explore her inner conflicts.

She clearly loved her sessions, throwing herself into them with wild abandon, and she risked falling in love with her clients. But she didn't like having to lie about what she did and wanted to be accepted as part of society.

Ariana had a Catholic upbringing and all those taboos made it more interesting for her.

Most of the women I interviewed thought the profession was unfairly stigmatized. When I got beneath the surface, I often found conflicting feelings. Several women used the term "revenge" to describe their motivations. Sabrina admitted that she told her mother what she was doing because her mother had been cruel to her as a child.

Many American women feel very threatened by escorts. **Ariana** told me a client's wife called her and said, *"Did you know that Tom is married? His daughter is named Jennifer and has the brightest smile."*

She felt a little bad about seeing married guys. Then her attitude changed and she didn't view it as being wrong. It was just people enjoying, sharing genuine pleasure and companionship. Her full interview comes later.

Many escorts told me they felt their work filled a legitimate need and they did not feel guilty. That doesn't mean they can be open about it, however.

Dr. Peterson wrote: "In highlighting the positive aspects of this business, providers who are able to pay their bills and subsist on their own, and hobbyists who find much-needed companionship and sometimes, genuine friendship, the crucial need for survival and human connection is underscored. In these cases, it is money that is the transactional 'glue' that holds both parties together."

THE CONTROL FACTOR

Sex workers of all kinds, from exotic dancers to escorts, usually love the control they have over men. That's the one thing they all seemed to agree on. The game is seeing how much money they can squeeze out of a hobbyist.

The escort's first opportunity to express control is in the screening process, pumping a potential client with questions to determine whether or not he's really a potential client or law enforcement, and whether he's someone she's willing to be intimate with. They demanded the real phone numbers, addresses, and references from other providers. Most independent providers spend far more time screening than they actually spend with clients.

The sessions themselves often include subtle power games. The provider can maintain control by pretending to be eager to perform a specific act rather than being domineered. They can pretend to climax when they want to end the sex. Just the fact of men finding them attractive can make them feel powerful.

Dr. Peterson wrote: "I am struck by the discussions of power games, again because these are not limited to the relationship between the escort and her hobbyist. Subtle power games are endemic in the majority of relationships."

THE FREQUENCY FACTOR

Sensual massage is less intrusive than "full service" sex, and sensual masseuses can see more customers. Some escorts can't imagine seeing more than one client a day. Others can be with four or five. I asked most of the escorts if they really had orgasms with clients. Some do and some don't, but the escorts that really climax are generally not able to see as many clients. Women who are physically and emotionally strong can also see more clients, but if they don't place limits on how many men they see they risk becoming burned out and jaded. My longer interviews depict women who went through the stages of learning this.

SUGAR DADDIES – SUGAR BABIES

Around 2015 there was a mass increase in young women and wealthy men meeting through a company called

SeekingArrangement. A 'sugar daddy' will financially support a 'sugar baby' through college or her early career.

It is much harder for young Americans to get started in their careers these days. It has become necessary to have a college or graduate school degree to obtain many jobs, but unless the student has wealthy parents, it is almost impossible to get a degree without incurring a huge debt that will take many years to pay off. States are no longer paying public universities and colleges enough money to provide low tuition rates. Even after graduation, it is difficult to find a decent paying job. In addition, employers want new employees to have previous experience, rather than training them as in the past.

SeekingArrangement.com claims to be the largest group facilitating these arrangements. They say they match wealthy men with young women for love and friendship. The sugar daddy may want a companion a few nights a week, on weekends, for travel, yachting tours, or friendship. To join you must agree to their contract, stating you are not using this for escort services or for locating an escort. The site has been featured in many of America's top news sites and is available as an app on prominent sites. There are many imitators.

The potential partners make sure they enjoy the same things and their schedules are compatible. The man might pay for the girl's tuition and books, her rent, deposit regularly in her account or whatever they agree on.

The website arranges for the two to read about each other, meet, see if they are socially compatible, and guides them to make written agreements, so it is all spelled out and there are no misunderstandings. They also give advice on how to make the financial transactions easier and more difficult for a third party to see. There is no sex described in the agreements, but some say sex is implied.

Most men find a sugar baby within five days. Some girls who have used this during college say they want to continue afterwards. To keep up with the times, even the sites that advertise for escorts now include "arrangements."

There is hardly anything new about a sugar daddy, and I suppose it's legal, but it's relatively new on the Internet, and SeekingArrangement.com says it grew eighty percent in the past year. One girl said she had two sugar daddies at the same time because of their different schedules. This sort of thing, in a more informal way, goes back thousands of years, has long been considered normal in Europe, and Asia, and is hardly rare amongst royalty and ancient hierarchies.

The *N.Y. Times*, CNN, and *Vanity Fair* have attested to this arena's amazing growth. It's also driven by the difficulties young people have earning enough money to move out of their parents' homes and live decently. When you consider how college girls are often mistreated by college boys in the "hook-up" world (see Chapter VI) this seems much more respectful, practical, and humane, though it's a long-term commitment, not a quick, single event.

CHAPTER IV: ESCORT AGENCIES

Escort agencies post on the same escort malls used by independent providers, plus their own websites. They also have private lists of referrals and past clients. Many of them demand complete control over 'their girls'. They might or might not allow them to be reviewed on review boards.

Some hobbyists mention in their reviews that they trust certain agencies to deliver very high quality escorts. The top agencies make sure that the providers follow a certain protocol as to what they will do, meaning that hobbyists know that providers from certain agencies will perform certain sex acts. Agencies are convenient for wealthy and busy clients. Once the client is established with an agency, getting a date is only a phone call and a few thousand dollars away.

Some agencies represent famous models and other ravishing women from all over the world. There is nothing new about this, except that the client can look at the escort's photo on his phone. There is no sex in quite a few of these sessions.

Before Yuki became an escort, she was financially desperate and answered an ad looking for a masseuse to work in a massage parlor. It was in an apartment but with lots of outcalls, so in effect it was an escort agency. The man who ran it was nice to her and taught her about the business. He moved to Las Vegas so she went into escorting on her own.

She said sensual massage was essentially the same thing to her. This is a little different from a previous discussion with her but they aren't really inconsistent. The last time I spoke with her she was facing a dilemma. She had witnessed a crime and reported it. The police arrested the suspect and demanded that she testify. She was afraid that friends of the suspect might harm her. Suki was highly emotional at the time. I'm wondering about some people being addicted to drama.

THE DARK SIDE OF AGENCIES

Taylor has done both management and independent escorting. She saw the ugly side of the business as practiced by some managers.

She said,

> *For awhile I rescued all the helpless little girls and worked them out of the business if they weren't strong enough. They are all damaged goods in some way. Nine out of ten, they don't have a prayer. Pimps and madams take pains to keep them down. A lot of weak young girls start out in massage and are okay with the seediness of rubbing up and down, and giving a hand job, with no kissing, not taking her panties off. Little by little, the walls break away, and she gradually turns into a prostitute.*

> *Sometimes a girl will start off earning four hundred or five hundred an hour for just massage, and think, "This is great." Then her madam stops running her ads so she won't earn anything. When she's desperate, they push her into full escort. So the girl does it.*

Alexis started in the business taking phone calls for an agency. She had an attractive voice and knew how to close a deal. The agency used her photos in their ads even though all she was doing was answering the phone. Eventually she decided, "What the hell," and started to work as an escort. She was given a pager and would sit around with other girls in a bar waiting for the agency to call with appointments. She soon went independent.

Sometimes an agency provides a driver who takes the money before the provider and the client interact. The agency takes anywhere from forty to sixty percent. The provider has no choice about whom she sees and is expected to make herself available at the agent's request. I've heard some horror stories about how certain madams treat their providers, but I've also heard of agents who were supportive and thoughtful.

If a provider is organized and confident it usually doesn't take long for her to learn that she can be master of her own fate by going independent.

Most of the agents I contacted did not cooperate with my research and a few gave rude responses. They might post different email addresses and phone numbers for each provider as if they were independent, but they all led to the agency. Some of their escorts wanted to give me interviews but an agency or their scheduler always intercepted the communication.

I sent a letter to Bee Jay, an escort who supposedly had her own email address. I said I hoped she received it personally. The reply was simply:

> *So??? $$$$$???*
>
> > *Nina*

'Nina' wasn't the name I'd written to, and I noticed the name 'Michael Wilson' in the Internet address. I thought it would be interesting to chat with Michael Wilson, but he wrote,

> *.....A more appropriate question is why should I?*
> *I am busy, she is busy and so are you but so far*
> *you are the only one benefiting, too one-sided for*
> *my tastes, good bye.*

One successful agent would cooperate if I gave up half the book, and when I declined went from very nice to hostile in a flash.

An agent or an independent provider has to be tough enough to handle business. One agent said she was helping her girls by providing them with an opportunity to salvage their lives and earn a lot of money.

ANITA

Anita is an independent escort now. When guys call and try to make an appointment she will ask, "What did you do, get my number off the bathroom wall?"

If they don't laugh, she hangs up. She will only see guys with a sense of humor.

Anita is twenty-seven years old. She spoke so fast it was hard to get it all down. She'd been in the professional world, but decided to "kick back and have fun." She got into escorting through her innocent-looking roommate, who made all kinds of money going to Beverly Hills homes on dates made through an escort agency.

Anita said the agency didn't care what might happen to her. She also said she never had real problems, but others might define it differently. When she first started, the agency sent her and another escort to a tough neighborhood in East Los Angeles. It was a big Mexican birthday party with a lot of drunken guys.

She said,

> *Guys told me 'you got to do this and that'. There was no negotiating with forty drunken Mexicans. They wanted me to jump out of a birthday cake. It was a mobster scene. I said, "Okay, let me go freshen up."*
>
> *She went into the bathroom and called 911 on her cell phone. Police helicopters came and their loudspeakers blared: "Let the girls out!"*

She got out and kept the money! Other people might have considered this experience a problem, but she was unfazed by it.

Her roommate had been there longer so they wouldn't send her to East L.A. but they would send a newcomer. The agency fed off Anita's ignorance. She's incorporated now, runs her own agency and said, "It's a cut throat business."

She doesn't have a college degree but her "street smarts" get her through. She only does what she wants, sexually and otherwise. She's not into eccentric sex, though maybe she'll try it someday.

She likes to see younger guys who are fun. Sometimes she will insult a potential client on the phone for an hour and a half in a teasing way. Anita said she doesn't want to disrespect the clients, yet she beats up guys verbally. It's part of the game she enjoys.

CHAPTER V: THE LAW

Dr. Peterson wrote: "There are clearly morality issues surrounding selling sex. In some places, the escort business is legal; in others, it's not. The overwhelming number of people interviewed for this book knew they were participating in an illegal act. If our legal system (in theory) exists to protect us, how should this topic be approached? For instance, speeding, driving while drinking and driving as a minor are against the law. The argument can be made that there are times when doing all of these things is technically 'safe', but the spirit of these laws is that they exist in order to make all of us more safe. Providers are often in risky and life-threatening situations, simultaneously afraid of being busted by the police for the work they are doing, and yet potentially needing the protection of the police. This is a thin line indeed for providers to walk on. What can be said about the morality of selling sex as it relates to our system of laws? There are two sides to this issue."

In 2017, the city of Oakland, California agreed to pay Jasmine Abuslin one million dollars, because up to thirty Bay Area police agencies in Oakland, San Francisco and other cities, had been sexually exploiting her for years when she was a minor, demanding sex in exchange for protection. Four Oakland police officers were criminally charged, and one of them committed suicide. The practice was said to not be unusual.

Law enforcement (LE) is a major factor in the lives of providers and hobbyists. The Internet helps police track down providers, pimps, madams and hobbyists. The fact that providers claim they are just being paid for their time really doesn't give them legal protection, and both providers and hobbyists are at risk of arrest or shakedowns by police, or people pretending to be police.

Police often enjoy these activities, and demand sex from women who are, or appear to be, prostitutes. This corrupts police, and sometimes lawyers and courts. Victims are loath to complain, because that would bring them disgrace and notoriety.

In California and many other places, prostitution is a misdemeanor, while pimping is a felony. There is a widespread assumption that authorities in some areas allow victimless crimes to take place so long as they have no complaints or the proper people are paid off. A victimless crime can become a crime with victims, the arrestees. An arrest can be a very terrifying event with lasting effects. Police and the courts have a limited amount of time and resources, which could otherwise be used for catching thieves and killers.

Having sex in a pornographic film is legal, because the producer who pays the girls isn't having sex with them himself. Pornographic films are considered a form of free speech. It's legal to have sex just for the fun of it or if you are married. Gore Vidal said, "Anything that turns you on is art." Porn stars are willing to accept limited public awareness of who they are and what they do. It probably helps if they are exhibitionists.

Of the escorts I contacted, **Marsha** was one of the most careful about law enforcement. She wrote,

> *You mentioned that you had enough info to portray the positive aspects of escorting, and that you needed more of the negative side. I have to admit, it's mostly been a positive experience for me. I enjoy working on my own, because I'm a highly motivated individual. But, I can think of two very negative aspects of the business... Law enforcement and the privacy involving my personal life (boyfriends, friends, dating, family.)*

> *I'm very well known for being one of the most cautious escorts as far as screening new clients, but this is because I have gotten "popped" (cops) 3 times... Once with a service (not my fault) and that's when I decided to go independent. The second time I got popped, cops used the reviews that clients posted on big sites like TBD, (thebigdoggie) to track down the clients at HOME, and force them to testify against me.*

> *I've never had an undercover sneak thru to me, so cops now trap clients in many different ways,*

and use that info to get to girls. The third time (ongoing) they made a dummy escort service incall...when guys showed up, they gave them a choice – either get booked for solicitation, or turn in any Internet girls you've seen. Guys always talk---even though a man will get a small fine, or get it dropped easily...whereas girls can and OFTEN do get up to a year in jail. So I have more than enough to say about the negative aspects regarding cops.

Much of what cops feed society (escorts spread disease, they are all drug addicts) is propaganda. If you do any research on escorts and STDS, you will find a professional escort is one of the MOST educated and safety conscious in society. There has NEVER been one instance of HIV in the legal brothels in Nevada. As far as our personal lives go, we normally live in secrecy...very few people in our realm of friends know what we do. We socialize with each other and 'talk shop' just like other working groups do. But the stigma of family and friends finding out is paralyzing at times. I've had both good and bad experiences with 'coming out' to friends. I've found that long term friends are way more accepting. Perhaps because they see 'me' first...whereas newer friends can't see beyond the word prostitute. Right now I am in a relationship and he knows what I do. He has his own job (AV tech) and film student. All of my long-term boyfriends have known. I'll end for now, and see if you have any specific questions or areas you'd like me to discuss in detail. Sincerely,

Marsha

I've added a few pictures, and yes, that's really me :)

Dr. Peterson wrote: "Marsha's discussion of the role in which law enforcement has touched her life, as well as the secret life in which escorts normally live, are themes that are often repeated. To accept these highly stressful and potentially traumatizing experiences as the norm speaks to a great sacrifice. It saddens me that any woman would have to bear this. Is this considered a 'victimless crime' because it is more likely the escorts who are being damaged rather than the hobbyists?"

An international escort named **Lara** told me that in Orange County, California, a woman who advertises as an escort could be arrested for intent to commit prostitution by just showing up. She was arrested herself and moved to London, where, she said, there is virtually no law enforcement against prostitution.

Chiksguy, a hobbyist ever since his wife lost interest in sex, wrote me,

> *Without even getting into the debate of whether it is a victimless crime, it is absurd to try to legislate, judicate, prosecute and penalize. The money we spend prosecuting and incarcerating those engaged in this act would be much better spent elsewhere. If it were legalized, the state would make revenue from taxes, and would be able to regulate and provide health care and attention, which is a very serious issue. As long as the trade is underground, those who earn money pay no taxes, and the public has no clue about the health safeguards that are or are not being used.*

Dr. Peterson wrote, "Chiksguy makes a good point about what the impact of having it legalized might be – if only the money spent in prosecuting and incarcerating escorts could be used to give these women better options early on in their lives."

CHEYENNE AND THE LAW

Cheyenne was an escort in Chicago. She is described as sweet and innocent. She left the business, and wrote,

I would be happy to answer your questions Jim. This is something that I would really like to share...

After being caught two times I cannot afford to be caught again because I might go to jail. The LE is the worst part of the business. The first time I was caught the officer let me do things to him that he should not have. I was arrested but the charges were dropped. The second time I didn't do anything but show up and stripped (not even fully naked.) This time I was charged with solicitation. I got the police report and to my disgust it was full of lies. It says that I did things and said things that never happened. But whom would the judge believe, me or the cops? Because of the reviews online, and because they took a Polaroid of me half-naked, my attorney has recommended that I don't fight it. I am still in court over this. If they need 3+ people to do a sting, and do so much work on it, why is nothing recorded? Why are there no hidden cameras? No bugs? It is not a fair game, and if they tricked me once before, they will trick me again, and one day, I will be in jail. I have lost my faith in our police force. When I would book dates for an agency off duty police officers would call to see girls. Also, both times I was caught the police officers gave me a speech on the dangers of the business, then also told me they really wish it was legal. I am sure you have heard many stories of corrupt cops...

Having a group of men bust down a door on you when you are half naked is one of the scariest things a girl can experience. I am thankful it was the police and I was not gang raped or something, but I still have flashbacks, and I am very afraid of hotels. Whenever I hear men talking outside of my door at home, or wherever I am, my heart begins to race. I hate them for that. Anyways, my perspective is this. I worked for a few agencies, and eventually became a call girl myself. There are more John's out there than providers to meet with them. On my own I would sometimes get 20 new contacts a day. This is something that will not stop because of the law, and I feel that what makes this industry so dangerous, is the law itself. The harsher the laws, the higher the price goes up, making the industry more dangerous, and leading to more organized crime because of the money, which in turn needs more law, and it's a never ending cycle. If this was legal, the service could be monitored, lowering the chance of disease being spread, and held in secure locations so neither party would be in danger. There will still be a stigma involved with this service even if it was legal, but at least the dangers would be nearly eliminated. It is okay for a guy to buy me dinner, drinks, jewelry, take me on a trip, in exchange for sexual relations, but not cold hard cash. It is also okay, if a third party pays me to have relations, and to watch and distribute it, but not if the transaction of money is just between two people. I just do not see the logic behind all of this. The law is causing a lot more danger, than the "murderers" and "guys that will beat me" the police warned me about. That danger does not have to exist at all."

Dr. Peterson wrote: "Another testimonial that makes clear sense – but the phrase, 'There are more Johns out there than providers to meet with them' speaks to how hungry so many are for the appearance of intimate contact the escort provides."

KIRSTEN AND THE LAW

Kirsten was also sorry she had to quit, but she got caught and was facing possible jail time. The case was still in court and there was too much at risk. She was living off savings, plus working as a personal trainer. She is physically muscular and was a sponsored athlete.

She was a lifeguard, then worked in the finance department of a big company, but she hated being at a desk and couldn't get time off from her job to finish school.

Kirsten has a very sensual voice. Like Alexis, she would be answering the phone at the office. Guys who heard her would always ask, "Who's that girl?" Everyone liked "that girl with the voice."

She worked info-lines, such as telephone lines for concerts, where people called for information. Someone said she should be a booker for an escort agency, so she worked as a booker (on the phone with men calling in) and doing the paperwork and advertising for ten percent. She also used her pictures for a girlfriend of hers who she booked.

She was curious about it so she decided to work on her own as an escort. She thought being an escort was just dancing. It sometimes does involve just doing a striptease or exotic dance, which is called 'a private dancer'.

She was very nervous the first time. They talked for about an hour. She had no idea what goes on and wouldn't go to bed with him. She did private dances for a while. How far they went depended on the clients and how she felt about them. As time went on, she did massage, then full service, from once a week to ten times a week. It was a good experience overall.

She said,

> *The clients were wonderful people. It wasn't very difficult. Most of the guys are great; city councilmen, church goers, doctors, anyone and everyone; normal, successful, hard working*

She had lots of regulars. Her clients were mostly single. She said, "The married ones go to call girls at hotels."

She mostly went to homes.

She also puts on musical events, is a concert promoter and professional musician, so she has no time for a boyfriend. She likes the athletics of personal training and works with top athletes. They offered her three times as much as other trainers. She said she is normal looking, but who can believe women about that?

I asked about her early family life. It was a close, suburban family. She was always sexual and flirtatious and always had boyfriends. Some of her former clients are still friends of hers and call a couple of times a week to talk. She always kept a day job. Kirsten travels frequently and has a lot of friends, none of whom know about the escorting.

Dr. Peterson wrote: "The 'good experience overall' evaluation over-simplifies the complexity for her. She is hiding one life from the other."

CHAPTER VI: OTHER SEX ON THE INTERNET

There is a huge amount of sex on the Internet. Historically, this has been true of other media in their infancy. Most of the earliest films were about sex. I advise caution placing personal information such as social security numbers on any website. On the mildest level, social networks provided by Google, Yahoo, or Facebook can show personal photographs, but no nudity or prostitution. Sexy photographs could be intended to get non-professional dates. Even before the Internet, computers were used to put together compatible people for dating. I co-produced a comedy TV film about it in the 60's. Friends of mine met this way and were happily married until one of them passed away.

Now there are social networks for almost any interest you can imagine. Some beautiful women call themselves "PUBLIC PERSONALITIES" and don't provide intimate or even personal contact; much less sex, but members of their fan clubs can follow their blogs for a fee. They might do personal appearances at clubs or bars, sell calendars with photos of themselves and list items or brands they like that their fans can buy for them. Fans follow their activities, recommendations for movies or music, or words of wisdom. Nice work if you can get it, and the fans obviously get enough of a sense of connection to make it worthwhile.

As of 2004 there were numerous legitimate dating services on the Internet, some of them with a global reach, used by people searching for serious relationships or marriage. Some women who are really looking for a relationship seem to want qualities in a man that are contradictory, a combination boyfriend/girlfriend; a self-confident, powerful, sensitive, aggressive, passive, outgoing listener, a sweet and gentle master of industry. This affirms Eugene O'Neill's point in *The Great God Brown* that women claim to want nice, sweet men, but are actually attracted to bad boys.

Adult Friend Finder (AFF) is a global social network designed for adults of all genders looking for sex. They don't permit prostitution, though a hobbyist claimed he found an in-call site there. As of February 11, 2004, there were allegedly over eight million members, and the site was growing by tens of thousands per day. They may have more competition today and merely clicking on a pretty lady anywhere on the Internet might take you to AFF, willing or not. Members had to verify that they were over eighteen years old. To explore this site, I had to join up. At that time they used avatars to represent people on a two-dimensional board, and the avatars moved closer to others who were saying something attractive. In 2017 they show sexy photographs.

Members might be looking for one-on-one sex, a couple looking for a threesome, group sex, S&M, 'cybersex', in which both parties hook up webcams and watch each other, a gang bang, or whatever they can imagine. Some are 'willing, to do anything with anyone'.

AFF is now part of the Friend Finder Network, with many subsidiaries throughout the world. They have online chat rooms and hookups for each community, and email service consisting of straights, lesbians, or people looking to explore new dimensions.

To become a member in 2004, I had to write something about myself, and they asked me to submit a photo. I only had two halfway presentable digital photos of myself; one in a jacket and tie, looking like a constipated bishop, and another picture proudly holding up a trout I had caught fly fishing. I didn't submit either.

Even after fibbing to make myself sound sexier, out of the 8.3 million members of AFF, not one person was willing to return any of my emails. My sex rating was exactly: "0,000,000.00."

An early description of Adult Friend Finder focused on the friendship and love possibilities, but now it is oriented towards sex. In 2017, the site appears with racy photos and videos, but there is no public nudity. Some photographs are close to the line, a fraction of an inch from a nipple. The free sex is either in person, or over the Internet through cameras and microphones. People can see each other or a number of people online, have 'remote sex' or meet up later. Users have to pay AFF for various types of access.

I also tried out **Eroticy.com**, a similar but even racier website. Same results. I still get spam from at least one of these sites, and probably will for as long as I have the same email address.

Some of the women on these sites were extraordinarily beautiful. I saw a girl in her early twenties who could have been a model in the *Sports Illustrated Swimsuit Edition*, without the swimsuit. Her photo revealed virtually everything her gynecologist had seen. She said she was, "Looking for daddy figures to spoil her." She never mentioned money, so it was legal, as far as I know. I never interviewed her.

One warm Saturday morning, Sandy described herself as nineteen, blonde, with a great figure and pretty face. She said she was going to the beach and wanted someone to set up an orgy for that night. She wrote, "Please be between 18 and 28 and have the place and everything ready by five o'clock. Your photo gets mine."

Many women on AFF were middle-aged or older, and up to two hundred eighty pounds. None of the conversations or anything else I saw on AFF, Tinder, or Eroticy implied prostitution or any other illegal activities, but they warned people to check their local laws, and sometimes warned people not to proceed if they are in certain states.

Most young people today have grown up seeing pornography on the Internet and watching sexualized popular media. Nudity and simulated sex are common on cable television and network TV dramas and dramadies after ten pm.

In the earlier version of this book I said that attitudes towards sex would probably change due to the way it was treated on the Internet and other media. Studies show that the average age for a girl to first view pornography on the Internet is eleven, whereas it is nine for boys.

Pornography is generally devoid of realistic feelings other than lust, with the performers faking exaggerated stamina. The sound tracks are sometimes added later. Some of them show women being taken violently, and pretending to like it.

It has become routine for many young boys and girls, from around nineteen to twenty-nine, to use dating sites like Tinder.com to decide whom to 'hook-up' with, but prostitution is not allowed. These sites are extremely popular.

Girls complain that many boys who 'date' this way are rude, disrespectful, unable to bring a girl to a climax, and an increasing number of them can't get an erection. Some writers say that young men try to imitate what they saw on porn sites, which is unrealistic. Because they spend so much time online, many boys never learn how to talk about feelings, much less make love well. The girls may be left unsatisfied by sex acts that are painful and brutal. Other women say they expect the men to approach them erect and ready to perform.

There's no reason this trend can't change drastically, as trends have in the past. At Pomona College, my undergraduate alma mater, during the peak of the previous feminist movement, girls demanded that boys sign contracts with them a day before a date, spelling out any sexual activity in advance, even a touch of a breast through her clothing. One girl had consensual sex with a boy, but many months later decided that she regretted it and sued him. Sorry, but I think that's ridiculous. Don Juan would have faced the guillotine, and it wouldn't be his neck on the block!

I read about a study that showed that men are more likely to stray from their moral codes when inebriated than women are. There's a widespread assumption that it's the boy or man's agenda, to prey on a woman by getting her drunk and having sex with her, but it's a lot more complicated than that.

During the hippy era, sex was exchanged pretty freely, and hippy boys were not trying to see how many times they could 'score'. Hippy boys and girls didn't seem to be in different camps. Perhaps they were more like people in Scandinavian countries, who have traditionally had much less of a taboo against unmarried sex, and are not crazed about it as they are in the United States.

The pornography video business is gigantic. Sex videos are fairly cheap to make and collectively earn billions of dollars annually. As mentioned earlier, performers in porn films usually aren't paid much, unless they own their own companies, but they are seen and desired by so many men that they can get headliner status when they appear in strip clubs, and make decent money that way. They can also form fan clubs like public personalities do, even years after they stop performing, and people pay for their photographs. The thing about being in a porn film is that it lasts forever, and may haunt performers later in life. I heard of one girl from Japan who did a single porn film, because she had to feed her child, and years later was terrified that her parents would find out about it and be ashamed.

INTERCONTINENTAL DATING

Women all over the world are displayed on the Internet, offering to fly to a city of your choice for a fee. A lot of them are in Russia or other parts of Eastern Europe.

WEBCAMS

Webcam sites show women called 'cam girls' lying around on their beds or preening for the camera, with computer keyboards nearby. Viewers type comments trying to get them to show more. These cam shows are free, but only show a minimum, until enough money has been paid so that they go 'private', where only paid members can see the more revealing video. `Paid members buy virtual chips, like in a casino, and spend them as they wish. In other private shows the performer follows a client's directions. Many of them are in places like Russia, Amsterdam, and Eastern Europe, as well as the United States. I never spent anything so I don't know what they do. I've been told some of them just dance. The attraction is that they're performing live for viewers, or theoretically following commands. Men can select certain cam girls as their favorites and follow their schedule. People will pay for the slightest hint of sensual fantasy.

I met one woman who seemed quite spiritual, and had a private web cam. She preferred it to working at a strip club, because she didn't have to meet anyone in person. She was so attractive she didn't even have to 'act sexy'.

MASSAGE PARLOR SLAVERY?

Many ads on the Internet lead to massage parlors. **Rubmaps.com** publishes reviews of masseuses at mostly Asian massage parlors, which have proliferated in Southern California. The reviews show that most of these massage parlors provide legitimate, non-sexual massages by trained masseuses. A few offer a sexual release, usually by hand, at the end of the session for an extra fee. A few offer anything for a fee. The majority of the massage parlors don't allow anything sexual, and good massages can receive high marks by reviewers.

I saw a television show (on PBS) about an alleged sex slave massage parlor in San Francisco, a 'sanctuary city' where local police don't turn undocumented aliens over to the federal immigration police (ICE.) The show claimed to show police 'liberating' sex slaves trafficked to the U.S. from Asia. The police allegedly found used condoms on the premises. They showed a bucket of what looked like used condoms.

An elderly policeman assured the women he was there to help them. They stared at him like he was crazy. He told a middle-aged woman, "You're free now. You can leave."

To his shock the woman just stood there and started to cry. She told him her entire family back home lived on her earnings here and they would have nothing to eat without her help. She wasn't a slave. After she begged to be left alone, the bewildered policeman finally arrested her for 'dressing improperly'. She wore normal clothing, medium-length shorts and a loose t-shirt, nothing sexy or revealing. It seemed to me like a false arrest.

There has been a huge effort by government and police to stop what they call a 'trafficking' epidemic of Asian 'sex slaves'. Politicians, including Senator Diane Feinstein, and police vow to close the massage parlors and 'free' the women. I've read in numerous places that the percentage of these massage parlors that use sex slaves is, if not totally false, grossly exaggerated for political reasons. They would have to operate off the Internet, getting clients by word of mouth, which would make it difficult to compete.

I've read reviews of a number of massage parlor workers at certain clubs that do allow some level of sex, negotiated between the customer and the masseuse, but the girls work by choice. I vaguely recall a newspaper article decades ago that described a house where undocumented Mexican women were allegedly forced into sex slavery. It was in a remote area away from the city.

Some massage parlors allow a sexual release to repeat customers, with private consent between customer and masseuse. One client on a review board stopped going because he heard or read about some Asian masseuses being slaves. Most Asian massage parlors guard against it. Once I went to get a legitimate massage and the masseuse was so afraid of being accused of something she wouldn't touch me below the waist. The massage parlors that allow in-house sexual contact are subject to arrest and can be shut down. Claims that the girls were underage have been challenged as well, pointing out that the statistics were only using a list of teenagers to start with.

On July 11, 2017, the San Francisco Mayor's Status Of Women Department completed its first annual report, and stated that there were NO known instances of sex trafficking of foreign girls in the city and county, even though a third of massage parlors suggested sexual services. They defined 'trafficking' as involuntary, as opposed to free choice, verifying the point I had made in this book nearly a year earlier.

There's one exception to this but it's offshore: the Mariana Islands, which are a U.S. Territory, and a U.S. Commonwealth in the Far East. When Mitt Romney was running for President there was a widely viewed video of a businessman at a meeting with Romney eagerly describing to him the cheap labor one could get there. The video cut off his speech. President Obama later commented on it publically, in a mildly amazed way, but not like he was going to do anything about it: Asian girls are recruited there by promises of good jobs. Their passports are taken away and they have to sign a contract, which many of them can't read. In addition to the cheap labor, the prettier girls were selected and forced into a whorehouse covered by barbed wire except for the entrance. The contract that they had signed stated that they agreed to have abortions should they get pregnant during their time there.

Traditionally, police in the United States have been known to exchange sex with sex workers in exchange for protection.

CHAPTER VII: ADDICTION TO SEX AND THE INTERNET

While it seems like everyone condemns adult websites and sex workers, tens of millions of people have secrets.

Taylor used to get angry when men would try to cut her fee until another escort pointed out that some of their customers were sex addicts who see escorts five or six times a week and can't afford it.

Many people spend hours looking at pornography or sex advertising at work, which is probably not what they are being paid for, unless they are writing a book about it. Internet addiction is a condition warranting treatment and it is linked with lack of sex education. Many men and women addicted to sex on the Internet have ruined their marriages or careers.

The government has admitted there are no reliable statistics on the sex businesses. The statistics that exist are usually out-of-date and worthless. Since it is illegal or frowned upon, sex workers use pseudonyms and often conceal their professions. The real statistics are probably a lot higher than what can be quantified.

Statisticians often lump together pornography with websites that run ads for sex. In 2016, John Lee wrote in Cybersex Addiction (online) that Stanford University did a study that speculated that nine million Americans were addicted to watching sex on the Internet. Family Safe Media estimated that in 2005 and 2006, the "U.S. porn revenue exceeded the combined revenue of ABC, CBS, and NBC. "

Websites claim that men are no longer the primary viewers of online sex. Women watch it equally. College-age students have twice as many hook-ups as traditional dates, and are not afraid to talk about it. They don't necessarily involve sexual intercourse, but they might, or at least have a B.J.

Being a virgin in 2016 made one somewhat less desirable as a date or partner. One prominent website recently said that anyone who tries to give you hard statistics on the sexual revolution is not using scientifically sound methods, and is probably trying to sell you a product or stay in the news. There is no way to know how many sex workers there are, since so much of that world is underground.

In 2003 I read on a government site that the sex industry earned fifty-seven billion worldwide, which was more than professional football, baseball, and basketball combined. That's small change now. There are a lot more people engaged in the sex businesses than in professional sports so the money is distributed more evenly.

Many escorts told me they were raised in puritanical religions, which seems to be true of hobbyists too. Promise Keepers is a Christian organization of American men who promise not to have sex outside of marriage. In 2003, a website reported that twenty percent of men and thirteen percent of women accessed pornography at work. Think that's high? Fifty-three percent of Promise Keepers accessed pornography in the previous week. Several providers told me that when Promise Keepers held a convention in New York it brought a huge increase in business. The more you tell people they can't do something, the more inclined they are to do it. Psychologists call this 'reactance', a human tendency to do the opposite of unsolicited advice. Maybe an escort ad should say, "You can't have me."

Many websites try to help people fight sex addiction and Internet-related sexual addictions.

DR. PETERSON ON ADDICTION

"The issue of addiction is potent – both for providers and hobbyists. Both are often tied into a world that can cause them shame, guilt and financial loss. What role does addiction play in joining and staying a part of this world?

"The term 'addiction' has come to include a vast array of compulsive behaviors, most with identified progressive stages in their development. Schwartz (1992) noted, 'persons addicted to sex rely on repetitive erotic fantasies and acts to provide an illusion of intimacy and connectedness, in order to compensate for the emotional voids in their lives, and their lack of intimacy with others' (p. 211.)

"The strict definition of an addiction involves 'a state of psychological and physiological dependence on a specific substance arising from habitual use of that substance and resulting in physical withdrawal symptoms when the substance is removed' (Coleman, 1986, p. 343.)

"In addition to many other researchers, Schwartz (1992), Coleman (2001), and Quad land & Shuttles (1987) argue that although sexual experiences may be 'mood altering,' there is no scientific evidence that physiological dependence occurs.

"On the other hand, there are many studies (Baker, 1988; Figueroa, 1992) that provide scientific evidence and attempt to explain all addictions as a biological phenomenon. It is understood that the rewarding system of the brain is responsible for producing a satisfying effect after natural events such as eating, sleeping, having sex or catching a prey. After constant stimulation, the rewarding system of the brain becomes dependent on one unnatural/external substance for personal and emotional purposes.

"Life can become a programmed and predictable entity for many. Addiction is an inevitable phenomenon based on our life situation and the kind of world we live in."

CHAPTER VIII: STRIPPERS AND PATHETIC LOSERS

Regular customers of strip clubs affectionately call themselves "pathetic losers", or PLs. In Southern California ZBONE.COM is the most prominent website for strip club listings and reviews, but they don't give specific details of anything illegal. Any club in California that serves alcohol is subject to stricter rules, and no nudity is allowed.

Nude strip clubs supposedly don't allow sex, but have areas for private dances. The amount of contact is determined by the club, the dancer, and the local police. It sometimes changes just before an election, with much fanfare. Many of the private rooms have cameras in the ceiling and bouncers walk into the rooms to make sure nothing is going on that could cause them trouble. Dancers will be fired if they go too far. The dancer might just provide an "air dance" with no contact, or rub herself on the customer. There are code words and abbreviations for all these activities. No matter what the dancer promises, there is no guarantee that she will deliver. Some dancers will wait until the song is ending, then start sensual contact and ask for more dances. The owners usually charge dancers to work there, and dancers must sell a certain number of drinks or dances, with kickbacks to the club.

I heard of one strip club in a semi-rural community that allowed full sex in their VIP backrooms. This is not uncommon in much of the world. The customers of that club formed an Internet user's group. I joined this user group for a couple of weeks, and it was a wild ride just watching the emails.

The club charged twenty dollars per song for a topless lap dance and forty dollars for a nude dance in the main room. To get in the VIP room the customers had to buy at least three nude dances ($120.) The songs were cut short so the total time was about eight minutes. Some dancers insisted on a mandatory tip just to go to the VIP room. The degree of touching or sex was negotiated between the dancer and the customer, and ranged from allowing the customer to touch her breasts, 'feeding', or sexual intercourse.

The user group had a database where customers checked off how far each dancer went and for what price. For example, a particular redhead would perform an unprotected blowjob for an extra sixty dollars. This website sounded like an invitation to a police arrest, but every time the police visited them, the club was notified in advance. The dancers who provided sex usually charged anywhere from $40 to $400 extra, averaging $100 added on. Most of the men only had three songs and paid around $220 including the house fee, or $31.42 per minute.

Dr. Peterson wrote: "The $220 for three songs or $32.42 a minute is one of the critical differences between paying for psychotherapy or for sex. I charge $225 for 45-minute sessions, or $5.00 per minute. If I charged $31.42 per minute, my sessions would run $1,413.90 (and that does not include any dancing.)"

On the message board, a PL reminded a dancer of the price they had negotiated; something like seven hundred dollars for sex during five songs, in addition to the house fee of two hundred. He wrote online, "I won't tell anyone." She confirmed the price. He might have ten minutes with her for nine hundred dollars. He could have gone to dinner and to bed with a beautiful escort for a couple of hours for that.

They didn't seem to realize that they would attract attention to their activities by posting them on the Internet. There was finally a big crackdown.

Not all dancers at this hardcore club provided sex, but if they didn't, it was hard for them to compete. Judging by the dancers' online photographs, many of them don't look like the type you'd take home to meet your mother or even date. This is hardly the pinnacle of the provider profession.

Some of the PLs made racist remarks. One of them worked at a fast food restaurant, earning less than eight thousand a year, and needed a better job to afford his dances. Many of the men are minorities, which may not be significant.

Dr. Peterson wrote: "Many of the men are minorities" is an intriguing comment – leaving me curious about why. One could write a whole dissertation on this subject, but does it boil down to our racist society in which minorities so often do not get the opportunities and privileges to be able to raise their children to become CEO's (and therefore have the resources to pay for highly priced escorts)?"

One Pathetic Loser wrote about the club,

> *The girls are usually not as hot as the ones at the other clubs, but I usually have a great time. The girls project a certain sexual confidence. In fact, I had a UHM experience. (UHM means 'ultra high mileage') with an African-American dancer on the day shift about 2 months ago.*

(They had sexual intercourse doggie- style (from behind) on a couch, each having one foot on the floor.)

> *The price and her enthusiasm made the whole experience incredible. I hope and pray that this type of UHM fun is still available at Club [deleted.] It's a funny thing, once you experience UHM in a club, it becomes the only 'lap dance' experience that is worthwhile or desired.*

He drove over a hundred miles to get there. He told me he had eight dances, which came to three hundred forty dollars. He tipped twenty dollars, which is not considered unfair because the dancers make much more for the sessions that last five or more dances.

One PL told me that he fell in love with a dancer. He'd talk with her for two hours, then spend seven hundred dollars in the VIP room, wanting to make sure she always had a great day. She borrowed thousands of dollars from him and refused to pay it back. She told him it was her job to rip him off.

One day this club changed their policy. No more topless, only nude private dances, which cost twice as much. Members of the user group started complaining and asking about other clubs or other ways to buy sex. They realized they were overpaying compared to seeing an escort.

Some of them still preferred the strip-club atmosphere, but because of their anger at the owner's new policy they started to talk about other issues. There was a post that the owner is Iranian and brings his Iranian buddies into the club, where they harass the girls. Allegedly, the owner coerced a particular dancer into having sex with the writer's girlfriend. The PL who wrote this said he couldn't reveal the details because he was sworn to secrecy, but, "It was sad."

A PL, who said he was from India, thought the owner's friend was "lucky" if he got her. There was a flurry of email about this for a week, and it turned into a frenzy of suspicion and name-calling. It turned out that the owner they were describing hadn't even owned the club for several years. The whole story was bogus. Someone was angry about something and getting even. This is pretty typical of bulletin boards and online clubs.

One person said he had touched a dancer's private parts with his penis, without protection, and now he was panicking. He asked if someone would ask the dancer if she had HIV and put her reply on the Internet. This post received many responses. Readers suspected he was a jilted fan, an idiot, or simply "trolling" to get everyone excited.

One PL said that even though it was expensive for the time he got, he loved being surrounded by nude women, having less expensive dances with several girls, than choosing one to take into the back room. PLs pointed out that seeing an escort could be more dangerous than having sex in this club. A couple of pathetic losers were robbed by escorts or beaten up by their drivers. One PL was a martial artist and beat up a driver who tried to rob him. They recommend TER to avoid rip-offs.

One dancer at this hardcore club agreed online to meet a customer at a motel nearby. As we've seen, stripping can be a transition point for dancers to become escorts. Just as I was feeling very judgmental about this group, a PL said that he was going to cancel his membership for a while because he's in the service and his unit is shipping out to Iraq. He hoped to read some good Internet posts about his favorite club while he's gone and enjoy a few lap dances when he returns. Several PLs and dancers wished him a safe return.

The club's user group conducted a survey of what qualities were most important to them in selecting a dancer. The PLs said they cared more about the degree of sexual contact than how she looked or how nice she was.

But another survey showed that the most popular dancer was a beautiful Japanese woman who wouldn't touch the customers. They said she was a great dancer, lovely, very sweet and friendly. One day all the members were up in arms because someone had published an Internet link on Zbone showing her in a hard-core pornographic film. She had done this at some point in her past, and now it was coming back to haunt her. She was a single mother and needed the dancing money to support her child, but now she was afraid her parents in Japan would find out about it, so she quit her job. Having once done porn, she now faces the possibility of exposure anywhere in the world for the rest of her life, and as a legacy for her grandchildren.

CHAPTER IX: FROM ECONOMIC DESPERATION

ERICA

This was added to my usual query letter:

Dear Erica, I saw your ad on Eros Chicago. Your donations are larger than others, and I'm sure there are several reasons for that.

Her first response:

> *Why would you assume that the image of a top-rated call girl needs to be raised? My image is sterling within the profession. See TER and (several review boards). I am not looking for approval from the masses, as I could care less about what middle America thinks of my business.*
>
> *If you are a serious writer, I may be interested in collaborating with you on this project. I have been keeping a journal since I started in the business and fancy myself a writer as well. :-) Seriously, I am a lover of the art of prose and poetry. When I am retired, I hope to devote more time to it.*
>
> *You know, I get letters like yours from time to time. As of yet, nobody has been really serious. Why would your being married be an issue if you are only writing a book? Doesn't your wife support your craft? This concern of yours shows me that your project is most likely fantasy.*
>
> *Prove me wrong*

By the time I finished answering her questions I had written my life story. Then I addressed her objections one at a time.

Dear Erica:

You may not care about the prejudices people have but lots of other providers do. Around sixty ladies are helping me to raise their image. You say your image is sterling "within the profession" and refer me to the reviews. It's the image of the PROFESSION that I'm trying to elevate, without sugarcoating it.

> *you know, I get letters like yours from time to time. As of yet, nobody has been really serious.*

In college I had produced and directed a little theater, co-produced TV films, written screenplays, and so on. Not a major player, but worked with many who were and had some successes. I was raised in Hollywood, (actually Beverly Hills.) My father was a writer-producer who was so successful they made him Executive Producer of Paramount Studios, a title that doesn't exist in that form today. He was in charge of selecting and overseeing production of all their movies, subject to telephone approval of any costs by the 'front office' in New York. He considered it a demotion from writing. If I told anyone that when I was a kid, which I almost never did, they thought I was a liar.

> *Why would your being married be an issue?*

Erica, you are over-analyzing. I sent the central body of my letter to a lot of people. I felt that mentioning my wife might indicate that I'm not just trying to get "favors." Besides it's true. My marriage is more important to me than my interest in this field. (Hearts and flowers speech, more autobiography.)

> *Prove me wrong...*

The challenge is good for me. In fact these letters back and forth might be an interesting part of the book. Do you want a resume or bio?

> *Jim,*
>
> *I didn't expect this kind of candid response and I thank you for taking the time to answer me at length. Hmm...I feel you are actually telling the truth. :-) I know a little bit about Hollywood's writer populace after living there. Some of the*

things you said rang true because you speak with the voice of experience. Forgive my skepticism, as I have trained myself to be highly cynical whenever I make a contact such as this via Erica. I am truly a romantic idealist in disguise. Yes, in truth I do feel the ugly myths about prostitution need to be dispelled; however, I have become jaded (or older and wiser) and no longer believe I can single-handedly change the world with words. There was a time I had my poems on my site until I realized I was wasting it on the wrong audience. Any verbal input I make regarding my profession would be given with the hope that something I say can make a little difference. I will put my words into your hands so the weight of their proposed impact will be off me. There was a time when I thought I had very much to say, so much that I had the dream of being published. That has been on the far back burner for a long time. Life happens and survival takes precedence over art when you get sick of eviction notices on Christmas Eve and bill collectors chasing you all over Manhattan. You may not believe me when I say this, but I have always wanted to find the right person to talk to about my story. My story is not all related to this business as I have only been an escort for 2 years. This may or may not interest you. We may not even like each other! At the very least, I have decided to contribute to your project on the sex industry as long I can confirm somehow that you are who you say you are. Like I said earlier, I "feel" you are telling the truth, however; I need to make sure so that I don't play the fool. Well, send me your resume and bio and I promise to answer all of the questions you have about my profession. The other personal project will either happen or not. Either way, on that it's fine. When it is ready to be born, I will feel it.

Until then,

Erica

Jim,

Thanks for sharing your resume and bio with me. Normally I would check your references if I were to meet you "professionally," but this is different. I will open up, take a chance and let you interview me with the belief that your intentions are honest. So go on and ask away! You have caught me in a good mood since I just picked up a large check from a friend who is helping to fund a new venture. :-) Yes, you caught me in a very happy mood. I will be here all evening checking email periodically while I work on some designs for my new site.

Erica

(More correspondence not included.)

Dear Erica:

I'm sending you a list of questions. So far, only one or two people have answered in writing, because it is a bit of a task. Thinking about your life and motives should prove valuable to you as well as me. I'm interested in the story of someone who was tired of things like being evicted on Christmas Eve. Here's the standard query, and if it's too much of a chore, don't worry, it's easy and natural by phone.

Xoxoxo and thanks again,

Jim

I also offered her help in her literary aspirations. She replied,

Jim,

I think your perception of me is not what I was aiming for when I mentioned those few facts about my life. I am not burdened by my story and don't see writing as a chore at all. In case you didn't notice, I love to write. I actually majored in English in school. Sometimes I get emotional in the way I express things as I tend to feel deeply.

I was not feeling sorry for myself, or looking for sympathy when I mentioned the eviction. The Christmas Eve thing was my fault. While in college I decided to go to Greece after doing a summer study-abroad in Ireland. When I got home my bills had piled up and I couldn't catch up or pay my rent. This was way before I knew anything about what I am doing now. Had I known then, what I know now - I would have bought the condo I was renting instead - with cash! Hey, that's a book idea, "Get rich quick by being a hooker." (that was a joke - and I don't really use the word 'hooker')

Erica

PS I will answer a few questions now. I am really up for this. :-)

Q. Any individual stories or episodes that would be interesting?

A. *PLENTY!!!*

Q. Any especially good dates or longer-term contacts?

A. *SOME...*

Q. How did you get started?

A. *I read* The Happy Hooker *when I was 12. My mother had it hidden in her room. I knew it was there because I saw her reading it one night and caught a glimpse of the title.*

Anyway, when she finished reading it, the book ended up in a pile in the back of the closet with the rest of the far less lurid paperbacks. I proceeded to fish it out from the recesses of her closet and read it in secret everyday when I came home from school. The book stimulated me and actually turned me on. I wondered about the profession and what it would be like. Of course, I never thought I would seriously do it, being the good little Catholic girl that I was. Later in life when I was 19 and in school, I started an entertainment agency with my boyfriend. I pretended I was much older and we rented a suite at the Marriot interviewing men & women who wanted to do bachelor parties. These women stripped for us as we sat there evaluating them. It was an incredible thing that I was able to pull this off from a small hiring ad in The Reader. *One time, I went out on a job as a French Maid to a mixed crowd party in Oak Park. My boyfriend never knew. I felt sexy in that outfit prancing around bringing out champagne. That was the extent of it for a long time. The entertainment business didn't take off like my other idea did, which was selling information about job opportunities by placing hiring ads. This other business really took off and I was in it from age 19 (1988) - 23 (1993.) Starting with borrowed money on a credit card, my boyfriend and I made close to one million in our best year. That business propelled me into many new frontiers. None of which had to do with the sex industry. We left Chicago and I lived in Malibu and in Santa Monica. I drove a red convertible Jensen Healy on PCH. Life was good. I had a PR agent who I met through my biological mother's (I found her at 21) ex-husband (he was in the band XXXX) and did two talk shows about my life...that part is a very long story.*

Before I fast track years ahead, I will say that the business was lost due to a break up with my business partner/boyfriend who I left for an eccentric German celebrity photographer who convinced me I was selling out. A mail fraud investigation and front-page article in the business section of the XX XXXX into my business helped me believe him. I divested myself from the business leaving what was left to my ex. I began taking acting classes and art classes and later moved to Europe with the photographer to experience the Bohemian lifestyle - while I spent all of my money. With that in mind (no money) I lived in NY and continued to live an artsy life while going to school and living on student loans with an occasional freelance graphic design job here and there. (While in LA after breaking from mail order I learned graphic design at UCLA...I did my "Erica" site) Life was good. All the while I was in NY I was in AA and had much success in recovery. I was doing well in school and though I was poor and getting evicted on X-mass eve, I liked my life in NY. I got invited by a female photographer friend, whose boyfriend was a doctor, to go to Monte Carlo. I was ecstatic. It was there overlooking the French Riviera that I had a slip. I started drinking again. This was a bad, bad thing. When I got back to NY I met an artist who claimed to be Salvador Dali's nephew - but turned out to be a coke dealer. I got hooked and left my studio apartment to move in with him. Fortunately that didn't last and I left him after five months to come home to Chicago to get sober again and stay with my parents. I was happy to be in a safe place, but my pride was wounded. I had traveled the world and now I was back in my old neighborhood. The neighborhood I couldn't wait to get out of, living on my parent's back porch on a tiny bed. I felt I had lost everything and all the experience I had was for nothing. Slowly I worked my way out of this apathetic state and started going to AA meetings again. This fixed my spiritual state, but I didn't like being broke in Chicago. In NY it is almost cool to be a starving artist – in Chicago it is not. Besides, I didn't have the art scene and friends I had in NY. In fact, I had nothing familiar as I didn't fit in Chicago at all. I left there so long ago... My thoughts of working as an escort came back - these thoughts always came when I was struggling financially in NY. I never acted on them in NY, but in Chicago, there was nothing interesting for me to try or do. I got a job at a small agency doing graphic design, but the projects were nothing like the fashion and art industry I had loved in NY. You know the cattle industry is big here and the jobs all seemed to revolve around ads for beef. I was sickened!!!!!!!!I began surfing the net and researched the escort business. I had always loved research and this was very exciting for me.

I soon went on an interview with a top agency and was offered a job immediately. I never worked for them or had any intention of working for them. I was merely collecting information. I took all I learned from that interview back to my research on the net. When I put it all together, I realized I could do it on my own. I created the 'Erica' image and the 'Erica' website. After placing a free post on bigdoggie.net, my email was overflowing. I was shocked that there were so many people willing to pay me for sex. It took me over a month and a half to go out on my first call. I was still not sure about this. It scared me and I was nervous to start. Finally, I decided to do it. On June 28th, 2000 I went out on a house call to see a computer programmer who I had corresponded with for a while via email. It was not the 'turn-on' I thought it would be from reading The Happy Hooker - and was nothing like the hot fantasies I had about doing it all those years. It was weird. I felt like I was an observer as I did the deed in his huge house in the burbs. I left with enough money to go out and get an apartment! I knew this was my track to getting back on my feet again and I needed a very fast-track. In only three months I outgrew that little dump apartment I was so happy to get and moved to a penthouse suite in a chic hotel in Chicago. There I saw exclusive clientele - no more going out to them for a lousy 1000 bucks.

Not long into this I got an exclusive Mistress arrangement with a guy from the Silicon Valley...it goes on from there. That apartment was amazing.

Q. How did your perceptions change over time?

A. I see this business as a spider's web that one can easily get trapped in. The money is ridiculous if you are good. How else can a woman make a six-figure income working way less than part time without having to use her brains (except in the marketing?) This realization has given me the impetus to begin my exit strategy. Obviously, I can't do this forever, nor do I want to. I don't want to be doing this a year from now.

Q. How did this world change your life?

A. I have become friends with other women in the business. These women are the most honest and real people I have ever met. I think we are kindred spirits. I am also financially secure and can do just about anything I would like to do with my life now.

Q. How do you feel about it? Things you like and things you don't like.

A. At first it made me feel wonderful because I loved having money again. I missed money! Now I realize I don't like the secrecy of having to hide what I do. This is a huge price to pay for $.

Q. .Do you plan to quit at some point? Do you have plans for what you will be doing in five years?

A. Yes, I am planning on quitting now. I need to have a business that will generate close to what Erica makes. This is tough, but I am trying some new things. In five years I would like to be married with a family.

Q. Do you tell friends, family, girl- or boyfriends about your profession?

A. Absolutely not!!!! My family thinks my graphic art business is finally paying off. I hate to lie to them.

Q. What was your family like as a child?

A. I had an idyllic childhood. I was adopted at birth by two very loving working-class Irish Catholics. All was fine until I hit my teens when I began drinking and smoking pot. My parents never accepted my acting out and there was so much turmoil and violence that I moved out at 16. I moved in with the boyfriend I started the business with at 19. My teenage years were not normal and I am sorry for this.

Dr. Peterson wrote: "When Erica describes her childhood as idyllic and then talks about drinking and smoking pot as a teenager, having such turmoil and violence that she was compelled to move out at 16, and struggling with alcoholism for much of her life, the concept of 'idyllic' is called in to question. It seems many of these escorts downplay the true trauma they have experienced as children. Perhaps the reality was so painful that they have authentically disconnected from the memories."

Q. Do you remember what you felt like just before your first date? A nervous "first time" where you felt butterflies in your stomach before meeting a client?

A. I was beyond terrified. I nearly turned back three times.

Q. How do different clients behave and how does that affect what you do?

A. Because I screen so carefully, most of my clients are so thrilled to finally meet me that they do nothing but dole out compliments and tell me I am a Goddess, etc. I still love the flattery!

Q. Ever back out of a date because you didn't like the person?

A. Yes, If I am grossed out by their looks I tell the client I just got my period! OOPS...BYE!

Q. Do you know of other providers who have had quite different experiences, including bad reactions to this profession? Any thoughts on how they might answer the above questions.

A. My GOD, my sponsor (yes, my sponsor is in recovery too - and is also an escort - another long story) is into a different marketing approach. She places ads in The Reader and sees men for less money, but sees many more men. Some of this lower-end clientele have tried to not pay her fee or have even stolen from her!!! She is very different than me in so many ways. She is a shrewd businesswoman and is a workaholic. Me I prefer not working at all! She told me she used to host a talk show in Florida. She sees her clients as guests. She loves to learn from each one, and when she is finished with him - "on to the next" she says!

Q. When an escort starts out, is it typical for an experienced escort or agent to tell her how to operate? What would they tell her? Not just 'take a donation up front', but safety, techniques, and how to build a clientele?

A. I think the typical story goes like that. A girl starts at an agency, or starts dancing or something. In my case, I think I am truly an anomaly. I read all about it on the net. There is so much out there that is instructional if you know what you are looking for!

Q. How does one avoid law enforcement? How much and in what way has LE harassed you or friends?

A. I am so careful that it is not a huge concern of mine - but I do assume any call or email could be a set up, so I grill everyone!!! My sponsor has been busted twice last year and had three close calls in the past two weeks from her ad in The Chicago Reader.

Q. Can you describe a particularly funny date?

A. I would have to think about that. There are many funny stories and nothing jumps out to me.

Q. How do you refer to clients, as 'Dates'? 'Customers'? 'Clients'? 'Johns'?

A. My dialogue has to be realistic. I call them 'friends' or 'clients' never 'johns' or 'customers'. I don't know anyone who uses the word 'john'.

Q. What do clients talk about:

    A. When they call for appointments?

A. They talk about themselves. I ask all the ??'s.

B. When they call and pretend they want appointments?

A. They don't answer my ??'s and I tell them BYE!

C. When you actually meet?

A. I usually ask them about their work and go from there. We can discuss politics, art, history, the weather...anything. One tenured philosophy professor friend reads Rilke poems to me. I really enjoy his company. I am not pretending to be interested like with some. Oh funny....yes! There was a guy who owned a company that made the equipment for upper GIs! Over dinner he told me all about these devices. I had to pretend that he was as fascinating as the best of them. When we were having dessert he warned me earnestly, not to ever be the last one to have an upper GI since the machine is never clean after the third exam of the day! I wanted to throw up over my crème brulee!!!!!

Q. Do you usually go to dinner, etc.? Like I can imagine them saying how beautiful you are, how rich they are, the weather, traffic, blah blah blah. Sports? Business or politics?

A.   Again, yes we talk about anything and everything. The difference between a paid date and a blind date is that I will always act amused and enamored even if I am really making a shopping list in my head.

Q.   Tell me about the first time you had sex.

A. That's personal!

ALEX – AN ARTIST

Alex is a painter, specializing in portraits. She is very sensual and accustomed to nudity, a free spirit. She also does sensual massage.

Alex puts herself in a different frame of mind when giving a massage.

> *No matter what's going on I slap self-acceptance on myself thirty seconds before I meet a client.*

She has to accept herself before she can be giving to another.

> *If I'm meeting a friend I might be self-critical about my hair or makeup, but not for sensual*

massage or escort, because no one cares about that.

You might think she'd be more concerned about her appearance with her clients, which is true of many providers.

As a teenager Alex was made to do things she didn't want to do. Between the years of eighteen to twenty-two she felt she had to do whatever men said. Guys would ask for something, and if she said, "No" they asked, "Well give me one reason why not." She couldn't think of a reason, so she did what they wanted.

Some men would even ask her to service another guy. Finally she got pushed too far. Other women helped her realize she could stand up for herself, and she finally realized she could say "No."

Long before she was an escort, the world always thought she was for sale. Men always followed her.

She said,

> *At twenty two I was wondering, "Why did old men think I wanted to be their friend?" There would be a guy following me in the park, and behind him another guy. I didn't know why they thought I was for sale. Cars would pull up with men making whistling or clicking sounds, trying to get my attention.*

Alex describing herself as 'very sensual' must be an understatement.

She started working as a portrait artist on the beach in California. It was hard to make a living as an artist. Her friends in the art world want her to work for free.

In her mid-thirties Alex saw a psychic who told her to study massage. She made a serious study of it and works on lines of therapeutic energy in her massage, but she always understood that sexual energy was a pressure that needed to be released. No talk was necessary.

She started by putting an ad in a paper. She is not an escort as such and her price is low, because she feels that with a higher price the man is in control, which she won't allow. She never worked for an organization and her glowing Internet reviews get her plenty of clients.

Alex charges a hundred per hour for massage or two hundred for escort. I presume 'Escort' means providing more service. She said, "Some men say things like: "Bend down," "Get down."

Alex doesn't want to be told what to do so she gets the more passive men who want to receive. She only does what's comfortable for her and will often turn down clients on the phone. She lets them know in advance what will happen and what will not.

Alex enjoys the work, the affection and appreciation, but she said,

> *Most women are doing it for economic reasons, even if they enjoy it. People work three jobs and still can't pay the rent.*

She finds it isolating and it makes a relationship difficult.

I asked if she was nervous when she first started, and she said she wasn't. She has always been poised.

She said,

> *You can be any age and any look. The world is looking for compassion and the feminine touch. You can do it till ninety. Superficially, the client wants compassion, love for a moment, the human touch, but it's really about being accepted.*

She isn't critical of her clients but she knows one masseuse who lectures everyone on eating and exercise. Another masseuse wants to be pleased exactly right.

She lives in two separate worlds, as an artist and a masseuse. She doesn't share erotic massage in the art world, although her art-world friends know what she does on the side. She says it is fairly common for artists to do escort work to supplement their income.

Alex keeps her life calm and her mind free. She has a daughter and is available for others' needs. She had a happy childhood, loving and accepting, with no traumatic experiences. She plans to get out of massage and into the pet business.

Dr. Peterson wrote: "She describes the work as isolating and '...it makes a relationship difficult', but she also says that she enjoys it. What a difficult balance of feelings this must be for her. I was powerfully touched by her comment that, 'The world is looking for compassion and the feminine touch'. It seems she can provide the appearance of compassion and love, and her clients settle for this, but there is nothing superficial about a human need for these things."

Dr. Peterson was also skeptical about Alex's happy childhood.

CHAPTER X: DEVON – A ROLLERCOASTER LIFE

Devon's interviews are partly by phone and partly email.

She is Canadian. I wrote: "Your clients have commented on your intelligence, so perhaps you can share some of that with me."

She wrote back,

> *I would be happy to answer questions for you, provided that you protect my identity. While my friends and family know and accept (with worries) my choices, I still require discretion for my clients.*
>
> *I'm glad that somebody is trying to round out the image of service providers. I am not trying to minimize the legitimate problems, which can occur, but there is certainly a more positive side to the business which is often not publicly recognized.*
>
> *Good luck with your endeavors, and keep me posted.*

Devon is an extremely cute twenty-seven year-old brunette. She speaks crisply, and, like most Canadians, is very polite. She was raised in what she says is a "typical family, slightly dysfunctional." Her mother drank and her father was physically abusive. Both were emotionally distant and cruel. Devon is reluctant to be judgmental and sounds very calm. Her mother told Devon that she, "should have shit her into the toilet instead of giving birth." Devon thinks her parents probably had an affect on her self-esteem.

When she was seventeen, she developed bulimia and anorexia. She left home when she was eighteen, got in a treatment program and overcame it. She had never dated and became a Jehovah's Witness, where she met her first boyfriend. He raped her. This was especially traumatic, since she was a virgin.

He apologized, promising it would never happen again. She believed him and stayed with him. After two and a half years of abuse, she went to the church elders and reported that he had raped her a dozen times. She was tiny, weighing a hundred pounds, 5'2" and he was 6'4". She hated it and had no other experiences with men. He used brutal force, leaving her unconscious and bruised.

The elders said she couldn't "pass judgment" and told her not to do anything about it.

She pressed charges anyway. She doesn't hold it against the entire Jehovah's Witness faith, just that particular congregation.

Devon met a man who helped her get out of that sick relationship and they became engaged. According to her religion you are not supposed to go to college, but she had broken away from the congregation when they would not support her on the rape charges. She is still very spiritual but not religious.

She wrote:

> *I began when I was 23. I was in University, and engaged to be married. I was working as a fulltime waitress to pay the bills (rent, food, etc.) I was fortunate enough to be on scholarship. We had recently moved and my fiancé was only able to find part time work, which paid about $200 a month. So the bills were being paid by me. I became very ill and exhausted and was barely able to muster the strength to make it to school, much less work fulltime. Our savings were running dry, and I was far too stubborn to take out a loan or accept government funding. (I have never owed a penny, and it would kill me if I ever did.)*
>
> *I was half-joking when I suggested to my boyfriend that I become an escort. I was expecting him to freak out and run out looking for work for*

himself. Instead he reluctantly agreed that it wasn't a bad idea.

I don't know if I made the call to an agency out of anger or curiosity, but I was asked to go in for an interview the following day.

My then fiancé was the only man I had ever been intimate with. I'm sure that a part of me was interested in experimenting a little before I settled down.

But partly, it was vindictive. She probably wouldn't have done it if she hadn't been so shocked and angry at her boyfriend's response.

She called an agency in the newspaper, went in the next day, and before she had a chance to reconsider she was being prepared for her first client. They brought her in to meet other girls. There were five in an apartment. Guys could come in and view them and decide whom they wanted to see.

She was terrified, but the other girls were supportive of her. They wanted it to be nice, so for her first client one of the other girls arranged for Devon to be with one of her own regulars. He was around twenty-four years old, in the military, and handsome. She didn't know anything about sex except what she had learned from her fiancé, but the clients told her what they liked.

The agency gave her no choice on what kind of clients she saw or what they did with her. They didn't care what the client was like. A man tried to strangle her and attacked her at knifepoint. The madam and the madam's husband were in the next room. She was fighting and screaming, but they didn't come in because they didn't want to be revealed as the owners of the place. They tried to book her with the same man again. Sometimes she had to see clients who were drunk or on drugs.

This was near Vancouver, where it is legal to work as a prostitute but illegal to run a brothel. She felt that the law is probably intended to prevent girls from being forced into sex.

As long as she was at the agency, she hated herself. The first month she would be shaking like an epileptic when she saw clients. She was so disgusted and nervous it made her sick. She lost so much weight she was skin and bones.

Then Devon decided to go out on her own. She changed her name and put an ad in the *Buy and Sell Newspaper*. She didn't post a picture, just an honest self-description.

> *Eight weeks later, I became independent. I despised the work, but the income was good. I was determined to set up a 'nest egg' for my fiancé and myself so that we would have something to fall back on if I ever became ill again. The agency had set the parameters of how I had done my job, and I continued in that manner. My self-esteem plummeted, and I began to feel that this was all I was capable of. I stopped going to university, and began to work up to 84 hours a week. I invested every penny in joint accounts, and lived meagerly. I wanted to get out of the business so badly that I would take any client at any time, just to be that much closer to my goal. I had absolutely no social life, and was completely neglecting all that was once important. I was focused on establishing a base for a good life with my fiancé.*

> *A year and a half later, I was in for the shock of my life. My fiancé had run off with another woman and completely wiped out all of the savings. The credit cards were racked up, and new ones were maxed out as well. Apparently I had been so busy with work (he booked the appointments), that I didn't spend any time with him anymore. He admitted to having a drug problem (heroin, cocaine, and crack), and said that he had seen over 70 different providers in the past 2 months. He had bought them expensive jewelry, trips, clothes and other gifts, and there was nothing left. In fact there were debts to be paid.*

> *I write this in part because rather than making me bitter (okay I was angry for a couple of*

weeks), it taught me something important. If I couldn't value myself, how could I expect anybody else to? We need to live for today. I had been sacrificing my life in the present for some abstract future. In the meantime, my fiancé took the exact opposite route. He had spent all my hard work in a couple of months. He had nothing to show for it, but I'm sure that he had a terrific time.

Gradually, her life went from black, to grey, to white. The main thing was leaving the agency, but later the Internet became important, allowing her to be much more selective, choose her hours, and screen out drunks, rude men, or men on drugs.

Devon became totally in control. She set her priorities, went back to the University, studied clinical psychology, minored in Women's Studies, and got a degree in Fitness and Nutrition.

She has a new boyfriend, who despises what she does. She wants to get out of it in time, because of him, but she likes her job. She's met good people and taken extended trips. Sex is a small side of it with her. Many of her clients don't have sex with her, and they have never even seen each other naked. They pay her strictly for companionship. She had offers from law firms and the government just to show clients around. They offered her two thousand dollars for eight hours, plus a thousand a day allowance for spending money, but she turned them down to keep her freedom. Devon likes having complete control; possibly as a reaction to the traumatic hell she went through when she first went into sex work.

She wrote:

I have had the opportunity to travel to some wonderful places with clients, and see many things, which I wouldn't have otherwise had the opportunity to. I have been to several countries, stayed in some of the finest hotels, and traveled via business class or private jet.

One of my clients makes a point of booking me for a full day or two every six months. The purpose of this is to spoil me and take care of me. I get to make the schedule and we can do or go wherever I please. There is no physical intimacy unless I request that he gives me a massage. These "dates" began when I was involved with a man, and was so busy working that I hadn't taken time off to go to a movie, play golf, or go hiking in over a year. This client wanted to make sure that I was getting out to enjoy life, at least a little, while still bringing in an income.

One of the best things about working in the manner I do is my independence. I schedule my work around my life. Family, friends, studies, volunteering, working out, and a wide array of other things can take precedence. I am not willing to give up that freedom at this point.

The majority of the men I see are long-term clients. I have been working as a service provider for 4 years now, and I still see persons whom I met in my first week. I have built up a rapport with most of my clients, and it makes the experience much more enjoyable. We know each other well, have terrific conversations, and even discuss problems we may be having. It is more of a friendship than a business relationship. (Yes, I know, I need to set better boundaries. But that just isn't me.) They do things like pick up groceries for me and giving me massages.

She has promised her boyfriend she will quit within two years. If it were more socially acceptable she might not have the pressure. Family and friends know what she does. She feels friends should know about it and she said she cannot lie. She also works as a fitness and nutritional consultant.

The actual sex isn't that enjoyable. If they have sex, she doesn't pretend to climax and she openly tells people she's not that sexual.

Escorting has helped her self-esteem. She said,

It is wonderful that they want to pay money to be with me.

She's not pretending to be someone she's not and enjoys making people happy. Her clientele includes people aged twenty to forty-five, all nationalities and social statuses. You would never have thought they'd utilize her services. The men are often business professionals, good-looking, successful, with very good personalities, caring. Her sessions range from half an hour to two days long.

She said,

> *You attract what you're looking for.*

Devon has evolved to the point where she refuses to be treated badly. A couple of guys tried to be rude to her and she put them in their place. They apologized and offered to give her a massage or go out and buy her flowers.

She knows that when she quits working as an escort she will need other things to substitute for the self-esteem she's used to getting on the job. Other than the fact it's not conducive to raising a family and a one-on-one relationship, it's ideal. She never works more than five days a week, and sometimes works short hours. Longer sessions are preferred, which typically include going to dinner or a movie. She worked three days the week I interviewed her.

After the interview I emailed her three questions:

1. TER says you have breast implants. At what point did you do that, and did it have an immediate effect on how you were perceived?

2. Have you always been a woman who men were obviously attracted to? Some women know they are physically attractive, but it doesn't help their self-esteem much.

3. You said you were shaking like a leaf the first month. I imagine that sex would have been pretty lame for the guys too. Would you agree? Or do you think they sometimes enjoyed it?

She wrote back,

> *In response to your latest questions, I actually got my breast augmentation several years prior to becoming an escort. The root of my self-esteem issues stem from my mother constantly telling me how ugly I was. I was by no means flat-*

chested; I just got tired of her always laughing that I was "A carpenters delight. Flat on both ends, and never been nailed." I was working as a waitress at the time, and didn't even notice much of an increase in tips after the surgery.

As for how I am perceived with large breasts, I actually find it a cross between humorous and irritating. From my client's point of view, they like them, but it is not typically an issue. My main complaint is the first impressions that I get. The stereotype of the general population is that large-breasted women are dumb. People often just assume that I have a substandard IQ, and are usually taken aback by the fact that I can carry on an intelligent conversation.

I still have major issues with the way I look. I suppose that work has helped me a lot in this matter though. I still never look at myself in the mirror, but I am a little more willing to accept the possibility that a man may find me physically attractive.

As for self-esteem in other areas of my life, I seem to be doing well. I know that I am competent and ambitious, and I have never not met a goal that I have set for myself. I have wonderful friends and family, and I know that I am a good person. People are attracted to my personality, first and foremost.

As for men always being attracted to me, I would have to agree with that. But I really don't think that it is appearance-oriented. Even when I was much younger (and through my anorexic stages where I was definitely not physically attractive), there was never a shortage of men. I do have a terrible time meeting females to spend time with though. I think that has much more to do with my personality. I am EXTREMELY low maintenance. I never wear makeup, don't own any hair products besides shampoo and conditioner (not even a blow dryer), and I love physical activity. I'm not afraid of getting dirty, and I love doing things like playing soccer in the mud. I think that the attraction with men is more of a "girl next door" or "just one of the guys" things, with a later realization that hey, she's a girl! I hate gossip, despise shopping, and only own two pairs of shoes.

As for shaking in the beginning, I think that some of the men did enjoy that. The agency had a knack for not attracting the type of men I would choose to see. Some of them really got off on the whole power/control issue. But that wasn't the case for all of them. Some (even at the agency) would just pay the fee, and not want to make me do something that I wasn't comfortable with. They were more the type of men who respected women, and yes I felt terrible, but they felt bad, because they felt that they were exploiting me or putting me in a bad situation.

I hope that this helps a little. And as always, if you have any further questions, don't hesitate to contact me again. As well, I would love it if you could let me know when you get this book/screenplay published, as I would love to see how it turns out.

Have a great week!

Devon

Dear Devon:

Thanks again, I'm glad you weren't offended by my questions. I will keep you informed about the book. It's hard to believe that you would doubt your goods looks, but I am reminded that anorexic women also see themselves as fat.

Later, she wrote:

I set limits on what I will do and never work when someone I love needs me. I have taken the time to complete my studies, go on vacations with friends, and I see a psychiatrist for 2 hours every week to help me keep my life in check. I rest when I need to, work when I should, and have re-prioritized my life. The clients I see treat me wonderfully. They have taught me that I am a worthwhile person who deserves to be loved, and is capable of whatever I put my mind to. They believe in me, which is more than I used to be able to say of myself. In a strange way, they have given me my self-esteem, rather than stripped me of it.

My clients tell me that the day I quit will be one of the happiest and saddest days of their lives. They will be so relieved and happy that I have moved on with my dreams and goals, but they will be sad at not being able to see me anymore. Many of them have asked whether I would be willing to accept them as clients in my new business so that they can continue to see me on a friendly and different professional basis.

My conceptions of this line of work have changed. Prior to beginning, I would have thought that the type of people who utilized these services would be the old/unattractive/social misfits and perhaps on the other end of the spectrum, the wealthy, looking to indulge in something taboo.

At the agency this certainly proved true. But I have learned that the type of clientele that you attract depends on you and how you advertise. Most of the people I see are 20-45 years old. They come from all walks of life, and if I were to look at them on the street, I would never guess that they would be 'the type'. They tend to be attractive, sweet, intelligent and a whole array of other positive qualities. The type of man who should have no trouble getting a date, or marrying the woman of his dreams. I have learned that many of them are lonely. They lack intimacy in their lives, or more often than that, they feel misunderstood. Many of them just need somebody to talk to. Somebody who won't judge them, somebody to listen. In a strange way, many of them are looking for a therapist to tell them that they are normal, that they aren't alone, that they are worthwhile. (Seeing a service provider and getting that seems more masculine and acceptable than going to an actual therapist.) Some long for a touch, though it isn't a sexual need anywhere near as often as it is just needing to be held.

On the flip side, a few men are just bored with a marriage. Their wife may be their best friend, but the sexual aspect is no longer existent. I have been told a number of times that this sort of thing saves their marriage. The men need the sexual aspect from somewhere. The other 95% of the marriage pie is perfect, but they need to fill the void, or they become angry, irritable, resentful and an array of other negative things, which destroys the remaining good parts of their relationship.

And finally, a few of the clients are just too busy for a "real relationship" and the head games that go along with it. They are looking for a "no strings attached" sort of thing.

Have a wonderful week!

I've spent most of my life as a dramatist in one form or another, creating fictional characters that face crises and transform themselves. That's the difference between fact and fiction. People rarely change, but Devon did.

Tennessee Williams said that the only unforgivable sin is deliberate cruelty. I think her mother's deliberate cruelty is unforgivable, but Devon's ability to forgive is the only way she will ever find peace.

Sometime later she wrote:

I can honestly say that I am happier today than I ever have been. There is a tranquility and peace when you begin to figure out who you are, and can honestly say that you like yourself. I wouldn't trade where I am now for anything. Nor would I change any of the less than wonderful things in my past. Those helped to shape who I have become, and serve to keep me grounded. My past also provides a stark contrast to where I am today, and without it I may have less appreciation for all the wonderful people in my life, my health and the world in general.

Dr. Peterson wrote: "If she defines an alcoholic mother and abusive father, both who were emotionally distant and cruel, as 'slightly dysfunctional' it would be like saying that Hitler was a little controlling. In the beginning of the interview her desperation spills off of each page. "I despised the work." "My self-esteem plummeted," seem to only hint at the intensity of her struggles. This woman describes her mother as saying that she "should have shit her into the toilet instead of giving birth," and later she says, "The root of my self-esteem issues stem from my mother constantly telling me how ugly I was." But as we read her comments and her insights she becomes far from superficial. She articulates beautifully the difference of the three types of men she encounters. The man who is lonely, lacks intimacy, feels misunderstood, wants somebody to talk to, wants somebody who won't judge him and who will listen is the same man who (or woman) who often comes into therapy. The men who are 'just bored' probably have other significant issues, and need more than this 'five percent' sexual aspect – but would never acknowledge this to themselves or others. The few men who are 'too busy' and want no strings attached could be just the opposite. That is, they are terrified of dependency and 'strings' but have an unconscious longing for a safe dependency. Rather than risk getting hurt, they deny any need at all.

"Yes, Devon seems to have gotten to the position where she can let go of hating and blaming her mother – she seems to have found some peace in spite of the trauma. She is the exception to the rule."

CHAPTER XI: ROSE – A TANTRIC GODDESS OVERCOMES GUILT

Rose was in her late forties and considered herself 'polyamorous', meaning she can be loving to many people.

I met Rose long after she started using Tantra in sensual massage. Tantra is a complex Eastern spiritual practice, containing many mental and physical exercises. Yoga is an offshoot of it. It uses concentrated visualization to prolong sexual arousal, one of many steps to reach enlightenment. It is probably best known in America as a method of prolonging sexual arousal for a very long time.

When **Goddess Rose** first started doing sensual massage she would lay down on the bed and cry with shame.

> *Dear Jim, You are a guardian angel to the goddess. We sisters pray for more men like you. Support the female energy and you will be empowered.*

> *Love, Goddess Rose*

Rose works out of her home and is not secretive about her profession. Her sixteen-year-old daughter knows what she does and was raised to think of sex as spiritual. Rose would be proud if her daughter followed in her footsteps but she wants to go to a university instead.

> *Dear Jim, I'm an avid endorser of removing our culture's ingrained programming regarding oppression against women and their powerful sexuality.*

She was destitute and depressed when she started doing sensual massage. She was divorced, had lost custody of her children, and was coming out of a religious cult. The company of men was therapeutic. She always thought potential clients were cute on the phone and loved to talk to them. Her heart goes out to nerds and fat kids. One man was four hundred pounds and his penis had atrophied to almost nothing. She worked on him a long time and finally he said, "Rose, you are the nicest person I ever met in my life."

I taped the interviews in her apartment in a gated community with waterfalls and lush landscaping. A natural comedienne, she often augmented her answers with gestures.

Q: How do you feel about becoming so prominent in Tantra?

A: *I always wanted to be an actress. I didn't get there but this work has turned me into a pseudo-celebrity. Maybe I wanted to be an actress because I wanted to feel important. I didn't feel important when I was growing up. I've always been a care-taker."*

Q: If people are in trouble, you try to help them?

A: *Yeah, I'm always taking care of people. I was a nurse. I was from a broken home. I was taking care of my first husband."*

Q: How did you fall into that?

A: *I went straight from high school to taking care of him. I was eighteen years old, having a baby.*

Q: How did you live?

A: *I cooked and cleaned and picked up all his clothes. His parents took care of us financially. Then I took care of Terry, my second husband. I went to nursing school and I went into acting for awhile. I had three more children with Terry and we were involved in a cult. We didn't believe in psychology so we didn't handle my co-dependency. I didn't even know that I had it.*

Q: Tell me about co-dependency.

A: *Well I learned about co-dependency from a book called* Women Who Love Too Much. *I fit right into the experiences and traits.*

Q: What are they?

A: *It's women that come from broken homes.*

Q: And you do?

A: *Yes. Alcoholic parents that I had to take care of. Co-dependent women had to think about their survival as children. You REVERSE the role and take care of the parents, so you missed out on your childhood. You'll find a lot of women in Tantra and sensual massage are co-dependent. A lot of women in the escort business might just be doing it for the good income.*

Q: You seem very comfortable with yourself.

A: Yeah. I wasn't at one time.

Q: Were you working as a nurse when you were married?

A: No, when I got married I stopped working. I was pregnant most of the time and I wanted to be home with the kids.

Rose and her girlfriend Angie decided to look into massage and wondered if they could provide massage "without the happy ending" [a hand-job.]

A: I put an ad in a paper. In those days you couldn't list your measurements or even use the words 'love' or 'I'm pretty', just 'therapeutic massage'. But if you advertised in the paper and it wasn't a chiropractic office, spa or clinic, the clients knew what was up. The phone was ringing off the hook. These were the days before 10,000 women were advertising.

Q: Is that an educated guess?

A: No, about five years ago a woman was trying to form an alliance and hired an attorney, and he actually did a census. And it was six thousand when the Internet just started.

Q: So it could be twenty thousand now.

A: It could. When you go on City-Vibe or Exotics, there used to be like ten women in escort, one or two in Tantra, and I'd be one of them. Now you scroll and scroll and there's these twenty year-olds that look like Penthouse models!

Q: When you started doing these massages your intention was that it would not be sensual.

A: Right. I had this very conservative side to me from the cult. So every phone call we'd get was, "Hi. I saw your ad. Do you give a really happy ending? Well thank you very much – click." We actually got a couple of sessions. They thought that they would come over and talk us into it. We would give them massages in our tight jeans, our boots and our tucked in T-shirts, fully clothed, and put the guy on the table. It was so clinical. They would offer twenty dollars or fifty dollars more for us to take our tops off. And I would say [in a sympathetic voice], 'Oh I'm sorry.

We can't do that!' [Laughs.] My nursing job was very depressing. I was taking a woman to get dialysis, being around all these people on dialysis and people dying. I was also very depressed because the kids were gone. I didn't know what to do, so I finally gave a sensuous massage.

Q: Were you nervous at first?

A: Yes! I was shaking. I felt like I was Eve in the Garden of Eden. And I was taking that apple. You know, as soon as my hand went down there it was like, "What am I doing?" And it wasn't so bad. It was like you go to the doctor and you go "Ah" and then the needle comes out. And you feel, "Oh that wasn't so bad." And then I did another one. One day Angie and I were talking, and both acting kind of nervous. I said, "Angie, I did it"' She said, "So did I!" [Laughs.] She said, "And I've been meaning to tell you."

I said, "Me too." It was like we robbed a bank or something.

Q: And she was seeing three guys and had a sugar daddy?

A: Yeah. Angie was really cute and she had all these guys she was seeing and was trying to hide them from her sugar daddy. And we were feeling guilty about sensual massage. There's the law, and whatever. You can have two sugar daddies, or three lovers in a week. But as soon as someone hands you some money suddenly it's evil. The only reason for the law issue is because they can't tax it.

Q: And from there?

A: She felt guilty and she stopped. She also had one of her boyfriends get on the telephone with her sugar daddy. I said, 'Are you out of your mind?' It was like $1,500 a month for that apartment. He stopped paying and we had to leave the apartment.

Q: Did you work at home?

A: Yes. I still didn't take off my T-shirt. They'd take their clothes off and ask, 'Am I the only one that's going to get naked?' And I'd say, 'Yeah'. [Laughs.] I was just too shy at that time. So I saw this girl Renée, who was a mortgage broker, and while she was waiting for a deal to go through she'd just do sensuous massage. She was classy, fascinating, poised, very pretty, and she worked in lingerie. I thought, my God, I can do this without judging myself. So I did it, and raised my price. The next level was, "Do you give massages on a table or on a bed" As more women got into the business a little more had to be provided because of the competition. Then I changed to Tantra.

Q: How did you get into that?

A: When I was doing sensual massage certain male clients said, "You should get into this thing called 'Tantra'. Tantra lovers were able to hold off ejaculation and last a long time, and I had a strong interest in it. I went to workshops, and came into my own style. I was one of the first. I had a picture taken with my face down. I was doing a lot of kickboxing, really in shape and tan. I would make them laugh. So I was kind of special. They were saying, "Oh, you're so beautiful." I'd say, "In ten years, my husband never made me feel this good." And it was true.

Q: How did Tantra differ?

A: In Tantra I went to completely nude, because I would offer something called a 'bath ritual'. You put the client in a bath. It's like a Baptism... a Tantric Baptism. I'm kidding. [Laughs.] That was in our workshop.

Q: Was the workshop for men and women?

A: No, it was just for women. The teacher said it's a nice way to start your sessions.

Q: Do you think the clients you see as a Tantric Goddess are different from the clients you would see doing sensuous massages, or that an escort would see?

A: The ones that truly want to learn Tantra are really open and relaxed. I've also spoken with escorts that tell me they get really nice clients and they sit and talk with them. Some of my clients can't even get erections. They're just really lonely and just sit and talk. I listen and I nod and say, "You do? Mmm." The other day I called my girlfriend and said, "I think I have died and gone to heaven." [This client had just gone down on her.] "I just had the greatest orgasm and got paid for it." [Laughs.] That's happening three or four times a week now!"

Q: With was the same person?

A: No!

Q: So you don't have sex.

A: *No, I don't have sex in my sessions.*

Q: When you first heard of Tantra, you thought this was an opportunity to use the spiritual...

A: *Oh! Totally. I was so excited because I still had a little bit of guilt! It was an evolution and I've learned a lot about men.*

Q: I'm sure there's diversity.

A: *Whatever type of woman there's a certain type of man looking for that. I'm the older-woman fantasy. I get guys in their twenties. I had somebody email the other day, he said, "Would you go out with me? I'm sixteen." I just wrote back, "No." [Laughs.]*

Q: You said you were in New York.

A: *In New York they're so guilty because there are so many Jewish and Catholic men there, and they're always in a hurry. I'll see a client, and he says [brusquely], "Hi'." He'll have his eyes down. I'll say, "Oh hi, How ya' doing?" And he'll say, "Fine." They put down the money and the next thing I know is we're going to have a problem. I'll have the towel ready [for premature ejaculation.] They'll say "Hurry up. I need to get out of here." Here, it's like I can't get them out the door. So I take off my top. "You want to touch my breast." They go, "Yeah!" They don't want to be caught looking. I say, "Here, go ahead, put your hands on my breasts" The minute they touch my breast they go "Au!" [Indicating a climax.] They get so excited! The minute they touch a woman's breast it's all over. It's so easy. I'm going back there.*

At the end of the first interview I mentioned that she never got into her deeper feelings so we did a second interview.

SECOND INTERVIEW WITH ROSE

Q: Tell me about the different emotional stages you've gone through in your life.

A: *There was a time when I had the little perfect world. Kids, a religion. I felt strong, because I could rely on the outside world to give me security. I didn't know it had to be built inside. Nobody ever said, "Hey you have to be strong in here" [indicating her heart.] I felt secure, but not happy. When my husband and I decided to separate, it got really nasty because he ran into a woman who was threatened by me. Everything was cut off to me. I had been living in a big, beautiful house and I missed it.*

Q: Why did you split up?

A: I felt alone. I did everything by myself. If you feel alone in a marriage or a relationship, you might as well be alone. I've learned since that you'll always feel alone until you fix whatever it is that makes you feel that way. I wanted someone like my Dad, who was always in the house and very into his kids. I had an attraction for Jewish men. Someone told me that Jewish men make the best fathers and the best husbands.

Q: That's true.

A: [Laughter.] That's 'cause you're Jewish, Jim. Anyway, I thought that if Terry and I split up, I was going to be free for awhile and then I'd meet someone and we would do things together.

Q: How did you split up?

A: It was very strange because Terry and I never argued. He was very unexpressive in his emotions and didn't like confrontation. So it was a really big shock for my son when we told him. He screamed and went under the table.

Q: Was it your decision?

A: It was me. I did a lot of crying and a lot of consulting with my older daughter, and with my best friend. I was scared to death. After what happened I can see why I was scared, because it was nice having a secure life. I went into a real scary time. We had a horrible divorce. He met a woman who told him that if he gave me any more than $500 a month she'd leave him. And he crushed [her son], who felt that he loved this new woman more than him. I was trying to survive out here with the kids. He had all the money for the best lawyers and took everything back.

Q: So what did you do?

A: I was in the car with the kids.

Q: Were you living in the car?

A: I had somewhere to go myself, but no room for the children.

Q: How did that feel?

A: *It set off some kind of strange anxiety. I thought I was dying. I got this extreme mental disorder, thinking that I had a different cancer every day.*

Q: Did he take the kids back at some point?

A: *I realized that I couldn't support the children and took them to his house. I'll never forget that night. I thought it was going to be for a short time, and the really sad part was my son was saying, "Don't go, Mommy, please don't go. I don't want you to go!" I regret so much dropping them off, but they needed a home. I dropped them off, and I watched them walk up those steps, and I'll never forget that sight. Now I was really alone. I was just screaming in the car. Crying. All the way down the hill and all the way out to the freeway.*

Q: Where did you stay?

A: *Julia, my older daughter's grandmother, was still alive. She was in her 70's, and had a house in Palos Verdes. She couldn't throw anything away and had this one room in back stuffed with years and years of her clothes. These ballroom dancing dresses were stacked on the bed so close together there was not one place for me to put a toothbrush.*

Q: She put you up there?

A: *I slept like this in the bed. [Pantomimes being scrunched in.] Yeah, she let me stay. Of course. I was the mother of her granddaughter.*

Q: And then?

A: *I went into a bad depression. I was there all day. I was looking through the personals, thinking maybe if I found somebody to go out with I could be a little bit happier. I met Ronnie, this young, twenty-two year-old Denzel Washington. That's all I can say. And I was forty-two years old. We talked, we hit it off on the phone, and we met at Thank God It's Fridays down at the Marina, [a singles spot] and we went to his mom's house, which hadn't been decorated since the 70's. He took care of me! We ended up in some cheap hotel on Western Blvd. He started going out and getting me things and just holding me. And I was just crying. But for some reason he just stayed through it with me. I was at my worst. I'd come from a religion where you're not supposed to see psychiatrists. He talked me into going to a psychiatrist, because his sister had a bout with depression. They put her on Prozac or something and she got better.*

He babysat me for three months, then he couldn't handle it any more. I feel like... [starts to cry]. I love this guy. [Cries.] He was like a... [cries at length.] He was like a little angel that was sent down to take care of me. And he was black, and he was taking care of me. If anybody had a stereotype about black people not liking white people and wanting to help, it's really not true. He took me to County Hospital and we sat in the parking lot, and I looked up at the gigantic, scary looking County Hospital and I said I couldn't go in there. I thought I would get a frontal lobotomy [laughs}, shock treatment or stuff. I finally went to a psychiatrist, and he gave me Zanax. And then Ronnie drove me up to Palos Verdes, and all the way up there, Jim, I was crying and begging him not to leave me. I said, "Not now. Let me get a little stronger so I can handle it. But please, not now." But he knew I'd be okay. He dropped me off, and I never saw him again. I took Zanax and for the first time since I dropped the kids off I felt like there was a little light at the end of the tunnel. Maybe I could function. I got addicted to Zanax. The doctor said, "Nobody can come off Zanax, taking as many milligrams as you are, without going to rehab." I said, "Well let's just give it a try." So we lowered it and lowered it. And I came across the Buddhists and started chanting. The one that says, "Nam Myoho Renge Kyo." I felt a little better and stayed at Grandma's a few more months. I wanted to get my nursing license back. They said that I could re-take the test. So I studied nursing, but nursing is so different these days and you can't learn it from a book. I learned as much as I could but I truly believed that by chanting and visualizing, for some miraculous reason I passed.

Q: And then you moved out and met Angie. How did you meet her?

A: *At the Buddhist temple. She saw a sign on the bulletin board, looking for a roommate.*

Q: So you moved in with her and the two of you decided to do a massage business.

A: Yes. She had done it in the past and made a lot of money, but she had been in a very sloppy, self-sabotaging place.

Q: Did she have a job?

A: She was working at some little coffeehouse and had the sugar daddy. I came from a family where we were always massaging each other, so Angie and I thought we'd place an ad and just do straight massage. They'd like being with two pretty girls at one time.

Q: How did you feel about that?

A: I had really mixed emotions on it. Massage was the perfect solution to my fear of being alone. I felt like I had ten or fifteen boyfriends at a time. I was LOVING it, but still fighting depression. I was a little less uptight if I took Zanax before the massages.

Q: Do you take anything now?

A: Yeah, I take Valium now.

Q: Do you only take Valium before a session?

A: No, I've been taking it for five years. My doctor said that I should continue until I get my issues on being alone settled, together with the tail end of the co-dependency. Co-dependency and not wanting to be alone go hand in hand.

Q: I see.

A: I've gone to psychiatrists and hypnotherapists. Until I can get stronger there's no way I'm going to be able to wean off the Valium. One of my goals is to work through these issues so that I don't have to take anything. If I stop I'll go into unbearable pain. In fact my neck's hurting right now because I didn't take any this morning. I didn't take any before you came, so I could feel, and not be numb. Valium gives you the endorphins that you should produce naturally.

Q: I see. How did you feel when you started sensual massage?

A: Because of the cult, when I first started doing sensuous massage I felt like I was doing something really, really bad. I had that buffet right there, with all the kids' pictures. And while I was massaging the client I would be looking over at my kids, because I missed them so much. It was almost like they were watching me. I wanted to go over and turn each picture around. I felt like, oh my God, if my kids could see me doing this, I'd be so ashamed. I felt a lot of guilt and I felt like my life had just gone downhill.

But what it DID do for me, is it really brought up my self-esteem. A little bit was about my looks. I didn't used to see myself as attractive but now I was being told all the time that I was attractive. And, actually, my clients were nicer to me than any boyfriend or husband had ever been. They would call me up and see how I was feeling, or if I wanted to go somewhere and get something to eat. Just come and spend time with me, because they knew I was lonely. Not ask for a session and not try to have sex with me. I've made so many friends through the years, from clients. I can't tell you how many times that clients have showed up when I was in dire straights. When I got back from New York I didn't have any money and a client showed up and handed me two thousand dollars to get this apartment.

When I started sensual massage, it was a strange time because I was missing my kids, and felt like I was sinning and doing something that was horrible to myself. But there was this paradox because I was getting so much love from my clients! I started to really think about it. If I'm doing something so horrible, why is it the first time that I'm really feeling loved? [Weeps.]

In a way, the business changed my life, because I felt like people cared about me.

Q: People do care about you. Obviously it's not just a session. A lot of these are dear friends.

A: Yeah! And to this day. [Choking up.] All my life it's always been men that have saved me. Emotionally, physically, financially, it's always been men. I grew up with brothers. My daughter will sometimes ask me, "What do women do in this situation" And I say, "I don't know." I only know about men. Ask me any question about men.

Q: What about Angie?

A: She was going through the same kind of stuff that I was.

Q: Did she have another career, outside of working as a waitress?

A: She had nothing going for her except that she was extremely beautiful. I eventually talked her into going back to work after I got rid of my guilt. I'll tell you, it was that book that I gave you. [Women of the Light, the New Age Sexual Healers.] *I sat down and read it in one night, and I went to see a leader in the Buddhist organization to get his advice. He asked, "Are you harming anyone?"*

And I said, "No."

And he asked, "Is it helping you in your life?"

And I said, "Yes."

And he asked, "Do you need to ask any more questions?"

And I said, "No."

Later:

A: The thing that had bothered me was seeing married men. I wondered, am I breaking up homes? Do they withhold things from their wives to see me? I felt responsible for how a wife may feel. But after having all the married men feeling better after seeing me, it didn't seem to be an issue any more. I didn't feel I was hurting anyone's marriage.

When I was still feeling a little bit of guilt I met a black lesbian at the Buddhist organization. We became friends and she'd come over and chat. She was always broke and couldn't get a job. She was going through a lot of issues with this woman she was in love with. She never tried to be with me. She was starving, and I'd say, 'How're you doing? Are you eating?'

Deborah would say, 'No.' So I'd just give her twenty or thirty dollars. Because now I was starting to feel blessed, like my God, I have money coming in. A lot, for me. A black person had helped me and here was a black person that needed my help. I would have acted the same if these were white people, but it was ironic, that here was this black person that needed my help. I said, "Deborah, if you're ever hungry, call me. No friend of mine will ever be hungry." [Cries.]

Q: Not bad.

A: [Tearfully] Yeah. I liked that. You know, when you've had a rough life, it gives you a good heart. One time, we were sitting in front of the Buddhist scroll and chatting, and she said, "You're so fortunate to be able to touch men. I would thank the universe if I could do that. You should be so thankful for what you have." Since Deborah said that I never felt shame again. With Tantra I became like a sacred healer, like a Goddess. Then the Internet came up, and people were calling me almost as a doctor, 'I've got problems with premature ejaculation.' 'I have problems with impotency.'

Q: You said at first you thought the men would come for spiritual reasons.

A: *At first, I was seeing what I wanted to see, which was that men were coming to me for higher consciousness through Tantra. Maybe a few were, but most were coming for longer happy endings. With sensuous massage we gave them the happy ending as fast as possible, because I just gave them a long therapeutic massage, and then wanted that part to be over with. You can't get away with that anymore with reviews on the Internet. There are too many women doing this in L.A. now. There are so many in New York that competition's intense.*

Q: I read some reviews and there are still some people who give a 'rush job'.

A: *And they get bad reviews. They'll call you a 'cock watcher'.*

Rose would like to do a television show that talks about Tantra and takes the shame out of sex.

Q: Give me an example of what you would do.

A: *The other day my hairdresser asked what I did, and everyone tells everything to her hairdresser so I told her I do Tantra. She said, "Oh my God, I need to know how to give oral. Can you explain that to me?" I happened to have a banana with me so I showed her. It was actually half a banana, so it was like a little guy. The nail lady and others were gaping. Here I was, with weird coloring on my hair, no makeup, this cape, looking like an alien creature, showing them how to go down on a banana. It was hysterical. I'd use humor in the show and if I could help even one person get over her fears and guilt, that would be wonderful.*

Dr. Peterson wrote: "This is slightly bizarre. I would have said that tantra is the antithesis of acting... as a spiritual discipline that is predicated on a radical authenticity. Tantric meditation practices are typically very empowering for women. Ejaculatory control is just one tantric technique – it's the same as the Middle-Eastern practice of *karezza* – but it is often the only specific technique that people have heard of. Hatha Yoga techniques were developed to open up the body's capacities to experience subtle energies, so yoga is an offshoot of tantra. She says nothing of meditational practices, which are the heart of tantric spiritual work."

Tugend: I've taken classes and practiced the meditative exercises at length, with remarkable results. Some providers offer Tantra as an option for a larger fee and are studying it strictly for the sexual benefits, but not the ones I've met. Tantra has helped Rose achieve a joyous life and I see her as a success story. Even when she wept, she wept for joy. She radiates happiness and humor.

CHAPTER XII: TEENAGE RUNAWAYS

TONI JUGGLES A RELATIONSHIP

Most of the providers who are married or have regular boyfriends are open about it. Toni is an exception. She is a college student and escort, who is very worried that her boyfriend will find out. She checks people out very carefully before giving them her cell phone number and instructs them that they must hang up if she says, "No" when they call; that means her boyfriend is there.

I interviewed her by phone. She was talking faster than I could type, so I've filled in the words as best as I can.

Toni was in a chat room on TER and the picture of her face was slightly blurred. In chat rooms everyone types whatever they want and everyone else sees it immediately.

From Toni:

> *I would absolutely love to answer some of your questions as long as I stay anonymous. I am busy tonight - but WILL get back to you, as I have been thinking of writing a book... called* I Know Your Husband. *hee hee! anyhow, we'll be in touch!*
>
> *Toni*
>
> *p.s. ironically, my real name is Love (1974 hippie parents) and you can email me*
>
> *I am intrigued... looking forward to it.*

Toni is a blonde bombshell. As to prejudice against escorts, she said, "How about a girl who goes out to a bar and goes home with a guy the same night? They are just being sluts."

I called later. At first, she thought I was a client. Then she said, "I've been talking to so many people, it's nuts. You know, I'm having one, two, three, four appointments, and I'll be drinking champagne and raspberries, so go ahead and give me a call after 8:30."

I replied, "All right."

She said, "Okay sweetie? Bye."

She really is working her way through school and has a regular job. She has one client who is a millionaire coke-head. He's so demanding she is probably going to stop seeing him. She has plenty of clients, but it's going to be hard to break the news to him.

As she was talking to me she was trying to drive an old, stick-shift car. The traffic got too heavy for her to shift and talk on the phone so we hung up and I called her five minutes later. She said she has been working as an escort off and on. We continued our conversation sporadically while she parked and went into her house.

She said she used to need the wealthy coke user's cash, but not anymore. While she was talking to me she was watching *American Idol*. Suddenly she shouted, "Listen to this guy! I'm a singer. This guy is amazing."

She told me she was on *Star Search* when she was sixteen years old and received an offer from a record company. Her dad took her winning money. He bought her a car twelve years later. Her father was an alcoholic and a hippy. She and her mother left him when she was nine but she moved in with him when she was sixteen. Her father went chasing after one of his girlfriends and he dragged her along with him. At this point in the conversation she said her cat was eating her roses and blocking the television. "Her tail takes up the whole monitor," she said.

I'm twenty-eight. I started out as a bikini waitress when I was nineteen, then did oil wrestling, followed by dancing in strip clubs. She said. Clubs started taking half your money. I'd go home with two or three hundred dollars.

So she started working for a company that arranged private dance shows. Not young bachelors, older gentlemen, who are more respectful. One thing led to another.

Her first real customer as an escort was the rich coke-head. She went to his mansion in the hills. He just wanted to sit there and talk with her. He had a brain-damaged child and needed to talk to someone. His wife was a flight attendant and had begun screwing a pilot. He drank booze too. They just talked for a few hours and he gave her eight hundred dollars. He couldn't have had sex if he wanted to.

She gave him her number and saw him on a regular basis. She'd walk around in lingerie, drinking his private branded wine. Now she takes away his drugs when he gets out of hand. She tells him she will give it back when she thinks he's okay. He's spontaneous too and will suddenly need to see her if, for example, his wife is on vacation or out of town. His wife won't kiss him or even touch him. He needs the attention. He can be good to Toni and bought her everything: clothing, computer, furniture, anything she wants. He owns a big company along with his father and brother, works his ass off, and is in charge of the company's money. He gave her a company gas card.

Sometimes he will call her every ten minutes and be a pain in the butt. Now, because of the Internet, she doesn't need to jump when he calls. When she did jump for him he would keep her there for hours, waiting around while he handled his own business in front of her. It was a control game, as if to say, "I'm taking longer because you need me." Sometimes he pays her eight hundred dollars, or a thousand dollars, but maybe only three hundred fifty dollars.

One night a nurse came on duty at his house at 11:30 at night to care for his child. He arranged to sneak out of his house and have Toni pick him up in her car. She told him, "Do not bring your drugs in my car. Do it in your house."

Now Toni has three websites she advertises on or manages. Despite her rules about not bugging her on her cellphone, a reviewer posted her private cellphone number in his TER review. She was at school and received a hundred sixty-three calls in one day. It was crazy for two days, but then TER took the phone number down.

She says she is doing really well, and is very, very careful. She won't see a guy if they don't hit it off and she won't see more than four guys a day. Toni says she has a strong mind.

I asked if she enjoys the sex with her clients. She said she doesn't like it. She only really enjoys sex with her man. Most of the time she fakes it with clients. This may account for her being able to see four men a day. That's my theory.

Then she excitedly blurted out, "I just saw a fireman on television who is gorgeous! He jumps out of a helicopter and rescues people."

She said some other escorts get more volume and better reviews, but she is extremely safe. She doesn't provide oral sex. That's for when she's in love. No tongue kissing. In fact she does not like kissing a client at all. She once had a fat old man who was stinky and had bad breath. She put her head sideways and swallowed vomit. Then she said, "Get off of me."

He asked, "What's wrong?"

"You need to have respect, brush your teeth, take a shower. Can't you smell yourself? If you don't clean up you can't see a woman."

She has more respect for prostitutes than someone who goes home with a different guy every night. Toni is not ashamed of being an escort. "They're doing it for school, to buy a house, to support yourself."

She likes the money and blocks it out emotionally. She's just doing it for a short time and is saving money to buy a house and finish college.

I asked about her relationship with her mom. She said, "My mom was a slut. Used to beat the crap out of me, and was jealous when I reached puberty."

Toni says her mother was a speed freak, and evil. Her mother went to medical school and took too many prescription pills. She tried everything, was controlling, and was promiscuous. When Toni was ten to fourteen years old she could hear her mother having sex in the next room. She repeated, "She'd beat crap out of me."

So she moved to her dad's house. He would beat up his girlfriends. Toni ran away with one of her dad's male friends when she was sixteen. The man was eleven years older than she was. That lasted two and a half years. She went back to her mom's but hated it so much she started bikini-dancing. She sounded very young, confident, intelligent, and charming. She came off as strong-minded. All her friends say she's amazingly together, considering her screwed-up family.

Later she wrote,

> *My life in this business has been filled with such bizarre and wonderful adventures that I can't help but want to share it with the world.*

Dr. Peterson wrote: "To have sex with four to five men a day and to not like it speaks to a powerful ability to dissociate or punish herself. And then to go home and 'enjoy' sex with her man calls for compartmentalization that would challenge the most highly defended patients I have ever known. Toni repeatedly refers to the beatings she underwent from her mother and the trauma she witnessed with her abusive, alcoholic father – and she says she has a strong mind. I wonder if she doesn't dissociate during sex as she might have during the beatings – in order to survive the moment."

JESSICA

From **Jessica**,

> *I am sorry it took so long to respond to your e-mail, I have been very busy with the Holidays and moving. Your e-mail intrigued me because I have read and seen many things about my profession, and have always been left unsatisfied. I would definitely be interested in answering any questions you may have. I have been in the Dancing/escort industry since I was 16 years old...*

> *I check my e-mail only once a week, so to reach me easier please call me at (XXX)XXX-XXXX. I look forward to hearing from you. I hope your Holidays were festive!*

Interview: Jessica was born in Washington D.C. to abusive parents. Her mother was uninvolved and un-motherly. By age sixteen the Department of Social Services was about to place her in foster care. Physically mature for her age, she 'escaped', got an apartment, and went to an exotic dance club, which hired her on the spot as a nude dancer.

She made enough money in one night to pay an entire month's rent, but because she provided fake Social Security numbers and had no other ID, Jessica was forced to move from place to place. Guys were soliciting her at the dance clubs and she would agree to see them privately for sex. She turned into a full-time escort. To find an agent she picked the first name in the *Yellow Pages*. The agency was run by a female agent and a pimp, both in their twenties. The agent had worked the street and knew that Jessica was younger than she appeared and scared.

The agency experience turned out well for her. They told her how to protect herself with condoms and also advised her to get health check-ups. Jessica describes the owner as 'real motherly', yet she also remarked, "The agencies don't care about you."

Her first time out for the escort service was with an older girlfriend. They would enter a bar carrying pagers and wait for calls. Jessica was so frightened her knees would shake. The girls would get paged by the agent, who gave them phone numbers to call. They would call the customers and say they were on their way, then hop into a cab.

Jessica and her girlfriend began to room together and after the sessions they talked about the clients they had met. Jessica was still frightened, but her friend was having fun and told her, "You need to calm down and relax." In those days she would just get naked and lie on the bed.

Jessica's older friend helped her with her outfits and advised her to take control of her sessions without the clients realizing it. She told Jessica to be enthusiastic and say, "I want to do this to you," before the clients took over.

She had a straight job but was always struggling and saving. Jessica can't tell anyone what she does. She enjoys the money and freedom but it's hard to establish outside personal relationships while working as an escort. She is a single parent and has had some PTA problems because of her work. She is not fond of the work but says she meets great people. Regulars sometimes become friends. When she is with clients she puts on an act, going into 'dumb blonde mode'.

When Jessica is dating someone it is hard for her to be with customers, because occasionally she has an orgasm with a customer, which makes her feel disloyal to her boyfriend. So if she's dating someone she puts her mind elsewhere while having sex with a client, perhaps thinking about what she'll have for dinner.

She once used drugs (downers) to disconnect, but when she became a parent she stopped. Some clients want overnights, but Jessica likes to be home at dinnertime so she only works during the day. Typically, she sees one or two clients a day.

She said, "I wouldn't want my kid to do it."

But Jessica enjoys the clothes, the makeup, the money and the freedom. Mostly, she loves the outfits and dressing up. She charges $250 an hour. She only works when she wants, does what she wants, and buys what she wants. She has lived in South Carolina, Jersey, Philly, and Pittsburgh. When she was in South Carolina, she saw many more clients, because the fee was less. Jessica said that overall, her lifestyle works for her.

Dr. Peterson wrote: "False lovers, false mothers. All in an inauthentic 'as if' role with little chance for a truly intimate exchange.

"She sees the owner of her first agency as 'real motherly' – her need to be mothered in some good-enough way likely helped her get over her initial terror and, ultimately, bond with this industry. If our ability to authentically connect in intimate ways with others is predicated on the kind of connection we had with our mother, then Jessica's story makes sense. Regarding the statement: 'When Jessica is dating someone it is hard for her to be with customers...' Her conflict is like the little girl who enjoys the physical sensation of being aroused by a molester, but knows that an incestuous boundary has been crossed."

CHAPTER XIII: VIVIAN – KIND AND KINKY

When **Vivian** was doing exotic dancing she was horrified at some of the things she heard. She said, "I'd never do that. Never say never."

Now that she's doing them, they don't bother her at all. But you have to be strong. Like any business, some can't take it.

Vivian's reviews all say she is a great beauty. When she was twenty-five she was married to a trucker who supported her. His truck broke down, and at his urging she started working as a stripper. He got back on his feet with the money she earned and then he told her to quit. She loved making money so she asked him to support her while she went to college. He refused. She didn't like the double standard and they split up. She was raising two children, now eighteen and twenty. She said that escorts won't admit it but most of them are raising children. She moved from stripping to massage and then to escorting. In her private life, she rides horses and is quite down to earth.

Vivian will perform 'golden showers', meaning she urinates on clients. She puts down pads or linoleum or does it in a bathtub. She will also beat up clients on demand. These clients are usually powerful professionals, including CEOs of major companies, who want to be abused. They are also usually gay or bisexual. She never does this with first-timers, but when she meets a client his desires come out in discussion.

Vivian thinks that half or more of the escorts hate it. Some aren't strong enough physically and mentally, or they get greedy and work too much. She said she hasn't seen that many weirdoes. One client likes being beaten with paddles. Another pays her to make threatening phone calls to him at work, demanding to see him. A deliberate 'Fatal Attraction', he gave her his boss's real name and all his personal information. He wants her to force him to go see her, probably to cover his guilt. He can say to himself that she made him do it. He's a black man and dresses up as a woman.

One client is fixated on her. She ignores him, which makes him want her even more. He'll watch her house and when she catches him he'll send her diamonds.

If a potential client says he wants to bring along a woman, Vivian declines, because it could be a pair of vice officers. One does the setup, the other one acts as a witness and does the arrest. She said an escort agency sometimes turns girls in to the police for a pay-off. (See the story of Sunny Monroe in Las Vegas in Chapter XVII.)

Vivian has a girlfriend who does massage once a month, but hates it. Vivian offered to ask her if she would talk to me.

Vivian and I agreed to meet for lunch near her home. At the time I had yet to meet any escorts in person. I drove to a restaurant where she sometimes meets clients. It was the most dismal, dark, depressing joint I've ever seen, and I've seen some bad ones. At noon, three or four cowboys were slumped over their beers, cigarettes cradled in their hands with ashes waiting to fall, drunk or just zoned out. Even the flies were listless.

She didn't show up. We had discussed meeting at her house so I drove to a funky community where people had horses and old wrecks in their yards. When she answered the door, we were both surprised. She had forgotten our lunch. She didn't have her makeup on and without it she wasn't as glamorous as everyone had described. She was getting ready for a date, but I had driven a long way and asked if I could at least have a look inside her house. Inside was a ravishing young girl, about twenty-two, who blushed with embarrassment and didn't say anything. She was obviously the girl who did massage. There was nothing unusual about the house except that her bedroom was especially well decorated and neat.

I phoned her later and she explained that her girlfriend has a mental deficiency or is bipolar, but can do sensual massage without the clients realizing her problem. She moved to a farm and meets clients once in a while at Vivian's house, but won't talk about it.

Vivian only works a couple of days a week and arranges her schedule so her children are never exposed to her profession. She was interviewed on television shows but stopped doing them because she couldn't express her opinions; the interviewers had their own agendas and wouldn't allow any other points of view.

Dr. Peterson wrote: "The customers who want to be abused make me wonder if she was humiliated, abused, beaten and threatened as a child. Perhaps Vivian takes on the roles of humiliator, etc. because those were the cores of her own relationships."

I don't know if I agree with Dr. Peterson. It's not like Vivian advertises as a 'Mistress' or 'Dom', and those clients were exceptions. Certain clients asked her to do kinky things, but it was my impression that it didn't particularly turn her on. However, Dr. Peterson sometimes picks up things that I miss.

CHAPTER XIV: GINGER – A CO-ED

Hi there,

It is nice to hear a voice of reason here; it is insane to view all providers as hapless victims of a horrible circumstance. I am an artist! I love what I do. I am an escort and Mistress. (A mistress dominates men or women, uses costumes, and sometimes spanks clients.) I am in the business of helping people live their fantasies in a safe, sane, connectional way. I know many of the Internet 'girls'. We are students, moms and others who need to maximize income and minimize hours. None of us are strung out on drugs or being exploited by anyone. This is a lifestyle that creates choices and options, not limits them. Many of us come from healing professions such as masseuse or nursing. The age range is usually mid twenties on to the 50's, not exactly kids being taken advantage of. The physical types are a wide range too. I myself am built like a 50's femme fatale. Petite and curvaceous. I know very thin, very heavy, all ethnic backgrounds. It belies the myth of "the American Beauty Standard." All women are beautiful and the industry reflects it. Don't forget the boys... There are many male escorts around too. They definitely don't fit the 70's gigolo or pool-boy stereotypes.

Legislating morality is a futile effort. Yet here, strippers are regularly arrested, or detained on solicitation charges. Adult Video stats and Mistresses all tell me horror stories of Child Protective Services Witch Hunts. People being convinced that because your clothes come off at work or you spank people you must be terrible parents. Irate parents trying to get

*deprogrammers to 'work' on their daughters
because they choose to strip their way through
school.*

*I hope that you will show things as they are
rather than the limited view that so many hold.*

Ginger got started through a girlfriend who worked for an
agency, and Ginger worked for the agency a little while too.
The agency didn't screen their clients. They would promise
anything the client wanted and didn't even turn down drunks.

Ginger said that some agencies are great. She is a
moonlighting student who works as an escort part-time. One
of the pluses for her is that she built a reputation for "role
play." She's noticed that after men reach a certain age they
sometimes start to enjoy role-playing more. She plays a
wicked schoolgirl, a cheerleader, a Catholic schoolgirl, a
secretary, and domination, within limits. She's not willing to
be a full-out dominatrix. She actually was a Catholic
schoolgirl. She acts out the things she wanted to do when she
was younger.

She's had no adverse affect at all from any of this. She has
increased her self-confidence, gained a more positive view of
herself, and is aware of her own strength, though she admits,
"Some of the scenes weren't that pretty."

She says she CAN have a meaningful relationship, but does
not HAVE to have it. She is not defining herself through a
relationship; she can be independent. She has learned to really
listen to others. Her boyfriend is still there and he knows what
she does.

Up to this point in the interview she sounded like an everyday
gal, but then it got more interesting. She was involved in a
polygamous marriage for five years. Her husband was in it
eight years; she was the third person to join, making it a trio.
They were not kinky. They'd do laundry together. They were
married, though not legally. They had a spiritual ceremony
and their families were present. The family had children and
this allowed the women to spend more time with them.

Before Ginger became an escort she was a music booking
agent, working eighty hours a week. Since she's been working
as an "entertainer", her hours are her own. She finds escorting

liberating and it's good pay. When I asked her about the negatives, she said there was a low percentage of negatives, even working with an agency. Contrary to the popular conception, she said 'druggies' might be able to dance, moving from club to club, but they are not reliable enough to work for an agency. Whether modeling or whatever, it's image, and heavy drugs ruin your looks. She works out and takes care of her appearance. She said some escorts try drugs but quickly learn it is not workable. She used drugs before she was an escort. She said maybe you could use drugs in the Goth crowd that doesn't think of the future.

She has future plans. She loves the adult industry, building websites, and is a photographer. Ginger is studying video editing, graphics and considering a career in the Internet.

She's been in Europe and Japan where she finds people are more tolerant.

Ginger's childhood was happy and she had loving, supportive parents and grandparents. She was over-privileged. It was a big, dramatic family. Women were not supposed to enjoy sex or use birth control. She has been very open with her mom, who thinks it's great, but her father never knew. Her clients are intelligent, wealthy, middle-to-upper class. Pleasant people. Men she would date. You would never meet these people in a singles bar. Some are married.

CHAPTER XV: AFRICAN-AMERICAN FAMILY

KAT

Kat is a twenty-four year-old African-American. She describes herself as 'Caribbean' on the Internet. She lives with her husband, three children and her mother. Her husband is having an affair and she's having one too. She started working as an escort, paying an introductory rate of only $20 for photographs and a two-week ad on an escort mall. She worked with a girlfriend who became jealous when Kat made more money than she did. Her girlfriend tried to come between Kat and her boyfriend. Kat told me that her girlfriend gossiped to her boyfriend about her (not to be confused with her husband.). The boyfriend told Kat everything her girlfriend had said. Kat never gossiped about her girlfriend (or so she said; she'd been gossiping to me. But I asked for it.)

She only charges $150 for full service. She had been working as a call girl for two months, paid off her bills, and had a safe full of cash.

Her parents and family have a pretty good idea of what she does, because she sometimes goes out at two a.m. They don't say anything about it because they appreciate the money. Besides, her husband is seeing someone else.

CHAPTER XVI: LATINAS

Amanda, a Latina, sees clients in her home. Some hobbyists on TER said it felt strange with her daughter's bed in the same room. Of course the daughter is not present when she is working.

It was difficult arranging an appointment so we finally agreed to meet at her home.

Amanda wrote:

> .....*bring a recorder and it would be much easier. It would be like a therapy for me. My story would amaze you if you really get to know me, since I have a debate between the good woman and the fucker bitch every man wants to fuck with, excuse my expression.*

> *Another time:*

> *I don't really have time to spare, since between my personal life, [there is] my dearest daughter's artistic life. She takes ballet, jazz and hip-hop since she was six, and with my "business" I hardly have time for the real woman underneath to relax and enjoy the roses.*

Dear Amanda,

I used to be sort of a psychological co-facilitator; not because of any formal training, but I could help people bring out their inner feelings. Practicing psychologists paid my way for multi-day sessions.

We finally met at her home, a tiny cottage in a middle-class neighborhood. Amanda was middle-aged and a little heavy set. She wore sweat clothes and no makeup. She appeared embarrassed, not for her looks but because of her work. I never saw the 'fucker bitch' side of her.

A: What do you want to know?

Q: How did you get started in this?

A: I was having problems with my ex-husband and I needed some money for lawyers. I had a good job but it wasn't paying enough to pay the rent and get custody of my child. It was actually visitation [rights she was fighting over.] So I decided to quit my job as an office manager and do this. I read in a Spanish newspaper they were looking for some escorts. I called the guy and he got me started.

Q: So at first they made the appointments for you?

A: Yes. It was an agency and they act like it's me talking on the phone. They did emailing with clients, and set up the appointments.

Q: Were you happy with that?

A: Not really. I wasn't happy. The lady, I think she sensed that her husband was trying to be nice with me. Too nice, and she sensed it and she was kind of mean, not giving me calls, not giving me clients.

Q: So having been an office manager, you could do your own email and phone calls. I see you have the computer system and everything.

A: Yes. When I was an office manager I ran thirty-five contracts and worked with around fifty clients, different types of personalities. I have ten years of customer service. So to me this is easy. It's a different kind of service, but it is still the same transaction, him trying to get what he wants, and me trying to get what I need.

Q: Was it difficult for you at first?

A: [Sigh] It was difficult to the point that I have to....put all my guts together to do it. Because I was brought up as a Christian woman. Going to church. I have very strong family values. And this is...not me, allowing people to come in here. Someone that I'm not attracted to, that I don't know, coming in and being in my house. It's not something that I really enjoy. To the point that I say, okay, I open the door to everybody. But you know at some point, I'm getting used to it.

Q: Do you talk to some people that you don't invite over? That you don't want to see?

A: *Absolutely. Yeah, I screen the people. I kind of sense the voice when they talk to me, the way they approach me. I learned that. When people call, sometimes they don't show up. Sometimes I get the feeling that this person is just looking for an opportunity to talk to a woman, or is not good, so I don't schedule an appointment.*

Q: When you work for an agency they set all the appointments, so you probably saw all kinds of people, right?

A: *Yes, but I didn't stay. It was a waste of time, so probably one month, is all I stayed with them.*

Q: And then, did you take out an ad on the Internet?

A: *Yes. I was browsing in it for adults. You know the adult plaything, the adult services. So in the beginning, I saw 'escort'. [I thought] what is this? That sounds nice. And then I started browsing, and checking out all kinds of sites, and I realize, whoa, this is what an escort does. And I started reading reviews, and getting really up on that kind of life, and I realized that the adult business is really strong.*

Q: What is the difference between 'adult' and 'escort'?

A: *Well it's about the same, but with an escort you don't talk about sex. It's like you are here. And we sit down, so whatever happens. Sometimes there's some special chemistry. It just happens.*

Q: It's expected that something will happen.

A: *Yes. Yes. It's expected. But not all the time do we have intercourse.*

Q: Right.

A: *Maybe there's a playful moment, and orgasm, and that's it. But not really penetration. That's the difference. Sometimes it happens, sometimes it doesn't.*

Q: So how is 'adult' different from that?

A: *Well that's really really like... uh, to me it's like cheap sex.*

Q: Oh. So you do the escort not the adult.

A: *Yes. The other is like, okay, I'm a hooker. You wanna come and fuck me? And what do you want me to do?*

Q: The escort's more what you feel like.

A: *That's right. Like, let's say 'sex with class'. I call it the 'girlfriend experience'.*

Q: Personal?

A: *Yes. Feelings. I really get to talk to people. They talk about their jobs, how a meeting went. Sometimes they relieve their stress. Most of them are businessmen so I kind of relate to them.*

Q: Are your clients of all ethnicities?

A: *Yes. I have to say that 90% of them are white. Maybe 10% black and just one Latino. But basically it's Caucasian people.*

Q: Not many Latinos.

A: *Only one.*

Q: Wonder why?

A: *They look for me, but Latinos don't see it like a job; they see it like this is dirty. Because this is part of our culture. There's no respect for the woman who's doing this. So they don't see it like companionship, or some kind of service, or take your time, they see it like...*

Q: They see it more like a brothel?

A: *Yes.*

Q: What would you advise a young woman who was thinking of this for a living?

A: *I wouldn't advise someone to do it unless they are really desperate. If they don't have a family it's okay. I think. To me, I'm still keeping my cultural things inside. And if you don't have a family, it's okay. I know there are some Caucasian ladies on the Internet that are married and are doing it, and their husbands don't mind. To me it's like [gasp] I don't get it. If they are planning to do it, they have to use the money wisely.*

Q: What about an older woman, who's been married, maybe divorced?

A: *Uh, yes. Maybe so. If she's trying to really get ahead. But try not to hurt the family. It would be painful if my family knew what I'm doing.*

Q: Is the social disapproval the toughest thing, particularly for a mature woman?

A: I think so. Sometimes when women get divorced they feel like they were on a leash, and when they don't have that leash they go crazy. And they probably enjoy it. But if someone were more family-oriented that would be difficult. Does that make sense?

Q: Sure. Do you feel that you are a pretty strong person?

A: I think it was the way that my mom brought me up. We are very strong. My mom was like, "This is your future and you have to take charge of it." I was talking this morning to my daughter. She wants to be a dancer, and yesterday something happened at the dance studio and she got kind of discouraged. I was telling her that women have to always be strong. Even stronger than men. The rain comes. The wind blows. Or someone tries to step on you. You have to keep on being strong. Try to support yourself. Even though I've been through a lot of things that brought me to this kind of business, I feel strong. I have a choice to decide who comes to my house. Who sleeps with me, who doesn't.

Q: Do you save money?

A: Yes. I've been doing it for five months and I'm repaying my credit. Because of my divorce and my husband's debts.

Q: You had to pay for his debts?

A: Yes. So to that point I feel that this has really helped me. I don't have a fat checking account but I feel accomplished because I have paid my debts.

Q: And once you've done that you can save a lot of money. And a teenager will have other expenses.

A: My priority is building a savings account for her college. I don't know how long I'm going to be doing this because I'm getting older and a man is always looking for something cute. I know I'm going to be at a disadvantage after maybe a year or so. Because there are fresh faces. There are nicer bodies and all that, so I need to do it now. And I feel like I'm famous. [Laughs)]

Q: You are well known amongst the review boards.

A: Yes, you can check on my reviews.

Q: I did, and you have a lot of very loyal customers.

A: Yes.

Q: Well that's good.

A: Yes?

Q: Is it a little embarrassing to read about it?

A: You know what? That I get mad. I get mad because to me, this is something very discreet, okay, and that is not a gentleman. I know this is business for them, I think they get credit whatever review they place, so I don't know if they get some money, or they get something from there. But to me this is so disgusting. Sometimes there are guys who want to talk about the other guy that came before. Or they ask, "How many guys did you see today?" Or, "How many did you fuck today?" And like I said, I don't talk about it. To me that's a lack of profession ethics, and that's not really respectful. And I feel the guys that come here, looking for a nice moment, maybe something that is missing outside, and they want to look for that in me, and if I give it to them, and they spread those things to some other guys, that's disrespectful. I don't see it that that's nice.

Q: All they get is a free membership. The membership is only twenty dollars a month. But I think it's maybe bragging.

A: Yes. Bragging over how many ladies they have.

Q: What they did, and 'I did this and I did that'!!

A: [Excitedly] You know they lie! They lie. Because sometimes they say that they did this and they did that, when they just lay down and they CUM!... You know, I don't try to rip them off.

Q: But they'll say that they did this, and they did that, and they did the other, but they really ejaculated and then they were finished?

A: Yes. Most of the time, they cum. They finish, the first time. We talk. And I give them a massage. I'm good with my hands. I'm really good giving a massage. And I relax them. Crack their back and everything, and sometimes, I'll try to get them back. And I do it. And I get them back for a second orgasm. Sometimes they don't cum. It's not my fault, you know, it's his body. (Laughs) But, yeah I try. And sometimes they write that they did this and that, like they're like super-machos. And I was like, (indicating boredom) Okay. To be honest, I'm very very sexual, and I can *cum a thousand times if you make me cum a thousand times. But (nervous laugh) I get really mad sometimes, when I read. But that gives me credit like you say, and brings me clients. So they are looking for the same as what they read. Fantasy. That's just fantasy. Everything is in your mind. That's why when we work in the agency we call them, 'The Show'. They used to call me, "You have a show coming at one." Because they're looking for a show. They don't see me like this. They don't see me with my hair like this. They see me with makeup. I mean like really la femme fatale. [Laughs] Like really sexy.*

Q: How do they dress? You see how I'm dressed. (I was in sweats.)

A: Sometimes they dress like that, or in sandals and shorts. When they come like that I say, okay this is not a future client. This is going to be a one-time job. But I know that...I have lawyers and businessmen.

(She has clients who work at a movie studio nearby.)

Q: Don't tell me the names.

A: I won't. Besides, they change their names. Like me.

Q: Some escorts require the real name, address, to make sure it's not law enforcement.

A: Oh, probably, probably with an agent. I take a lot of chances. Every time that I open the door, I shake. That's why I started to stick with the same customers.

Q: Yeah, because you don't know, it could be the law.

A: That's right. That's right.

Q: That's why many escorts want to know their work and home phone numbers, and real names.

A: That's why most of the time I try to do it on the Internet. We email. I try to get to know them. What they do. Sometimes from the very beginning they tell me, "Well I'm a so-and-so and this is what I do, and I like to know more about your service

Q: Do they behave well?

A: [Slowly] Yes. Yes. Yes. I've been lucky. I've no complaints. Most of the time they are gentlemen. And very respectful.

Q: It's interesting, and maybe it's the difference between men and women, that you can climax over and over, and yet you don't like doing it in a way.

A: *No, I do!*

Q: Oh, you do.

A: *Yes. I do. I do.*

Q: So the tough part of it is just the reaction of other people. So do you like being in this business?

A: *Uh…*

Q: Just honest. Be…

A: *No. I don't. I like it… okay let's say fifty and fifty. I like it because it's fast money.*

Q: And it feels good.

A: *And to some point, it feeds my ego. Some point.*

Q: Feeds your ego?

A: *Aha! Yes. That guy finds me attractive. I keep getting paid. Instead of meeting a regular guy and going out. Anyway, it's going to happen, if you want to. It's dinner and a movie and that's it. This is different. You know, getting paid for something that's…*

Q: You said you could climax a thousand times… but the physical element is not a big motivation?

A: *Uh. Mmmm. No. Not really.*

Q: That's what's different about men and women.

A: *Yes. Yes.*

Q: Women can climax even more, but it's not their motivation.

A: *No. I enjoy being with someone. But there's a big difference if I have a boyfriend and I enjoy being with him, and I touch him and there's something building up, than being with someone that I don't know. Maybe it's a fat guy, maybe it's an old guy, could be an old guy or a fat guy, but very nice. You know sometimes that happens. Or it could be a skinny guy or someone that I'm not attracted to, and doesn't make me feel good. So it makes me feel…*

disgusted. Disgusted. So it's not really like I do it because I'm a sexual maniac and I want to do it with so many guys.

Q: Did you ever meet a guy and say, "No, I'm not going to?"

A: No. No I haven't. I don't think I could do it, ha ha.

Q: You couldn't do it?

A: I couldn't do it because I couldn't discourage someone.

Q: Do you know other providers that you sometimes work with or know as friends?

A: No, well, uh, not really friends. I know someone who was an escort when she was twenty-two. That's what she told me, and now she's married. She started, her brother actually, he started his own website for escorting. And we started emailing and became a little close. Now I know that she's doing it again, and she's married. So we talk about it and all that, but it's not like we're friends."

Q: Is it easier to talk to her?

A: Yes, she's just fine about it, I mean, it's not like me, because I feel guilty. My family knows that I do massage. That's what they think I'm doing. But this lady she is doing it because... this is her. You know?

She looked exhausted.

Q: That about does it.

A: Good!

She looked relieved the interview was over. I felt that confronting her conflicted feelings had been painful for her, but probably beneficial, because it forced her to face the fact that this life was really not for her.

MANDY

Mandy describes herself as Caribbean. She is exotic, intelligent, and beautiful. She advertises that she does sensual massage.

She had a sexually repressed background, raised with heavy religion. That was twelve years earlier. She rebelled against the religion, drank a lot, but then sobered up and went on a spiritual path. Her boyfriend suggested she look into sensual massage. Mandy didn't know what it was. She had been working as a receptionist and when she found out her first reaction was, 'Oh my God, I could never do that!'

When she broke up with her boyfriend she thought it over for two days, then checked into an agency and discovered that she liked it, and, to her surprise, was really good at it. Mandy stayed at the agency. Eventually, because of her reviews on TER, she was able to work independently. She doesn't need a website ad anymore and is no longer a member of TER, so she doesn't read the reviews. Providers can still be reviewed on TER without being members, and it's her best asset.

She said,

> *My work is more about undoing damage from being told sex is bad. I found it was good for me to open myself up. It's had a hundred and fifty percent good effect, an amazingly good experience. I had been insecure before becoming a provider.*

She meditates regularly, and practices spiritual breathing exercises. She particularly likes appointments with other meditators.

> *Men who are spiritually attuned. Society says you have to be in love and it takes lots of time, but you can reach a high spiritual plane with anyone, if they are willing. We are all one.*

Mandy is a strong person. She says she's one of the lucky ones, with no negatives. She has a loving relationship, which makes it possible. She had only been doing sensual massage a few months and charged four hundred per hour.

She let's customers talk about themselves but some clients don't want to talk. They give one-word answers and it's exhausting when they are cold. In these instances she thinks to herself, 'When will this hour get over?' She won't see clients below age thirty. Young guys just want to 'get it' and have no idea it's a mutual experience. She feels the guys should do something in the session.

She gets incredible reviews and says she is authentically into it. She admits she's a horrible actress and couldn't fake a climax. She said,

> *Be into it or find another profession. The provider*
> *should let go and give herself permission to enjoy*
> *herself. Don't be run by voices of repression. A*
> *woman is not supposed to only want one man.*

She feels no inner conflict about her profession, loves it, and finds it fulfilling. She can't imagine some other line of work and sounds youthful, calm, and relaxed. Apparently she sometimes goes a lot further than the sensual massage she advertises.

Her friends say, "You must meet weirdos," but she hasn't encountered any, just received some emails from them. She has a lot of long dates and only sees someone when she wants romance, sex, etc. Then it's an evening, not necessarily including sex.

I notice that providers who were raised with a strong, repressive religion often maintain a strong sense of spirituality after they drop the religion. This may be equally true of the general population.

CHAPTER XVII: LAS VEGAS

Every month around twenty of Las Vegas' leading escorts have lunch together at a nice restaurant. They are dressed like any group of women, and conversation centers on things like their children, fashion, and new homes. My wife, a movie producer, suggested this would be a good way to start a film. The escort business is so rich in Las Vegas that escorts often visit there from other states. I've selected a couple of women based there.

SUNNY MONROE

It would have almost been a crime against humanity if Sunny Monroe had not become a model. She was a centerfold or feature model in numerous men's magazines including *Penthouse*, and often worked as a featured dancer. She has the kind of full figure and face you'd expect in a men's magazine. She provided escort services in Las Vegas and other major cities. She replied to my email.

> *Thanks Jim:) I will do my best to keep in touch. Just email me if you need to ask me something and if I can call you at that time I will, always include your number. For now I will keep my number private... .sorry :(no hard feelings, I KNOW your book or movie will be great! The best of luck!*

Sunny called me on my cell phone while I was at the carwash, so my notes are not extensive. She was already a celebrity but was not an escort yet when an agency offered her two thousand to dance for a private group in Las Vegas. She walked into a hotel room and had barely begun dancing when she was arrested. A Las Vegas lawyer said she would have to pay five thousand to stay out of jail: twenty-five hundred to him and twenty-five hundred to pay off the city. She said that the sting was a set up by the agency. The agency's regular girls were safe from law enforcement as long as the agency 'gave up' a few girls every month to the police and prosecutors. Other providers in Las Vegas told me almost identical stories.

Sunny did not have the money and the only way she could stay out of jail was to become an escort.

She said that despite Las Vegas' drive to become more family-oriented around the year 2000, it was still a prime location for the sex business. It was 'Sin City'. Many people went there for a wild time or for conventions. Men attending conventions away from home often have time on their hands and money to spend. Prostitution was illegal in Las Vegas but legal in nearby communities.

Sunny said,

> *Sometimes men get carried away with the Las Vegas nightlife and forget that they had made an appointment. I have found that a large, nonrefundable advance deposit is a wonderful cure for this particular kind of memory impairment.*

Sunny's website provided her with multiple sources of income, including video games featuring herself. Once a woman reaches that level of popularity she can keep selling photos and other items to her fans for many years.

Laura was a voluptuous brunette in her early thirties. Five-feet, nine inches tall, 38 or 39D cup. In her photos her hair fell gracefully on her shoulders. She had an exquisite face with high cheekbones.

Laura started dancing in Las Vegas thirteen years ago and was married at the time. She was an escort when we spoke. Her former husband became impotent. Maybe that's why he was 'former'. She said it was difficult having a relationship under those circumstances. She made very clear what kind of behavior was unacceptable from clients. A man was expected to be freshly showered, polite, truthful about his identity, and respectful. If a client made explicit requests or asked for anything unusual, she would leave. She toured the Western world and published her schedule on the Internet.

Her Internet biography said she was Latina, which was not apparent from her pictures. Laura made public appearances and sold products but I gather that most of her work was seeing clients privately. Laura planned to switch careers and was studying for some kind of advanced degree, so potential clients were advised to book an appointment or appearance before she retired. It was best to apply two weeks in advance.

I asked her about the Las Vegas scene. Laura was afraid of violence and said it could be a scary town for providers. She said the agents would send you anywhere. She was sent to bad parts of town or to see violent men. Bodies had been found stabbed to death. An agent told a client she was a Linda Carter-lookalike, which was true. The guy was crazy, and thought she was the real Wonder Woman. He grabbed her by the neck and she fought him off. Then he thought she was a green monster. Another client wanted to have two girls, so he could make himself a sandwich, but Laura didn't work with other women or couples.

She told me the Vegas agencies did bait-and-switch schemes. They would tell the client that it was going to be a hundred fifty to two hundred fifty plus tips, but this didn't include anything. It just got the girl to the room. When the girl arrived she said, "That doesn't include my tip." She'd ask up to $1,000. Whatever the clients wanted, the girls kept saying, "You have to give me more money." She quit the agency.

Most of the Las Vegas escort business was run by email since the clients were from out of town, often coming there for conventions. Nothing by regular mail. Cell phones were a big part of it. Being a successful independent escort required lots of work, mostly corresponding. She worked from nine to five creating advertisements, updating her website, and paying for ads. An ad cost $100 per month. She typically received sixty emails per day.

Asked how she reacted to being an escort, she said that when she first started, "It was exciting." She preferred dinner dates. She sometimes felt anxiety going to a place to see a client. The clients stayed in hotels and it was a challenge to get into the hotels and up to the clients' rooms. The hotel management harassed them. At some hotels, they followed girls they suspected might be escorts.

She used fake or expired hotel keys to pretend she was a guest at the hotel. There was often a question of how to get up the elevator. Vice cops arranged set ups – basically sting operations. She was busted when working for an agency. She used the wrong wording. It cost her fifteen hundred to her lawyer and another fifteen hundred to the city. She had to go to court and might face sentencing. That was stressful.

Cops checked purses of women who were alone in Las Vegas and they would arrest a woman for carrying more than one or two condoms, so some girls didn't carry them. They also didn't carry lubricant or antibacterial ointments. Harassment was a problem in Las Vegas.

Laura said, "Prostitution is never going to go away. The police should spend their resources elsewhere."

Some girls had been known to put Mickeys in drinks and rob the clients. [A 'Mickey Finn' is a knock-out potion.] Laura felt discretion was better than dressing like a sexpot in public.

She had no problem with the sex. She established a rapport with the clients and they were nice men. She would date them if they weren't clients. She would never have been able to meet such fine men outside of the profession. She admitted to two or three bad judgment calls.

> *Independent escorts are home owners, they pay taxes. Escorts spend their money, have their share of community involvement, vote, and are scout leaders. The cops are hypocritical. The escort business supports fine clothing stores, hair and nail salons, and so on. They bring a lot of cash to town.*

Regarding guys on drugs she said,

> *Drugged-out guys can't stand to be alone and have no concept of time. Some girls will get two hours pay for five minutes.*

Laura refused to be around drugs. Her normal rate was five hundred per hour but she sometimes took four hundred per hour to work more often. A dinner date usually came to a thousand and encompassed four hours. On dinner dates the clients really wanted to know the girls. She said,

> *The most trouble is with compulsive clients, who have a string of precise expectations. They will have it all planned out in their heads. The two of us will stroll down this street, then shop here,*

> *then dine there. The whole evening is planned out*
> *in the client's head, including exactly how I'll*
> *behave. These are overly neurotic, unhappy*
> *people who are compulsive and usually end up*
> *disappointed. Some of them will risk their*
> *personal and professional lives to see me.*

Women usually started the conversations and she'd "become a great bull-shitter." She said they always talk about their trip. They might talk about their dogs, where they used to live. Topics include foreign policy. She said she doesn't talk about the split between Democrats or Republicans. One guy was bashing Bill Clinton for his 'immorality' for having sex out of wedlock. She said she didn't care, and the guy went nuts. What hypocrisy! Laura was no longer based primarily in Las Vegas and was moving on to a new career.

Many women, like popular singers and exotic dancers, can accept sexy dancing in revealing clothes in front of a group, but wouldn't provide sex for money. If these stories were true, the stings would have happened years earlier, so I have no idea who was allegedly involved. Dancers also had to have a city license to dance in Las Vegas, even for a day, or they will be arrested. What the women described depicts the police, judges, and agencies turning victimless activities into crimes against victims – the dancers.

CHAPTER XVIII: PROFESSIONAL WOMEN WITH OTHER OPTIONS

TANYA – A BUSINESSWOMAN

Tanya was of Asian/Hispanic mix. She was one of the highest-rated escorts in Southern California because she was personable, attractive, and willing to do just about everything, with gusto and flair. In a discussion board someone asked what her favorite sexual position was. She said that should be obvious from her pictures on her website. Her pictures featured her butt.

When I interviewed her by phone, she turned out to be the opposite of what one would expect from her photographs and reviews. Tanya broke all the clichés. Like most of the escorts I interviewed, she was outspoken, businesslike, and very intelligent. She made good money as a marketing expert in the entertainment industry and inherited considerable money from her grandmother. She was also a published author and sometimes modeled, so she had to keep her face out of view in her ads and didn't escort people in show business.

She started being an escort because she felt dates were a waste of a time and money. She said,

> I don't drink, smoke, use drugs or eat meat. Dating is therefore difficult. You have all the phone calls. Three dates cost the man a hundred to a hundred fifty dollars. Why not just one date, maybe an hour, and get to the point?

She charged three-fifty an hour, which was low for someone who was so highly rated. Perhaps this was consistent with her principle of not wasting men's money.

Instead of learning about the escort business from a madam or another provider, she did extensive marketing research on the Internet. Then she posted an ad on a website called 'Eros', saying that she had never done it before, which intrigued a lot of hobbyists. She received numerous calls even before she got a picture posted on the site. She was nervous at first, but her clients taught her the ropes.

The Erotic Review went wild! She said she quickly became a legend and one of the five top-rated escorts in L.A., receiving a hundred to a hundred fifty calls a day. She chalked it up to her marketing skills and great reviews on TER. When one well-known hobbyist wrote a glowing review, others had to see the girl he was talking about. On TER, Tanya was classified as a "girlfriend experience" (GFE), which means warm, friendly, not just a piece of action.

She didn't care about a client's looks but she did care very much about the person she would be with. She could tell what they were like by talking with them on the phone first. She turned away a lot of people through her screening process but she believed in giving the client everything she could, the best service. She told me she really liked doing it. At one point she lowered her donation so she could see more men, like Kelly.

Tanya wouldn't see men under thirty-five years old. She said she might see women under thirty-five, for variety. She wouldn't see foreigners and preferred Caucasians. She wanted her clients to be married or attached. "Attached" could mean that he had an important job or a girlfriend. This was for her protection. A man with an important job, wife, or girlfriend had to be careful, because he had more to lose. (If he were really careful he wouldn't have seen escorts at all.) It also meant she had some recourse if he were to give her a bad time. She only worked with one other girl and didn't associate with other escorts. She said they could be too cutthroat.

She had recently lowered her profile and cut back her workload to no more than two or three clients a week and gotten herself removed from TER.

Tanya had a graduate degree in marketing and was studying for another graduate degree in finance. Being an escort had been 'great networking'. Tanya developed a bunch of regulars who were close friends. She almost married one client. Her clients often became mentors, highly successful men who taught her more about business than she learned in graduate school. They included MBAs, lawyers, and other professionals. She had an agenda, but it was not really about the money, because she made good money otherwise, plus her inheritance. She invested all her escort money and owned property, real estate and otherwise.

Several months after my interview with Tanya I looked her up on the Internet. Her ad showed nude photos of her body, featuring her ass and legs. Her dark skin was glistening with oil in an erotic pose, a surprise after the interview. I had remembered how professional and focused she was but forgotten what a sexpot she looked like in her ads.

SCARLET – AN ESCORT FOR SEVENTEEN YEARS

Scarlet also sounded very professional on the phone. She was thirty-nine years old and had been in the sex business, in one capacity or another, since she was twenty-two, but it didn't feel long. She had a law degree, and joked,

> *If I become a practicing lawyer I'll not really be changing professions. I'll still be fucking people for money.*

She'd been independent since 1992. Before that, she was with a really good agency. They were nice, and discriminating about clients. She thought being a sex provider was great and had no regrets, but said it was not for everyone.

Before the Internet, the agencies got the business for the escorts. Advertising on your own was too expensive and you couldn't screen clients.

She was dating someone who had used escort services so she knew what was involved. She was in dire straits but she had other options, because she was a college graduate and had an associate degree in mental health. At one point she did psychological evaluations for the county. She started by answering an ad in a newspaper. They were working out of Orange County, California, which was the one of the toughest in terms of law enforcement, and her original madam ended up in prison.

Scarlet worried about girls going straight into it without learning service. She said,

> *Journalists are the really biggest bad guys.*

She had some sex abuse history, but doesn't think it affected her.

I asked if she had been very sexually active before becoming a call girl. She was promiscuous, which made it easier. Before she tried it, she thought it would be difficult. On her first call, she was nervous beforehand and didn't know what to expect. A friend drove her and waited in the car. He was worried. The client was a small man. Afterwards, she was okay, and said, "Let's go make some more money." It's not been dramatic or difficult, although for the first few years she was nervous asking for the money.

She said,

> It's all about sex and conversation. You have to be physically and mentally strong, and open-minded. If you are judgmental, it will turn on you. It helps if you accept the clients for what they are. Otherwise, you won't feel good about yourself.

She talked about it openly and always had. Her boyfriends all knew what she did. Her family knew too. They didn't like it, but accepted it.

Escorting was difficult and did cause problems, (I realize this is contradictory.)

Generally, the men seemed a hundred percent normal. In the 1980s it was people using drugs. She immediately left clients if they used drugs. Men on cocaine would spend tons of money and keep you there, offering more and more money, but it was depressing. She felt bad about them.

Scarlet had other friends who worked in the escort business. She said that occasionally you would find one with a mental problem, but they were mostly typical women, normal people, from normal backgrounds, and very well adjusted. People who were confident and had healthy sex lives did better with it, as did people who were unconcerned about what family or society thought of them, people who were inner-directed, independent thinkers, who didn't get caught up in what people thought of the profession.

Brothels were interesting too. She mentioned an escort who worked at the Chicken Ranch, a legal brothel in Nevada. Scarlet was there herself and met a number of interesting people. There was no stigma at brothels. It was very safe. The brothels said they never had a case of HIV.

Scarlet supported decriminalization. Casual sex wasn't against the law. You could have sex with whomever you want. The morality was up to you.

She said,

> *Women always place conditions on sex. They'll have it after three dates, five dates. When we get married. When he buys me three drinks. Women withhold or reward men with sex all the time. If a wife is mad, no sex. Or if the husband buys her something good, you will have sex.*

One thing bothered her. When she saw on discussion boards that people wrote, 'sell their bodies' it really bothered her.

> *They rent them out for the hour. You're not someone else's property. You still own your body.*

ARIANA – A MID-LIFE NEED

Ariana was a software engineer in Washington State. She planned to visit Los Angeles, so she went online on the L.A. chat section of TER to meet people, which is where I found her. She seemed very hostile to the men, and defended the women from imagined insults. She said she was "ready to rip somebody."

She worked for a very moral and upright firm and was thirty-seven years old when she decided to become a part-time escort. She was full-bodied, stylish, played Billie Holiday on her website, and loved everything French.

Ariana had "lots of reactions" to being in the business. Escorting was amusing sometimes and she enjoyed it. She'd been escorting for about a year but it felt like five or ten years because of the wide variety of emotions.

She'd met great men and regretted not seeing them again. She'd also been degraded and was beaten up once. It could have been the police. She found no screening process was reliable. Her own screening was not much better than random.

The Happy Hooker intrigued her in the seventies and she was always interested in the idea. She was married once, but she was not in a relationship when we spoke. She'd also lived in Amsterdam with a famous author. She loved the movie BELLE DE JOUR and had a collection of movies in this field. Before she was an escort she always thought the women were exceedingly brave.

She liked the idea of a secret life and the overall control; something about the power. She was very much into women's lib, was bisexual, and against spiritual or physical discrimination.

Ariana started because she had a friend who told her she was a lap dancer. At first Ariana was upset when she heard about it. She thought that her friend was going to end up hating men.

Her friend was much more beautiful than she was and Ariana got this huge sexual energy hit off of it. She realized she had been revolted and putting it down because she was jealous, and decided to become a lap dancer herself.

First she did phone sex and then got dance lessons and tried lap dancing for free at sex clubs. She enjoyed rubbing her boobs all over people's foreheads. She said,

"I was okay at it, and one thing led to another."

She wanted to be a professional DOM (dominatrix) but did not always have the desire to go that far with the pain threshold.

It's a huge learning process. A studying process.

When she first started, she had to figure out the business. She met a provider at a sex club, a "place where different activities go on." It was not really underground and nothing illegal was done. The provider gave a talk and Ariana talked with her afterwards. The provider said, "Independent escorts start out in their own little worlds."

Ariana took part in a lot of chat rooms, one of which was for emotional support. She and other girls talked and shared information. Prostitution was legal in her community but they still hid it. If two girls got together and started talking, that could be considered 'conspiring', which was illegal. It could also be considered 'pimping'. You had to be professionally guarded. The more well known you became, the more LE would be looking at you. Ariana hired an attorney and put her on retainer. The lawyer briefed her on what to say if she was busted.

She said, "I have been able to handle it."

But she was affected by whomever she met. It made a big difference whether her clients had respect for her or not. If she couldn't really share with them, she found it a little painful. She didn't want to think of herself as being used as a physical device.

> *If someone just wants to get off or get a blowjob there are places they can go for that.*

She had someone infatuated with her and was stalked once. She did reasonably well but didn't earn enough to afford a separate apartment for her work. Because of her corporate job, Ariana only worked evenings and weekends, but she was thinking of doing it full time.

She said, "It's more honest than working for a corporation."

She worked for a big escort agent once. He was a good agent but he told her she needed to do it full time or not at all. She enjoyed the people she met and the sex too. Ariana had a need to be alive, engaged in the moment and with the environment. She needed to plan things. She didn't think she knew how to do a good blowjob at first, but attitude was important and she learned.

Against her own better judgment, she told her friends about working as an escort. She was having dinner with a lot of her friends and at a giddy moment she blurted it out. She lost a lot of friends that night. She said, "It confronts their self-image of sexuality and who they are."

The married women considered her a threat.

Her website was all real. No false images. On the phone she sounded like a serious person who enjoyed it. She told guys the rules: they could be friends, and talk, go on dates, but she was not going to become their girlfriend, or someone to date regularly if they hit it off. If that's not what they want, they shouldn't call her, because it's not going to be permanent. Her best clients and the most fun ones were from out of town and had learned about her from websites or referrals.

Some guys were in love with her and wrote glowing reviews. Men bragged on their reviews. She'd received both good and bad reviews, some about sessions that never even happened. A bad review affected her too much emotionally, but it was hard not to read them. They could be painful or wonderful.

She thought that maybe she was a little paranoid. She saw a low volume of clients. She showed her face in her ads, but that didn't cause her any trouble. She didn't see young men. When she was just dating, some young guys said they were in love with her. She met nicer men and women escorting than she ever did dating, which was awful. There was no structure for it. This way, the results were fairly easy to anticipate.

She got lots of men who were inexperienced. Some men saw her as exotic, and she met men with similar tastes. Many of her clients liked a French or European style and someone with whom they could talk. She saw a lot of older men. There weren't as many long dates as she would like, because of her other job. A married executive at a major company wanted her as a mistress. She thought, 'I can do this'. She would not be exposed to unknowns, but the more she talked with him the more she realized their personalities were very different and she'd lose her independence.

Ariana had a humorous personality. She was shy but inquisitive. She was glad of what she was doing, appreciative of the opportunity, and said she enjoyed meeting the guys when they weren't creeps. Sometimes, they were AWFUL, selfish. "I want this!" "On your knees." "Suck this cock, bitch!"

When I asked her if she'd walked out on people she said she'd only walked out a couple of times and probably should have walked out more. Her perception was that if she walked out she was not giving the guy a chance.

Ariana had a ritual. She tried to look as good as she could. She went to the top salons, and they knew what she did. She had her hair done, her nails done, a facial, a body wax, and a scrub.

She completely redecorated her house, creating a beautiful environment for these sessions and even had houseboys clean her house. She cooked extravagant meals for her clients. She charged more for all that, but most of her earnings went to paying for the lifestyle. She hardly made a profit, but money was not the object. It was something she did for passion. She didn't count the minutes.

She said she was a good person, believed in karma, and provided pleasure. She was learning Tantra, which she considered a wonderful mental model. She didn't regret escorting, only that she didn't do it when she was younger.

Ariana wanted to do something with art. She wrote a little bit and had a great website. While at work she was always looking for erotic, suggestive things for her house, stories for her website, or outrageous, wonderful recipes to cook.

She described a fantasy in which she seduced a whole room of people at once. First, she came out with things to eat, in small amounts that balance each other, sweet and sour. Disarming everyone. Always more. Whatever they were thinking about before, whether they were mad at their wives or work, it all went away as their palates were exposed to new tastes.

She felt some kind of change coming on. Maybe she would move to Los Angeles, which would mean a complete change in her life. She had to decide if she wanted to make this radical step. Or maybe she would go to Europe again, possibly Paris. There were adult attitudes in Europe.

Ariana said that before she was an escort she spent years putting up with relationship problems. She thought she was unattractive and was emotionally unable to have a relationship. They always broke up because she was too demanding. She felt that she was acting stupid, wanted her life to be completely different, and it was.

She felt younger than she used to, and somewhat less prone to depression. She was lonely, not happy. She still yearned to be a lap dancer in a strip club. She liked the attention and loved doing it, but she couldn't compete with eighteen year-olds. They could do things physically she couldn't do, but she still had that desire. She also had tummy tuck scars, which would be a problem.

As for the upcoming Los Angeles visit, she read about a place called Club Starlite, a taxi-dance club. Hostesses dance with customers for a price. From what I've read about Starlite it sounded like they were strict about preventing sexual contact.

She said, "Dancing with the men and having them feel me up is hot." The taxi dancers were mostly Hispanic, as were their customers. Many of them didn't speak English. By modern standards it was considered old-fashioned, low end, and barely mentioned on the Internet.

She said she was really living in the present, though it sounded to me like a lot of fantasy, complex feelings about men and perhaps fear of aging. It was important to Ariana to be aware of her own feelings. She felt she had gotten a little blasé, and needed to upgrade her goals and make a move. She repeated that Tantra was her goal, and she wanted to share that with men.

One word that was never mentioned in any of Arianna's interviews was 'vanity'. It's a word more frequently associated with women and gay men, but it's just a word, not an explanation. It must have had something to do with her wishing she could get paid for lap dances.

Perhaps my first instincts were right about Ariana preferring women to men. When she came to Los Angeles she only met with women.

She seemed driven by her feelings and needed to be seen as erotic and attractive. I wonder how that affected her inability to screen clients well, or end unpleasant sessions. Some providers seemed to be able to handle that much better than she did. I think her perception and intuition could be clouded by her needs and feelings. However, some very intelligent people are unable to judge people correctly by watching their faces, while other people are good at it. I've read that some lawyers aren't, but that people with IQs so low that they are institutionalized, what used to be called 'morons', have an uncanny ability to tell when someone is lying.

CHAPTER XIX: A DEAF WOMAN FINDS MEANING

I read on TER that **Kimberly** was a deaf woman who gave sensual massage. Her website said this work was especially meaningful to her as it provided means to communicate at a deep level.

From Kimberly:

> *Thank you for reading my HOT TER! And your nice compliments.*
>
> *As being profoundly deaf since birth, I'm so happy to serve my magic hands to all walks of life. Men (even married), women and couples. I have a life to live and I have a real purpose for my decent being as a masseuse professionally and personally.*
>
> *OXOX~Kimberly*

Dear Kimberly: Thanks for responding to my query. Would you be willing to answer some email questions for my book and/or movie script? As I said before, your identity would be concealed. It's wonderful that you are able to share your special gift

Jim

> *Jim~Very warm welcome. I do believe in giving and receiving theory to share from each other. What will I expect from you? & I want the whole world to know who I am! This is our 21st century and I have so much more to share with my heart open wide. An opportunity to be an actress? Anything possible?*
>
> *~Kimberly*

My next email reiterated that all contributors would be anonymous and unpaid. No response.

CHAPTER XX: TAYLOR – A SAGA WITH A TWIST

Taylor was quoted several times earlier in this book. This is only a small portion of the actual interviews. She was suspicious at first that I was pretending to be a writer...

> ...in order to gain access and favors of loose and gullible women.

She also wrote,

> I have an incredible perspective that defies imagination...and literally begs for an award of some sort.

> So...lay it out. What are you really looking for?

We wrote back and forth and after one letter I added,

"P.S. If you happen to be near a TV tonight, watch 20/20 on ABC. My wife is the beautiful Chinese-American woman who produced FREE WILLY and then worked for years to rescue Keiko the whale."

Taylor included an apology in most exchanges. She replied,

> Is the whale ok? Hoping so. Ok. So you convinced me. Please don't blame me for skepticism. It is both intelligent (given the environment...and necessary!) How rare to find someone who is actually who they claim to be, for a refreshing change!

> I did my research, and found your credits... And here you are wandering about in my world. I would love to meet you and talk about all sorts of things. I would love to meet Keiko. I'd be open to a lunch meeting with you, and Keiko if you'd like... I'm intrigued by this project that you are proposing. You don't seem to come from a "crass sensationalism" background, and I am dying to find out your perspective.

Thank-you for screening yourself out as a "cheap thrill" seeker. I hope I didn't offend you with my skepticism........ I'm guessing that we would both be enriched at the very least by meeting.

And if we can help each other...well...God bless America.

I am a single mom, with two children I adore and will not compromise for any reason on earth.

Dear Taylor: Thanks for responding and offering to help. Hopefully I can help you as well; most of my writing students were produced, published, or sold. I've mentored a lot of people (blah blah blah.)

The whale is okay, but I don't think he can make lunch. He's in Norway, trying to adjust to living in the wild, and having a smashing time. (You asked if you could meet Keiko; that's the whale :-). Jennie worked for years to save him.

Thanks Jim! And please, my sincere apologies to your wife Jennie...I had no intention of calling her a whale! Doesn't that just figure? Here, I finally encounter somebody in this silly town who actually can back up their story, and the first thing I do is to confuse his wife with a two-ton mammal? Nice going.

...I may be able to share a few pearls of insight into your subject. You mentioned that the women who are "not happy" about this business are hard to pin down or communicate with. That's because they are either on drugs or whacked to some degree, or they wouldn't be here. Myself included. (And I wouldn't have it any other way, because being normal is too damned dull!)

Looking forward to meeting,

Taylor

She later wrote,

I have an interesting few weeks coming at me...I am a State's Witness in my ex's criminal trial for

*'terrorist threat and stalking' ...so bear with me...
There is something compelling about this chance
meeting that makes me want to know a little
more.*

*Perhaps it's that I see in you (collectively)
something that I have reached for... but didn't
know where to start in order to make things
actually happen. For some reason I am compelled
to not simply, "blow this off", because the timing
didn't work as planned. I simply sense in you, a
sort   of...uncanny   competence...practical
application aptitude, that I lack, admittedly;
coupled with what appears to be a relatively
kindred spirit and outlook which is far too rare in
my experience, and thus I do appreciate it when I
see it.*

*I am curious, and interested... hoping that you'll
forgive me my delay in response...Graciously.*

Taylor

TAYLOR'S PHONE INTERVIEW

Taylor was raised by poor and ignorant parents. They'd
already had two children a dozen years before she was born
and wanted another baby. Her mother couldn't conceive, so
they adopted her.

Taylor was much smarter than her mother, who was jealous of
her. Her sister also resented her. She was the apple of her
father's eye, which made them even more jealous. To this day
her mother is still putting her down with backhanded
statements like, "You're not so fat." Or: "Maybe you're not too
old to attract a man."

When she was sixteen years old, she was pretty and had
thirty-seven inch DD breasts. To this day, she says, "I never
met a man who could tell me the color of my eyes."

She said she wanted to get laid in high school, but couldn't.

She thought boys her own age were too stupid so she dated
thirty year-old men, but they were afraid of getting involved
sexually. She was very aggressive and they thought she would

be trouble. She said, "I was willing, but I would get what I called 'the kiss of death', which is a kiss on the forehead."

Taylor had an excellent business selling gift items in resort communities. She was earning good money and taught sales techniques, but she was married to a 'nut case'. He was certifiably insane. I asked her why she married him and she said it was because he couldn't function without her. We discussed the 'Florence Nightingale syndrome', where some women seek out men who are useless or even abusive, because they make the women feel needed.

She went through an abusive marriage and had two children, eight and two years old. For fifteen years her husband told her she was fat, ugly and undesirable. Her husband had cancer and they went through bankruptcy. They thought he'd die, but, "Unfortunately, he lived."

Then she realized her husband's insanity was manifesting itself in her children and she was determined that this was not going to happen. She couldn't just leave or he'd kill her. She had to live a lie, make him believe she was accepting his abuse, while setting up a backdoor to escape.

He was spending all the money she earned on their house, which kept him off her back a little bit. She kept journals and tapes so she could prove his insanity. She was sleeping with the enemy while investigating him.

She escaped and came to Los Angeles under the protection of the City Attorney in a witness-protection program. She was still legally married. Her husband was facing criminal charges for making a terrorist threat. He found her, stalked her, broke into her house, kidnapped her kids and took them to a remote cabin with no water or electricity, then came back into town without them to taunt her with the knowledge that they were alone in the woods.

She coaxed him into bringing them back. These legal battles continued during the course of our interviews. Despite years of abuse, she was still having a tough time bringing herself to testify against him in the criminal trial.

After she moved to Los Angeles she started having a romantic and business relationship with a man who gave sales seminars. He was a magnetic speaker and his theory was sound but he could not actually sell anything. She went through fifty thousand dollars during their romantic affair. She said he was the first person she had even kissed in fifteen years of marriage. (Maybe there was no kissing but they did have children.)

She finally kicked him out, but her life was a mess and her business reputation was trashed. This caused her to lose even more self-esteem. She needed to feel attractive as a woman so she became promiscuous, proving over and over that she was attractive. She was living with a life-long girlfriend who secretly hated her and eventually kicked her out. (Several of the escorts I interviewed had been betrayed or kicked out by a girlfriend.) After that she was living out of her car.

Three years ago she saw adult employment ads in the *LA Weekly*, selected an ad for massage, and met with a pimp. She told him about her marketing techniques and how to apply them to his business. He was a well-known organized crime person but was blown away by her grasp of how to fine-tune the adult business. She explained sales techniques like writing out scripts for girls to use when answering the phones. They advertised for in-call massage on an adult Internet mall, describing it as "a very sensuous session, full of body to body."

Whoever answered the phone would say something like, "Hi, this is Jackie, are you thinking about an appointment for today?" Then: "Well let me describe myself a little bit." She would get right to the point. Nine out of ten times customers are calling for someone whose picture they saw on the Internet, but that person is not there. The girls might say, "I'm (so and so's) roommate. I'm five feet four inches tall, a petite brunette, 34D, all natural. I'm very attractive. Does that sound like your type"?

They charged a hundred fifty to two hundred dollars per hour. They usually booked for an hour, but the sessions typically lasted only twenty minutes.

Taylor worked for the pimp as a madam, though she refers to it as "management." They weren't lovers but she was intrigued by him. She invested her remaining money into renting an apartment and opening a sensual massage "pad."

She refined her marketing techniques and got the place up and running.

Taylor was driving down the street in sunglasses, feeling great, thinking, 'I'm a Hollywood Madam'.

But her criminal partner stabbed her in the back. He strong-armed her and kicked her out, giving her thirty seconds to get out of the house she had paid for with both her efforts to improve his business and her own savings. He turned it over to his girlfriend. This was the third man she had chosen to help who had screwed her over. It was just business this time, but she had allowed herself to trust him because she was infatuated with the dark underworld.

When she got kicked out of her "pad" she had nowhere to live. She was staying in hotels, working off her cell phone, and seeing clients in the hotels. Her children would stay with her parents.

At first, Taylor was just doing massage, but it quickly became obvious that without several girls and an apartment, it was not going to pay. You usually need four to eight girls for one pad.

At first her quoted price was a hundred dollars plus tip, but then the client had to pay another twenty-five for her to take her top off, and another twenty-five to remove her panties. She would lure them in, then the price would get up to three hundred, four hundred or five hundred. She could end up with two hundred fifty or three hundred dollars for a hand job. The danger is that anytime you verbally claim that certain acts will be performed in exchange for money, police can arrest you.

But doing massage alone didn't pay. Besides, Taylor would usually end up going further. She said,

> *Sensual massage is unnatural, strange, very procedure-ized. You walk down hallways, show him the room, ask, 'Why don't you get yourself comfortable?' They are naked, face down. A cursory massage, then, 'Why don't you flip over?' Get them off and out the door. So silly and impersonal. You take him halfway there.*

So she turned to being an escort or 'full service'.

When she started in this business she would spend all her earnings on expensive clothes, a nose job, fancy cars, giving money away, and buying presents for boyfriends. She handed a man a thousand dollars because she wanted his love. She said, "You fall into a gigolo situation to compensate for what you're subjected to. You get the money so easily you can replace it tomorrow."

After a year and a half of escorting she got over the need to take care of guys.

TAYLOR'S ATTITUDE TOWARD MADAMS

She said,

> *Most madams are willing to sell anyone down the river and are vile human beings. They have no souls. I didn't thrive as a madam because I wasn't willing to rape an innocent child and destroy her, and if you don't act like that, that child, struggling with her demons and fears, will stab you first. She will lie, steal, and hand you over to cops. If they are aware of your boyfriend they'll come between you if he's worth it to them. In many ways we are all innocent children at first but a young girl raped by her father becomes capable of anything."*

Shayne, a young girl who worked for her, was sweet, soft, needy, and let attractive, abusive men control her. She seemed so innocent that Taylor wanted to hug her. Taylor asked her if she had a boyfriend before she agreed to manage her, because a girl like that with a boyfriend is bad news. He'll become jealous and cause problems.

She said that she didn't have a boyfriend. But Taylor was at Shayne's apartment when Shayne started having a fight with someone over the phone. She handed Taylor the phone and said, "You deal with him."

Taylor asked, "Who's this?"

Shayne said, "My boyfriend."

"You told me you didn't have a boyfriend."

It turned out he knew all about Taylor and they were both in grave danger. Shayne pleaded with her, "Please take me away, he'll beat me again."

Then Taylor said, "If you come with me, you are doing it my way. No going back."

Shayne agreed. They ran out of the apartment and jumped in Taylor's car just as Shayne's boyfriend peeled around the corner and chased them. Taylor managed to ditch him and asked if he knew where Taylor lived. Shayne swore to God that he didn't know, so Taylor drove home and they went inside. The next thing she knew the boyfriend was kicking down her front door. He'd secretly been through her house with Shayne before and even been through all her stuff. Taylor asked more about him and learned that he was a Mexican gangbanger!

Taylor said,

> *Shayne is like Jekyll and Hyde. She will lure you, knowing she is feeding you to the devil.*

Shayne and her boyfriend would beat each other up, then make wild love.

> *Some people are adrenaline junkies and get off on the drama. Escorting is show business in a way.*

When he was kicking in the door Taylor called the cops, but he broke in, grabbed her and threw her down the stairs.

Another time Taylor had a run in with a madam. She did a threesome with a girl that worked for the madam. The girl was neither intelligent nor able to handle her affairs well. The madam was keeping her destitute so she would be subservient to her.

Taylor took her in and told her she could work on the side, keep the money, and improve her condition. But the girl was too weak to keep quiet about it. She confessed to the madam that she had gone behind her back with Taylor and seen clients independently. The madam retaliated against Taylor by having a bunch of phony negative reviews posted about her on the Internet. It ruined her business for a couple of months. Taylor was eventually able to show the review board that the reviews were phony and they were removed, but in the meantime she lost thirty-thousand dollars worth of business.

Taylor was arrested. The first offense is usually a slap on the hand and she got probation, but it made her custody battle more difficult. She won full custody in spite of her conviction, because her ex-husband is far more insane than she is.

She didn't have moralistic ideals or guilt about the sexual activity. She said,

> *I was willing to go there (all the way.) And sometimes enjoyed it. If you can get a little excitement out of the deal, God Bless America. Some new girls say, 'Oh how can you stand to let someone go down on you? That's so personal!' I tell them, 'Oh please, that's part of the payment plan'.*

> Taylor is thirty-seven years old. I asked about her future plans. She doesn't have much savings. She said she has business plans involving some of the wonderful clients she has met. But her main focus is on severing the relationship with her ex-husband.

I asked her about other providers who say they mostly see regulars. She feels that's an exaggeration.

> *If you went out to dinner a lot, would you always go to the same restaurant? The thing to remember about escorts is that their lives start over around every two weeks. Whatever they are planning and working on changes around that cycle.*

Taylor has lunch with other escorts once in awhile and one will ask, "What do you like best about men?"

> *Answer: The oversized bulge on the back of their butt. (Their wallet.)*

Question: What's the ideal client?

> *Answer: Small, quick and grateful.*

> *Or: Small, quick and generous. And when you*
> *get older, small, quick, grateful and nearsighted.*

Taylor also said, "For some clients, this is their game and they try to milk every possible (sexual) position out of a session."

LUNCH MEETING

Taylor and I were meeting for lunch. I didn't know what she looked like because her face was blurred in her ads. All I knew was that she was around five-feet four inches tall with really big breasts.

I waited at a table out front. A striking brunette, about five-feet four inches tall arrived, obviously looking for someone. We were both studying the menu outside, trying not to look flustered. I wondered if she was Taylor. I looked closely at her breasts and they seemed too small. Then I realized that the woman was aware of my staring at her breasts. I didn't intend to be rude, but she apparently thought I was leering at her and walked away in a huff.

A statuesque blonde in a tight-fitting top appeared. I stared at her too. She gave me a naughty smile, but walked past me into the restaurant.

When Taylor arrived her knowing smile made it clear who she was, but she did not look anything like what you would imagine a call girl looks like. She wasn't dressed conspicuously; her outfit was less showy than the other two women. She had a strong demeanor and moved briskly. We sat down in a large booth inside the restaurant and I asked some questions.

Q: When you started out doing massage, and usually ended up going further, was it because you wanted to, or because the clients talked you into it?

A: *I was desperate to be acknowledged as desirable, and had always been a horny woman, so I would often end up being talked into having sex while nominally giving a massage. Someone said, 'She definitely has 'CBP', which stands for 'come-back pussy'.*

Q: Did your childhood prepare you for victimization or the compulsion to be needed?

A: My parents were 'Oakies'. Ignorant, not very intelligent, religious fanatics.

Taylor says her IQ was in the genius category and she was highly intuitive as a child. She once had an intuition and said, "Mommy, someone is going to die."

That day, their preacher died. The congregation held her down and laid hands on her to get the devil out of her. The effect was to objectify her and remove her from any faith. She had been pretty skeptical anyway.

She always masturbated and wore out four Teddy bears when she was a little girl. She still masturbates, and enjoys doing it on the 405 freeway on a long, steep hill where truckers can see into her car.

Q: How did you meet the girlfriends who also work in this business? Through ads and working together?

A: Girls I meet with are associates, not girlfriends. We sometimes see clients in pairs. Myrna and I are seeing one guy tonight.

(Myrna is a top-rated escort on TER.)

Q: What happens to the helpless girls you were unable to save?

A: They end up with terrible self-esteem, on drugs, or being abused. For example, one girl applied for a job working with me but I felt the girl was too scattered to take care of business. She wouldn't be discreet and would get caught. She ended up with a pimp who had her set up to see twelve guys downtown. She would see each guy for half an hour, then on to the next, personally earning $100 each time. She didn't realize she would burn out from that, and could make the same money with three dates.

Q: The few you can save, what happens to them?

A: Some I would either take care of (make it work if they are strong enough for it), or transition out of the business. If I just rejected them that would make them feel even worse; they're not even good enough to be a call girl. I couldn't save everyone and didn't want to be arrested because of their mistakes.

Q: Has this profession made you stronger?

A: My personality has not changed. I was always strong. The basic nature of men and women is different. Any woman can walk into this room and get laid in five minutes. No man can do that. Men are stronger and more aggressive in other ways. Call girls provide the same thing as a relationship, sex and passion, except that it's confined to one hour. A real relationship, but with no strings attached.

In retrospect, this sounds like a rationalization.

Every time the waitress came up we stopped talking mid-sentence. The waitresses and busboys seemed to be dying of curiosity.

Q: If I were to see an escort I might not be able to perform, because I love my wife and I would feel awful.

A: That happens. When I sense that the man is feeling terrible guilt I try to make them feel okay about what they are trying to do. I tell them, 'As long as you are discreet, it's all right to see someone else for your special needs, or if you aren't having sex at home.' It's ridiculous to think we're going to be monogamous with one person forever. It's natural for the passion to fade. You may lose that friendship and love, by resenting the other person. So using the services of an escort in a professional and discreet way protects your spouse from the embarrassment and pain of having love fade.

I visualize a cartoon with a middle-aged man in bed with a young, voluptuous woman. His wife has just walked in with groceries and his shirts from the cleaners, and he says, "I'm doing it for you, Honey."

When she talks to a potential client on the phone she tries to reel them in with her voice. She sometimes finds herself talking to them in a high, little-girl voice. Taylor suggested I call, don't tell her who I am, and try to get a date. She said I probably will hear a different kind of person.

I asked Taylor if she fakes her climaxes, and she said she really does climax, and easily, whenever she sees someone, so she can only see one or two guys a day. If she did it five times a day she would die. There are those who can do it all day long, but they just lie there; they don't give or feel anything. She glowed when talking about it, like the thought of sex was getting her hot.

She also has a trick, which she has told other escorts about, but not her clients. If a client keeps going for position after position, time after time, she has a controlled pee, and the client thinks it is a massive climax.

I asked her if she wanted to have a real, lasting romantic relationship or marriage. She said she would love to, but she doesn't want to have the balls in the family.

She said,

> We know too much. We are the keepers of the secrets.

She is still a romantic and would like to find the white knight.

Q: Do you recall a particularly unusual date?

A: *Oh yeah. [She blushed.] A guy named 'Fred' had a friend named 'John' who was in the hospital, recovering from knee surgery. Fred bought me a complete nurse's uniform and took me over to see him. As Fred guarded the door, I went in and said I was there to give him a sponge bath. John had no idea that I was not a real nurse. He was probably a bit drugged. I pretended that I had certain fantasies I'd always wanted to explore. I found him VERY cooperative! Fred was splitting up laughing outside, while I did an acting job. I don't know if he ever learned the truth.*

I can imagine him checking himself into that hospital for all kinds of flimsy reasons, hoping to get the same nurse.

> *Dear Jim:*
>
> *You had asked me earlier to elaborate on my comment about all sex being paid sex. All men pay for sex. They may pay with different currency, but make no mistake, they all pay. Some men pay with cold hard cash on a dresser. In my opinion, it's the most convenient, beneficial and honest method available......*
>
> *Women rarely pay for sex, because they don't have to. That is not to say that women do not value, desire, nor would not otherwise be willing to pay for it if necessary. (Especially really good sex!) It is merely an established fact that women*

don't have to pay for it. Blessed is the woman who gets to use sex as valuable consideration, and wouldn't have missed the chance to do so for the world!

Women pay too...but not for sex. Women pay with sex for whatever else it is that they need to make their world work. For some, it is financial security, stability, marriage, and children. For others, it is attention, affection. For some woman, the trade may involve bargaining for a big enough dose of pain, abuse or heartache, which, sadly for her, is the only thing she's ever known that feels safe and familiar, like home. Men, in general, have very simple, straightforward needs and requirements. They want sex. Period. And maybe some food and a beer. On the other hand, what any one woman is trying to exchange sex currency for is unclear. Usually even to her. Always so to her partner. And it is subject to change without notice. As a friend once put it, 'If it weren't for sex, women would have a price on their heads'. He's probably right.

I have heard many a protest from my more highly evolved male friends who take exception to the idea that women don't get just as much out of the pure, isolated act of sex for it's sake alone, as men do – and thus, find themselves offended that males alone should be expected to pay for it. Ha.

Women may indeed enjoy sex to levels never imagined by the average male...I know I do. But here lies the litmus test: No matter how much a woman enjoys it, if she were offered the chance to have great sex with you or get to attend a private, incredible clearance sale of outstanding Italian shoes...your chances are fifty fifty... Make a similar offer to a man, involving something he really likes vs. a chance for truly outstanding sex. I rest my case. Women will throw you off like a cheap suit for Italian shoes...not because they don't love you...but because they're pretty sure they're going to end up with both, if they play it right.

So in light of this theory, here is my recommendation: This is the way things are. Embrace it...Enjoy it...Utilize it....And finally, if you don't agree with it, at least never let your stubborn desire to change the way things are, get in your way of having truly outstanding sex.

On a predator:

I just got a phone call that you might find highly interesting. Another provider was calling to warn me of a predator client who had been troublesome before, and is up to his tricks again. He sets an appointment, comes in, finishes the session, and then flashes a phony badge and hits the girl up for $500 then, and $500 a week as extortion not to 'turn her in'. A lot of girls fall for it, and at the very least are forced to move and change identities.

This time, he picked the wrong girl. He had already hit this girl before, and when he showed up, she knew whom he was. She blew him off, but was smart enough to set him up. She followed him and watched him as he parked his red truck, and switched license plates from California plates to Alaska ones and she got the number. She has his phone number and she's burning up the phone lines letting other girls know. She has apparently gone ahead and reported him this time. This guy could be arrested and outed for this!

I was sparked on a few angles....the story of a predator impersonating an officer, who uses these women's fear of arrest to blackmail them...the women, so fear laden that they can't see the irrationality of a real police officer who would be so unafraid of HIS own arrest and prosecution...a virtual department publicity fest if his claim was true... The angle of a virtual underground "phone tree"...and girls who are normally suspicious of each other...even nasty to each other...uniting and overcoming the normal obstacles, to reach out and protect each other...strangers... from being the next victim...

My wife and I had been trying to help Taylor write. She had pitched a movie idea that seemed excellent and salable. All we asked was for her to put it in writing, just as she said it, but she always came back with useless digressions.

I saw this email as a plea for help:

Sorry for the delay...and as you know, there were pressing reasons for it, both practically and emotionally, as I have withdrawn a few of my boundaries while sorting out the flood of honest revelations. Being a grown up is grossly overrated. Avoid it whenever possible. I have been a little lost over the last week or so. I'd really love to seek your input on a few things. I'm always very shy about drinking from any well that I come across...careful not to take more than my share...but an honest word and a true direction is so rare to me...I am finding that writing damn near anything is the only thing that sustains me, and I am in serious need of learning there and embarrassed in my naivety and lack of polish.

would you help me?

Family tragedy:

I wanted to let you in on my current status, in hopes that you will opt to remain in contact and warmness with me...over the miles and time distance...rather than write me off as one more lost soul who doesn't respond.

My father's massive heart attack and all of the drama that entailed, spurred yet another dimension in my life. You, of all people that I know in the universe, I judge as being specifically sensitive and in tuned to my gist, when I say: "Just about the time you think you've got it all figured out...your mother calls."

We really don't fall too far from the tree that bore us...try as we might! Your initial initiation of contact, and reason to do so, was based on my underground activities. The reason I have chosen to spend time pondering, considering, and choosing to take steps to keep communication and contact going with you, no "hustle" on the line...no easy money to be had....is very clear to me now....

I understand why you are so intriguing to me....You are a pure journalist. You're incredibly pure, in fact. You possess an unbridled curiosity that simply demands satisfaction and discovery, without being presumptuous. You seem and feel neither opportunistic, nor threatening, almost safe - and at the same time, warm and compelling. Perhaps I'm mistaken, but on gut feelings alone, I feel convinced that by bearing my soul and soiled linens before you, I risk nothing more than the sheer usefulness of journalistic sensationalism. You had no other agenda or desire to harm me. To make my illustration clearer: In divulging delicate details to you I feel that I might need to consider that some of the things I say might actually appear....embarrassingly even...in print, but beyond that I am in no additional danger of having my weak points exposed, only to be exploited for other gain or additional, concealed agendi against me - from you, at least. You feel safe within reason - considering that you are the enemy. [Reference: ALMOST FAMOUS.]

We all push the envelope in our own way. The only thing that determines what is in my envelope, as opposed to your envelope is the level of risk that we have allowed ourselves to experience. The same exact desires exist for every single person. Our differences exist in the manner in which we address those impulses.

We want to be safe and comfortable, but we also want to be sparked, intrigued, and challenged. For some of us the choice is to switch from channel 12 news and watch that wild HBO. For others it means sneaking out of bed, after watching the clock, and knowing that your lover is solidly asleep at 12:30 am, and, tiptoeing downstairs, high heels and black dress in hand, to catch the end of the 2am last call...pick up a stranger...have a wild tryst...shower, pull yourself together, and be home by 5:45am...so that when he rolls over at 6:30 and nuzzles up to you, he's none the wiser.

Same core emotion.

I'm assuming that Jennie has gotten used to your antics by now, and that she isn't going to be simply appalled at me. It's my guess though...She isn't easily appalled at anything. How could she be by now?

Taylor

I asked her about girls who just give a massage and a hand job. She finds that hard to believe.

In the hand job massage arena, they'll never admit it. They all say, 'These guys pay me just to take my top off'. You can hold that line if you are gorgeous (like Mary.) No girls will say they've never given a blowjob or let the clients rub on them. The more expensive, the better the clients. The $150 guys are disgusting.

The sensual massage reviews show that many women provide sensual massage but place strict limits on what they do. I think she is projecting her own inability to draw the line onto others.

TAYLOR'S GROUP DATE

Taylor told me that she had an enlightening experience over a three-day session in Las Vegas with two other providers. One of them, Dana Michelle, is world-famous and gets all 'tens' in her reviews. Taylor said the session was with terrific clients, three married men in the medical field and three girls. Taylor's client had been with only four women in his entire life. She said,

> *They were green, and paid way too much. Their ages ranged from thirty to thirty-five. Each couple had their own hotel suite. Our rates were agreed to separately and I received $600 in spending money plus $1,500 a day, for three days. We were taken to the best shows, including the Blue Man Group, and we had expensive dinners. The men worked together.*

Taylor expected that there would be some kinky swapping, but there was none of that. They were perfect gentlemen. She started out on her guy with a blowjob, but didn't finish because they stopped to get ready for dinner. After that, he chickened out. They never had sex, just companionship. She slept in the bed and he fell asleep on the sofa all three nights.

> *It was a revelation watching Dana Michelle. We each have our own style. There are a lot of emotionally damaged women, angry, and striking back at men. They see a man as a mark and they need to even the score. The air conditioner would blow and she would ask for help. One of the first things she said was, "I notice we haven't been paid yet. Is there a problem with the money?*
>
> *She had no fear of being a bitch, but the men are bullied by her and she gets a lot more money than the nice girls. She was asked to leave on the second day, but was paid extra to find another room in Vegas. She walked away with all the money as if she'd finished the weekend, and completed only half the contract. She was ruining his time and being such a bitch that she was intolerable.*

Dana Michelle wasn't competitive with the other women, but she scared the hell out of the men. After an argument with her client, she said, "I know you are married and I know where you work. If you cause any trouble for me or write a bad review, I'll call your wife."

Taylor was amazed how open the men were with their private information.

> *They emailed us with business names and titles. These were prominent citizens, married, and they gave out their cell and office phone numbers. They were so afraid they would not be accepted as clients they made no effort to protect their identities. I find that all the time. These men are thinking with their penises, not their heads. I can't tell you how many times, at least twice a week, I get messages and I call back and get an answering machine with the wife's message on it. What were they thinking? For men to be such strategists in life, they certainly don't think this one through. If there were an argument or problem, I could cause them trouble. An old joke is 'God must be a woman, because why would a man create another man with two heads and only enough blood to run one of them at a time'? It's almost a suicidal attempt. Maybe we become depressed and take chances. Maybe for men and women this is a category – taking chances. Why is it more interesting than what we do for a living?*

Back on the three-way date: before Dana Michelle got kicked out, whenever the girls got together they became girlfriends.

> *But when we went to the bathroom the boys became suspicious that we were up to something. If one of us was left behind, she would be drilled about drugs or pulling something. They thought we were conspiring together. They kept accusing us of taking drugs, which was not at all true. And yet they were privately asking each of the*

girls if she could go locate some Ecstasy – which we would not.

They seemed to be afraid the girls would get together and deny the men their due access to them. It felt like, 'We can get disrespected by women for free. We're paying for this'. The men were not needy but they wanted to control how the women acted, they wanted to direct the play. They were scared to death we were going to break up their fantasies. Most hobbyists come into a situation with a script written in their minds and their satisfaction is based on whether or not the performance followed that script.

The women were selected from their reviews. Taylor said, "I haven't advertised in over a year, but for this client to write a review he would have to lie."

He was not angry and they left as friends. Maybe he felt grateful that she didn't make a big deal out of him not performing.

I asked about the guy kicking Dana Michelle out.

The argument started during night clubbing. He flirted with the waitress and we were flirting with him. It was his birthday and he wasn't having a good time. He was not happy with Dana and it escalated. Finally, at three in the morning, she confronted him like a jealous lover, shouting, 'How dare you flirt with everyone else? I was supposed to be your date'. He had had it, so he said, 'This isn't working out. Why don't I just give you some money and you can get your own place tomorrow'.

Taylor said,

I would guarantee Dana Michelle doesn't have the regular customers. Are the men looking for their mother? Someone who makes them feel like a little boy? I try to be a child with them. I become their partner in crime. Other women become their judge, the one that finds fault with them. I've seen such a range in how girls behave. I was such a mess when I first started. What I needed was to be accepted, to be adored by men. I needed to see myself pleasing them, so I worked hard to win their approval. I told them stories about my life and gave up intimate details that were none of their business, hoping to establish an intimate friendship that was bigger than the business exchange. And I carried the illusion that I had close personal relationships with a good number of these men, in the sense that they would care for me beyond the realm of their personal fantasies, and me being there with them in the room. It's much more than the money. My rude awakening was when I won my battles, put my ex-husband in jail, got my kids back, rose above my battles, and called these men. Eight of the ten were happy for me but said, 'I didn't realize that you were married before'. I had sat for hours drinking and talking with these men, but once I left the room, they couldn't even recall that I had a problem. A long time ago, when I was needy, I would have been destroyed by that. But by this time it almost seemed humorous. We take ourselves too seriously. Your value to anyone in this business or any business is based on how you make them feel. And that's not a bad thing. Our job is to take care of ourselves, because nobody else is going to do it. So when we are concerned about someone else's problem, that concern is pretty much how that person's problems affects your enjoyment of them. When they were with me and expressing their concern, they were being genuine in the moment. It's just that the nature of what's so beautiful about this business is that it's an agreed upon, isolated moment in time. It has a beginning and end. It's not continuous. We're not responsible for each other in the spaces between. When escorts and clients come together

they heal each other. So are we defined by the
things we do together, or the spaces between?"

It is a coping mechanism, and compartmentalization.

Taylor said that a lot of people are in this business because they can't handle a relationship, except for a short period of time. Men have asked her, "You are so perfect. Why hasn't someone grabbed you up?"

I've been told that I'm the perfect woman for
three days. After that, don't ask.

She doesn't trust herself to not fall into the old patterns if she were in a full-time relationship.

I can hold myself together for a certain amount of
time, to not become a doormat. And thank God I
get paid for it too.

TAYLOR EPILOGUE

We had lunch a few months later. She had given up the business and had never been so happy in her life. She said she had been a cocaine addict and was probably high at all our previous discussions and meetings. Taylor said that the philosophies she had espoused were mostly bullshit, denial, to help her cope. One thing that rang true is that for providers the sex business is 'mostly an expression of control over men'.

She was in the process of rescuing a young lady from the business. I asked her what drove her to clean up her act. After equivocating awhile, it came out that shortly before her final custody battle in court she had been arrested. Six policemen took her to jail.

She felt that her husband may have used an investigator to set her up, but she wasn't sure. On the day of her custody trial she didn't know if the opposing lawyer was aware of the arrest. She was on the witness stand, and he asked, "On the day of November 10, 2004, were you placed under arrest"?

She admitted it and told the complete truth, how it had saved her by forcing her to clean up her life. This is a good argument for law enforcement. The judge ruled that she would maintain custody of their children because her husband was so crazy that she was the better parent.

I asked if she had a boyfriend. She did, someone she had known a long time, who never dated her while she was in the business and on drugs. I told her that I figured she would have to have a boyfriend because I know how lusty she is, and you can only drive up and down the 405 freeway so many times before your car wears out. Neither she nor her boyfriend regret the sexual prowess she has gained.

Taylor said that the other day two women were discussing something, maybe the weather. Previously, she would have excluded herself, feeling that it must be apparent to others that she is a prostitute, but now she entered into the conversation, and it was just three gals chatting.

As she admitted the whole truth, I noticed that her eyes are brown. It wasn't because I had been staring at her chest during the previous meetings, it was the first time she was really looking me in the eye.

Dr. Peterson wrote: "Providers often deal with a past that included abuse, abandonment and conflicted relationships. A common theme is an abusive parent or parents, a competitive relationship with their mother and leaving home at an early age. These women were affected by these formative experiences in a variety of ways. A conclusion to be drawn from this could be that fundamental survival skills trump higher levels of development, leaving the abused child to do whatever seems necessary to live in this world."

CHAPTER XXI: INADVERTENT INTERVIEWS

One interview with an escort took place by accident. An escort mall showed a picture of a very sexy girl named Lucia. I sent her my email query and she wrote back that she'd love to talk to me. When I called, the girl who answered the phone said that she was Lucia, but she had not agreed to give me an interview. Two or three girls often use one name and picture on the Internet. This was obviously her roommate or working partner. She was very polite and I thought it could be valuable to get an interview from someone who hadn't planned on giving one, and therefore had no agenda.

The Lucia I spoke with sounded young and open and was quite candid that being an escort had made her jaded. Unlike the other girls I had interviewed, she had never refused to meet a client because she didn't like the way he sounded. I told her that the providers who had positive attitudes towards their profession were very selective about whom they would see. She'd never considered that.

This next 'inadvertent interview' was in person, a long time ago. I was between marriages and too shy to get anywhere with girls, especially girls who were easy.

I had a curly, natural Afro and a beard that concealed my weak chin, so I looked cooler than I was. I'd shown up for two dates with women who answered the door nude, and in both cases I didn't make a pass. Another time I was walking down a sidewalk chatting with a pretty girl wearing a pink cashmere top. As she got into her new Porsche convertible I reached out to shake hands and she did something with my hand that was one of the most erotic experiences of my life, and she invited me over to her house. We were lying on her bed. I was hopelessly trying to make small talk, and mentioned that I love fly-fishing. (How's that for a sexy line?)

She said she went fishing once and liked it. Her fishing consisted of taking three Marines to a beach and staying with them in a tent while they took turns… 'tending crab traps'. She said she was famous for her oral skills, and the U. S.

President's buddies had asked her to service him. She agreed, but said, He's a prick, so I wanted to catch syphilis first so I could give it to him. I told them to do it, but they wouldn't!

She was still shocked. Believe me, I can't make up stuff like this. It says a lot about the power she thought she had.

As she started to get amorous I made a clever joke and she was turned off. I think she was at the top of her profession but not an intellectual.

QUICK REPONSES

Hannah Love describes herself as: 'A film star turned performance artist'. She is well-known, and can pee when climaxing. I'm not sure she intended to give an interview. She said,

> I've been doing this twelve years and have no complaints. I've had some dramatics but I'm not up to reliving it. Whores have the ability to share their most private, sensitive body parts with total strangers. They are adventurous and dare to live dangerously. They have patience and tolerance for people who others couldn't put up with. Most would never be doing it without economic distress. The world really wants women to have to bend over and do something for them in the back room.

Jasmine, a porn star, must have put me on her mailing list without reading my query letter. She emailed me,

> HI!!

> Just writing to tell you of some of the great things happening with me right now. As always, there have been plenty of updates on [a website] including LIVE sex shows. You really have to check these out – you won't believe what you see. We have also added ADULT games to play. The better you are – the more you see. Coming up in future updates you will be able to see me drinking piss right out of a sippy cup. Every last drop! For those of you that have been coming to (a show

and time.), you saw the sexy SADIE fist me last night. I love the feeling of a fist deep inside my pussy. Don't forget to watch next Monday when I will be fisting SADIE.

And don't forget to check out my appearance page. I will be in Las Vegas this month. Hurry and make an appointment to see me. I will be there for a short time. And next month, I FINALLY get back to NYC. Make your appointments quick — I would love to see you!

And on February 13ᵗʰ — come chat with me at (another website) Check the site for details!! I look forward to talking nasty with you!

Well, that is it for now. I hope you enjoy all the new things going on. I am working hard to give you everything you want!!!

Jasmine

ALICIA LOOKS BACK

This was Alicia's response to my original query letter:

Hello Jim, Thank you for your kind words and interest in what intrigues a young intelligent woman to become an escort. I think it is obvious the main reason is the money and the other several reasons are being your own boss, easy work and having control over how we want to make a living, or let me put it in another way, control of our sexual preference. I never knew it would be so easy and fun. I can be anyone I want to be; it's sort of being an actress.

I can be this sexual predator or a goddess or even Miss America. I did not realize that I would still being doing this, I always had one or two jobs. I was a survivor from a little town in Ohio, who had big dreams. But I think this is the closest I will ever get to becoming someone important or famous. Don't get me wrong, I did not want to be an actress, but just someone who would be noticed or have a comfortable life. I know it's not a career and I am now too old to do anything worth making a career of, being forty and all and boy, if my mother knew she would kill me but, most of all be disappointed! You see I am from a large family, four brothers and one sister. I was the one who was going to make my family proud, which I have done, until the unfortunate death of my only sister, who meant the world to me. But I was the example of making it on my own and doing the right thing. As you can see now I think I am stuck in a fantasy world of glamour and sexual events, which, I have grown, accustomed to. You see, men to me are just a money machine and nothing else because of what they do to their spouse, girlfriend etc... How they cheat and the kinky things they want done to them, you just look and say, "I would not have a man like that" until you start believing in yourself. Don't get me wrong I love having sex and I am usually too much for most men. I do believe I can say I enjoy doing it......

But enough of my life story, I just get carried away sometimes and forget what the main reason was that you contacted me. I would answer some of your questions and hope that it would be of some help to you and your book. You can call me. I'd hope that some of the information I gave would be of help to you. Have a blessed day and good luck with your journey on the life of an ESCORT.

Alicia

Without realizing it, she'd already given me an interview.

CHAPTER XXII: A SOCIOLOGICAL PERSPECTIVE

AMBER

Amber, a sociologist and author as well as a provider, found that a majority of escorts had bipolar disorder, whether diagnosed or not.

Jim

I would be more than happy to talk to you about many different things. But I have to give you this caveat. I am a published author and I am in the process of writing a book about my experiences in this life. This will be the 4th book I have internationally published and a slight change in my normal genre. I have many pieces of information I have written on a local review board I would also be glad to share with you. You will find that I am very verbose about my opinions. The works I have now are already covered by copyright, but anything more I can add I would love to. Even if it is to give you my perspective with regard to this life and the reasons why I am in it. I have an extensive education, presently hold a RN, BSN with a Masters in Social work (MSW) as well, so I can offer a very wide base for you to draw from in reference to not only my experience but the girls I deal with on a regular basis. I currently run a "providers" board in this area as well, so I can possibly give you more subjects to help you gather your research.

See you this evening in chat!

Hugs

THE INTERVIEW

Amber was thirty-seven years old and had been an escort for two years. Before she became an escort, she was working a forty-hour week, but didn't have enough money. She had been an Army wife for ten years, married to a green beret who was gone two hundred days a year. He was an active philanderer and felt he was not married when he was out of town. What hurt her with her husband was that he loved another woman.

Escorting gave her a chance to have a sense of control. It felt like payback for being used. She was always giving and giving, and was now getting something tangible in return. She felt the business gave escorts independence, finances, and freedom to take care of their kids, because she didn't have to work eight hours a day.

She also got a sense of satisfaction out of it.

Amber was previously in the Air Force. Before she was married, she was very kinky. Open sexually. She did some porn – which got her kicked out of the Air Force. She'd been in *Oui* magazine (of Schwarzenegger fame), and performed in two videos (probably not with Arnold.) She and her husband met when they were six. He had seen the videos.

She said,

> *You have to have a nurturing attitude, an open mind, be accepting, and a phenomenal actress, pretending to have great sex. Escorts have to have a life experience to call from. The same is true in business. And an ability to 'be there'. If you are not comfortable with your body, it's hard.*

Amber still didn't think she was attractive but her self-esteem had been built up. Some women got into it with low self-esteem. It filled that hole.

Gradually, I learned more details about her background. She had been raped as a young girl and raped again in the Air Force. When she got married she became sexually repressed. She went two years without sex. Her husband said she smelled bad and would only allow her to give him oral sex.

She came out of the marriage feeling like "a piece of shit." (Presumably they had sex earlier, because they had children.)

After her marriage ended she repeated the same pattern and found the same kind of unloving men. She was not open to being loved at that time in her life.

She would not have started as an escort if she were seeing someone at the time. She searched the Internet for dates, and found alt.com which founded Bonded Domination SM. She said to herself, "Wow, some of this kind of turns me on, not necessarily sexually." It was just talking through AOL messages. There was less identity, so people could communicate more freely.

She had been working full-time, receiving no child support, no bills were being paid, and she was going to lose her house, with three kids to support. She was working as a nurse and a bookkeeper for a corporation.

One night, she started looking at profiles and stumbled upon "girl - indie – escort", with a link. She searched escort links and review boards over three days. She thought, "What the hell."

She made up a screen name and as a profile entered "Indie Escort, big boobs with pretty face." A boyfriend had taken naked pictures that she included. She said, "I got so many IM's [Instant Messages], oh my God, asking for an appointment."

She didn't know anything about screening or about safety. Only safe sex. They asked, "What do you charge?"

She didn't know what to say, so she started at a hundred fifty dollars. She was terrified at first, and stupid. The kids were with their father and she had the client come to her house. When he showed up she was shaking. But she loved it. It was a massive adrenaline rush. He became a regular. He had been very nice online and was the same in person. He showed her a review board on her computer.

She had never taken drugs and didn't drink. She felt a strong connection between sex and power. She had never been told by her husband she was beautiful and how much he wanted her.

We discussed the psychological aspects. She said, "It's like professional acting where you immerse yourself in a role and project what you feel."

I have studied acting extensively and, without going into the details, she knew what she was talking about. She said, "You project sensuality and relate to his mood and what he's looking for."

She explained that escorts are not in their role when they are not on a date. You were literally leading a dual life and had to switch back and forth.

For her, the line between the two lives was starting to fade. "Amber" was starting to overrun her other personality. She said,

> *You are conscious of what you are doing, so it is not schizophrenia. Schizophrenics have breaks with reality. The other frequent factor is bipolar disorder, also known as manic depression. It consists of periods of mania, hyperactivity, an almost narcissistic, impulsive outlook, followed by periods of depression.*

She had done surveys and found that sixty percent of escorts were suffering from undiagnosed or self-medicating bipolar disorder. While they were manic they would research the boards, post, meet clients, and then disappear from the boards when they were depressed. During depression their sexuality fell into the toilet and some turned to methamphetamines.

Being an escort was a great way for these women to work because they couldn't hold down a regular job. Successful escorts were statistical abnormalities. Most were in this as a last resort, were not always able to keep appointments, or were self-destructive.

I asked about her parents. Her father had pornography all over the walls so she saw women as sex objects and became desensitized to it. She stated several times, in different ways, that providers become desensitized. In denial of the facts, they say they are not desensitized.

Her parents knew what she did. I asked if her parents were desensitized.

> *"They have to be desensitized. They are horrified...."*

They can't imagine her doing what she did. "The norm is monogamy."

Her answers seemed inconsistent, but both sides were probably true.

I asked, "Where did it begin?"

> *It became a fantasy. The underlying psychological things, ninety-nine percent are control issues. And this overlaps with bipolar disorder. Where did it become acceptable? For the artist, you can break the conventions, not conforming, and you can be public. Here you can't. Clients can't go public either.*

She had been studying clients.

> *If women would look at their husbands as sexual beings, not just a breadwinner, it wouldn't flourish.*

In Europe it was acceptable for men to see escorts or have mistresses.

Clients said, "I've never had oral sex like this."

Their needs were not being met, so they would see an escort, who was safe, but not emotionally involved. Eighty percent of her clients were married. She was not a PSE (porn-star experience) the sensuous dance, and so on. She was a GFE, (girlfriend experience.) Her clients wanted a physical and mental connection. They wanted to feel that first kiss, infatuation. When they were with her there was mind-boggling sex and the fantasy of love.

She usually worked two days a week, but the week of our interview she saw three clients on Tuesday, two on Wednesday, and four on Thursday. She usually chose a location, staying at different hotels. She had also done in-call two days in a row, seeing six or seven clients a day.

> *Making an appointment is like buying a car. You type their phone number into Google and get their address. Make the customers prove who they are. You have screening techniques. I keep them secret, so the cops won't know. Cops know that*

> *clients don't like to give out work phone*
> *numbers, so they will say they are insurance*
> *workers. Girls have started talking to each other*
> *and trading references and secret methods, which*
> *they will not reveal. Most of all, screen by gut*
> *instinct. Talk to a potential client a couple of*
> *times. If he brings up money, he's gone, because*
> *they can look it up.*

The clients can look up prices on the Internet, so there's no reason to ask.

I asked if the reviews were true. She said they were usually true, but the perception was the clients' reality. Sometimes a client would put something in a review she didn't want written. She might have performed a certain act with one client because she wanted to, but didn't want all her clients to expect that. She said that TER did a great service by allowing the providers to take things out in that kind of situation. Some clients were referred by the reviews, but seeing what people said about their sessions could be degrading for the provider.

Everyone had his or her boundary. She usually wouldn't get naked with a client. But there was one client she liked, and she just had to get naked in the shower with him.

I asked, "How does a girl handle relationships?"

She was engaged to a client. He had booked five hours and before he arrived she thought to herself, "What am I going to do for five hours?"

> *The minute he walked in the door it was like*
> *being hit in the back of the head with a baseball*
> *bat. I completely lost control. I said, 'Let's order a*
> *pizza'.*

She said she doesn't believe in love at first sight.

I said, "But you just said it happened to you."

> *You're right. The minute he walked in the door.*
> *He's never been a client since. He's a*
> *psychologist. A widower. His wife died of breast*
> *cancer.*

This is her two lives blending. She's finding it difficult. Amber and Carol (her real name.) She is very much in love, but as Carol, not Amber. It's hard to reconcile.

It bothered her that her work didn't bother him the way she thought it should. She said, "Crazy people are the most comfortable around the insane."

He was forty-seven, had been married twenty-two years, and widowed six years. After his wife's death, he went to escorts. Amber was the second one he saw. He had a decent marriage. Men don't grieve, they replace. He was into therapy over his lack of grief and dealing with issues surrounding death.

Before Amber saw a new client, there was always the fear, 'What if he doesn't like me'? She had to figure out what he wants and how to rock his world. And she does have to rock his world.

> *Drop dead beautiful women get shitty reviews if they provide poor service, or are focused on themselves.*

Amber used to train people for customer service. She described the Pike Street Market customer service program, which has three main principles: "Be there, make their day, and have fun." That is the key to success in anything. Escort service is the ultimate in customer service. Identify what the client's fun is.

I emailed her a news report:

Saturday, February 22, 2003. L.A. Times pg. A-22. Twelve female cadets in the U. S. Air Force Academy said they were raped, and then reprimanded for reporting it, according to Sen. Wayne Allard (R. Colorado.) The men who performed the rapes were not disciplined. The Air Force responded to one rape allegation by charging the woman with "drinking, fraternizing with upperclassmen and having sex in dormitories."

The implication in all this is that the rapists get off, while the victims are penalized for reporting it. Was this part of your situation? I believe you said that they also discovered something about your past.

xoxoxo

Jim

MELISSA

I wrote a series of emails about the issues Amber had raised to Melissa, a nurse and escort in Arizona. I had interviewed her previously and wanted to know her opinions about bipolar issues and escorts using amphetamines.

Melissa was a blonde, very statuesque Scandinavian who enjoyed sex since she was a young girl. She was born in America, moved to Amsterdam and did some porn movies, then moved back to America and became an escort. She'd had a fairly trouble-free life, especially because she loves having sex with different men. The only down side of her profession was that she was not as close to her family as she would otherwise be, because she didn't like having to conceal her main line of work. She continually updated her website with new photos, sometimes wearing goofy costumes in very theatrical sets.

Hi Jim,

Thank you for the compliments to my website. I have a lot of fun being creative!

I do know that a lot of girls do some form of drugs from time to time and speed is very common as it gives you energy and helps you lose weight - as it is an amphetamine.

Some providers do not enjoy their work, but do it for the money. They live well beyond their means and without formal education to fall back on, they decide that they "have" to do this work to make the money to pay their debt. They take drugs to "numb" their mind so they can do their job. While they are under the influence of the drug, they are happy, numb, whatever, so it makes what they are doing (which they despise) doable. When the drug wears off, then they are depressed, down, etc. because now they are feeling "reality." It's a messy downward cycle.

I do know of a few providers who are extremely "moody." One day they are bubbly, the next time you talk to them, their affect is flat. They also make poor decisions (hence the influence of drugs) and happen to have a lot of baggage.

I'm doing well. I have been doing yoga (my drug of choice!) 4-5 mornings per week and cardio 5 days a week. I am currently reading The Fountainhead *by Ayn Rand. I finally finished* Atlas Shrugged *- was that ever deep! and long – 1,158 pages. Anyway, I hope you are well. I hope that I was able to help you with your questions. Good luck on your book. If you need anything, let me know - I'll be happy to answer questions as best I can.*

Have a great weekend!

Kisses,

Melissa

I wrote back to Melissa,

Do you, or any providers you know, have a serious relationship with a man going on while still working? Does this cause an internal conflict?

One provider found that nearly sixty percent of the providers she surveyed seem to be bipolar, what used to be called manic-depressive. This profession provides a good way for them to make a living, because they would have difficulty holding down a full-time job. This is similar to what you described in your last letter.

A few providers had some sort of issue with their parents, or were raped when young. I know this is a cliché, but sometimes it is true, though less often than most people think. I believe in your case, you always liked sex. I wonder why some girls are naturally open to sex and want it, while, others aren't.

Hi Jim,

Well, I am not in a relationship, so I really cannot answer your first question. I prefer not to be in a relationship while I am a provider, as it would be too difficult for me. I do not get involved in other provider's personal lives - it's more of a "casual working friendship" between them and myself. I prefer it that way.

I am not aware of the bipolar survey. I would have to see actual statistics from medical studies from reputable medical journals to form an opinion regarding the relationship between bipolar disease and providers. I do not place value in a "survey" conducted by a layperson.

I have always been comfortable with my body and felt comfortable expressing myself sexually and otherwise. I do believe that it may be true that some girls have been sexually abused as children/adolescents and perhaps that is what led them to become providers. I think that there are several reasons why girls do not want sex. Some girls think that sex is for procreation only - due to their upbringing or religious beliefs. Some girls think sex is bad or dirty. Perhaps they do not feel comfortable with their bodies for whatever reason.

Thank you for the compliment to my photos. Check out my cave girl series on my gallery page. I just finished it last night.

Kisses,
Melissa

CHAPTER XXIII: HOBBYISTS

I interviewed the hobbyists later. Just as the providers who took the time to give interviews may not represent the majority, the men who chose to give interviews might find a more profound meaning in patronizing escorts than other hobbyists.

I contacted most of the hobbyists through a TER message board. They were as diverse as the providers, but there were some common themes. They find it a powerful turn-on to read reviews about a provider and comparing it to her Internet advertisement with its text and photos. Most earned over a hundred fifty thousand a year. The single men would marry an escort if they fell in love, but conceal her background from their families.

Unlike the majority of the providers, most of the hobbyists were willing to answer a list of prepared questions in writing.

Dr. Peterson wrote: "I went on a chat room associated with TER. I asked those there what they thought the psychological benefits were to the providers and/or the hobbyists. I got immediate responses – all from hobbyists. They all identified intimacy, human touch, and the 'appearance' of being special and cared for as primary to the actual sex.

"Other than the monetary, they couldn't come up with other benefits a provider might get from the exchange."

Chiksguy is married. His comments on the law are in Chapter V. He wrote,

> In my opinion, even if it is just rationalization, seeing providers has saved my marriage and helps keep me sane. Abstaining, even for short periods, makes me very irritable. When my wife slowed down (drastically), I didn't. In fact, I was really ready to kick it up a notch. I can't see altering my needs to suit hers.

His general impression of the hobby is:

It's an indulgence and an attempt to realize fantasies, which is a lot like chasing rainbows.

It doesn't give him a sense of fulfillment. As to the element of danger:

There is somewhat of a rush at the thought of getting away with something and that adds to the sexual gratification.

Asked if it is an obsession:

It can be obsessive. I think I have it under control as far as the expense is concerned, but the time spent in the overall pursuit is excessive. I probably see providers a little more than once a week. There would be a greater frequency if it took less time performing the due diligence.

He earns over a hundred twenty thousand a year and spends around three hundred dollars per session.

My best encounter wasn't necessarily the best sex, but the overall experience, where I really could suspend reality and believe she was into me, and me alone, and that we connected on a mental, spiritual and emotional level, as well as a sexual level. When I finally realized that she had no more connection with me than any other guy, that she was just a really good actress, the illusion disappeared, the bubble burst, and I quit seeing her.

His advice to a woman who was thinking of becoming a provider:

There are numerous books and essays on the subject that I might refer her to, that indicate what a hard life it can be. I doubt she would pay attention, if she were already seriously considering it. I would give her advice to save money, spend and invest wisely, don't get caught up in the darker side of the lifestyle that usually goes along with the trade, don't lose your sense of self worth, or your sense of humor. As with any

job, if you really don't like doing it, for your own
sake and for the sake of your employer, get out!

Unlike Chiksguy, **Sailor352** is transported into a world of
fantasy when he visits escorts. He says he feels the excitement
of instant romance, intimacy, and acceptance. Sailor admits
that he has trouble separating fantasy from reality on this
subject. He is attracted to an imaginative, intelligent website
ad, even though they could be written by someone else. He
feels that he has helped providers with his advice, which gives
him a sense of fulfillment.

Snazy loves sharing escorts with his wife. Many of his
responses have a competitive edge. He wrote,

> *Not many guys can say they have done what I*
> *have (threesomes.) Many go to their grave*
> *wondering how it would have been. I feel*
> *complete and ready for death...lol.*

> *I love the girls we see regularly, as does the wife.*
> *We have built good relations with some that even*
> *extend outside of the hobby. I do, however, see*
> *many of the girls as lost souls, hating what they*
> *do, and it shows in their performance.*

He and his wife love the danger.

> *We enjoy walking past hotel bell desks with an*
> *escort in tow, past the valet driver or security*
> *guard that has that silly smirk on his face*
> *knowing what is happening. One of my best*
> *experiences was going to a "ranch" in Reno for a*
> *session with a prostitute. As we waited in the*
> *bar/reception area for her to be ready, many of the*
> *guys stared at my wife and I. When she came up*
> *to greet us (barely clothed) and led us into her*
> *lair, I looked over my shoulder at the staring guys*
> *and gave them a smile. You should have seen the*
> *looks on their faces. This question also reminded*
> *me of a situation we had once. We were seeing a*
> *19 year-old provider quite often (2-3 times a*
> *week). She was working with us exclusively. She*
> *didn't need any other business because of our*

frequent long sessions. She missed her next period and her tits began to swell. She said she thought she was pregnant, and so there was no doubt I was the father. I never bare-backed her but I had a few overflows. This scared the hell out of me but turned my wife on beyond belief. I thought this was a strange reaction and still don't understand it.

At one time the hobby was very obsessive and overpowering. I almost ruined myself financially by seeing providers as much as 3-4 nights a week. One time was with the same girl 6 out of 7 nights in a row. It was bad. I have since put it in check (thanks to my wife). I spent around $50,000 since last June. OUCH!!!

It has improved our sex life beyond belief, even without a 3rd party.

As for law enforcement:

I am scared of being caught, not for myself but more because we have small children. Would they take my kids? I'm not sure.

He got introduced to the hobby through the Internet:

Got robbed the first time. Got lucky after that. The thing I love most about our hobby is doing a girl or two at a hotel, leaving the room and hi-fiving my wife as we leave. She is my partner in crime and we have a blast. I once called our most regular girl and she came over to our home and brought a strap on [dildo.] Next thing I know she is fucking my wife in the ass with it while the wife gives me head...omg!!! Another favorite memory is this very cute redhead doing me cowgirl (riding on top) while my wife was on her knees behind the girl with the girl's ass in her hands, guiding her up and down. I prefer not to relive my ROB experiences (it raises my blood pressure.)

The wife and I share a secretary, who knows what we do because she saw a charge on my credit card once. She thought I was alone with the girl and it became necessary to come clean. Actually, it made her (the secretary) horny and wanting my wife.

His advice to a friend thinking of becoming an escort:

First of all I would ask their rate...lol (just kidding) I would tell them some of the horror stories I have heard. LE (law enforcement), getting beaten and robbed etc.

I've gotten so aroused writing reviews I've had to call the girl to come over.

BigJohn's wife developed a medical condition that made sex extremely painful. She slipped the phone number of a provider into his overnight bag when he was going out of town. He doesn't see providers in their home state and doesn't feel it has affected their marriage.

The positives: The women. I have found many of them to be sincere, fun, bright ladies who are enjoyable to be with. I enjoy the erotic aspects, but I have also found that I enjoy the company of many of them outside the business aspects.

The negatives: Two things. The fact that it is illegal (mostly from the point of view of how it makes the work more dangerous for the women, but also because it roughly doubles the price when compared to a similar quality experience in Canada.) There are also a number of clients who are first class jerks. One lady whose significant other, also a provider, was murdered a few years ago. The day of the funeral a local guy posted that it was unprofessional of her to have gone to the funeral because he had already scheduled a session with her! This is probably the most callous case I know of, but many of the posts I've seen confirm that a lot of men in this business are jerks.

As for a sense of fulfillment:

> *Yes, in two related but different ways. I have
> made several very close friends out of women I
> met in this business. There are three women I
> keep in constant contact with (several times a
> week), and we discuss essentially everything
> except sex. We decided to drop the provider
> relationship and progress the friendship part. I
> am not saying this happens to all people. One I
> met on the TER board and have never seen as a
> client. We wrote back and forth for months, and
> then we met for dinner. A second I haven't seen
> professionally for at least 2 years. The third I see
> every chance I can, and if our laws allowed
> polygamy, I'd pursue her to marry her. I also
> have been in a position to help a few providers
> out, either financially or otherwise. These
> situations have been very fulfilling because as a
> group, I think these are some of the hardest
> working and most open (often resulting in their
> being taken advantage of) people I've met, and
> they work in some of the toughest situations.
> Almost all of them that I have gotten to know
> personally (I'm counting 8 or so in my head)
> would truly prefer not to have to do this the way
> they do. Many say they enjoy the sex, and enjoy
> some of their clients, but almost without
> exception they have told me that they would like
> to be financially secure enough that they could
> stop, or at least be more selective than they are.
> It's their job, and as with most of us, they would
> rather have more control over it. Essentially,
> every one of them has men they do not enjoy
> servicing, or men they do not completely feel safe
> with. When I have been able to make them a little
> less dependent on their escorting income, and
> therefore more selective, it is a very rewarding
> feeling for me.*
>
> *I take enough precautions that the danger to me
> is minimal. It is a negative, but not enough to*

cause me to stop. The danger is significantly greater for the women.

I see women in the hobby once or twice a month, almost always for 2+ hours. I only pay for about 2/3 of the meetings. Total expenses, about $8K last year. If I had more money to spend on it I would do so. I fund it by having stopped some other things I used to do, saving money by frequenting less expensive hotels/restaurants when I'm not seeing a lady on that business trip, etc. When the hobby money isn't available, I go without. (Though if one of the ladies I see regularly knows that I'm broke she often throws one in for free. That makes me feel uncomfortable so I try not to let them know.) While I wouldn't classify my situation as obsessive, addictive or overpowering, I would also say I definitely enjoy it and do not plan on stopping in the foreseeable future.

Law enforcement has affected him in two ways:

First, I'm very careful who I see. Second, it becomes a frequent topic of conversation with the women, and a personal irritation. I continually get frustrated when the women have to hide from LE instead of being able to count on them for the kind of normal protection everyone else takes for granted.

As to his general impressions of what providers are like when not working:

I have been to some of their homes, cooked dinner for them in their kitchens, met their friends/kids, gone shopping with them (not just when I'm buying them something), picked them up from the airport, vacuumed their apartments, walked their dogs with (and sometimes for) them, and driven out to change a flat tire for one. She was on her way to see a different client and it was 11 PM; she wound up spending the night with me instead. Now if I could only figure out how to remotely cause flat tires!

Usually I get my first interest in a woman either from a reference by a provider I know, or by reading her posts on TER &/or TB. At this point I'm looking for some hints about her spirit and if she is a fun person. Then I go to her reviews to get a more complete idea about what she is like. If I'm still interested, then I go to her site. This is more to see if there is some reason not to see her based upon her looks rather than to convince me I should. For me, personality (fun, sensual, interesting) is 2 parts of the attraction, her looks are one part. I try to e-mail back and forth a few times so we get comfortable with each other.

If I enjoyed the company of a woman the first time, subsequent meetings are invariably even better because we are more comfortable with each other. After several years I have now gotten to the point that there are enough women I enjoy being with that I see fewer and fewer new women.

Probably 20% of the time I have hired a lady with the understanding there won't be sex involved. About half of those times we wind up having sex off the clock anyway (in these cases, always at her initiation.) I only do this with women I have seen before and with whom there is a certain degree of friendship. Several times I hired them on their birthday to only take them to dinner and a show as a birthday present. Typically these non-sex dates are much longer and very relaxed. If one of these leads to the bedroom anyway, it's at her initiation and is usually some of the best sex ever because it truly is a GFE (girlfriend experience.)

The law allows those few guys who are scum to prey upon the women with little fear. A guy who threatens an escort, robs her, or beats her shouldn't feel that she would be too scared to go to LE for protection, but that is exactly what has happened to several women I know.

I've seen a very small number of women who use drugs, and I either walked out or stopped seeing them. None of the women I have gotten to know personally use drugs, though most drink & smoke.

BigJohn said that writing a review is more a matter of helping out the women and thanking TER than excitement.

If I have enjoyed my time with them and it helps them, great. What's amazing to me is the difference in the women.

He's not kinky or into extremes. He is particular about the providers' personality, looking for fun people to be with, not necessarily wild women, but women he would go out with for coffee. They'll go out to dinner, then maybe go back to bed or maybe not.

Viking got into the hobby through escort malls.

For the most part it has been a big blur. For some reason I keep looking for something that isn't there. The Internet got its claws on me. I think it was EROS. I think it is a statement of human necessity. People get into it for all reasons, but for me it is a way to get physical relief. People need contact mentally, spiritually, physically and emotionally. I think it relieves pressure on the social system. It keeps people from breaking other laws. It is potentially harmful to those who cannot distinguish between reality and fantasy. Mostly, it makes me sad about the human condition. I wish we could all not feel so puritanical about our bodies.

I find it addictive, and it seems to lead to escalating amounts of danger. From FBSM (full body sensual massage) to FS (full sex), to PSE (porn star experience) to multiple partners. Do I have it under control? Good question... I guess I am still doing it, so no. I may see one once a month. It hasn't been a financial problem, but I can see how it can be. If I started to go on longer "dates" or see more than one provider a month, then it would be. I am married and I am sure it lessens my integrity somehow.

I think escorts are regular women. I know that they portray something different, but I assume that is all part of the fantasy.

I had one lady just talk. She did nothing. TER let me post the review, but since then it has been pulled and some other guys may have been burned because she no longer has the negative review.

I have seen a couple of escorts repeatedly. One disappeared the other became a little scary for me. I wrote a positive review for her, but she thought it was a little too honest. She did not actually threaten me, but there was a little innuendo. She has since apologized, but I am a little scared of her.

Roadie *wrote: "I'm single. No wives or ex-wives, no girlfriends and no kids. I work in the computer field and make a 6-figure salary. With the popularity of the Internet, many aspects of the "hobby" have changed. The hobbyists have been able to establish a rapport with the providers through websites in a way, which can enable them to seek ladies for reasons over and above physical attraction. At the same time, the hobbyists have been able to give a much different spin on what is actually going on. Everyone knows it is prostitution but a new vocabulary has been developed to almost hide this fact. Terms like "provider" and "hobbyist" are much more palatable than "hooker" or "prostitute'" for the lady and "john" for the guy. Even the term "The Hobby" steers attention away from the fact that* *we're still paying for sex. To me, this partly indicates that a number of hobbyists still aren't comfortable with the idea of paying for sex and use this vocabulary to describe prostitution in a much more pleasant manner.*

At first, I was scared of seeing a prostitute for fear of arrest, of contracting some disease, or just not wanting to violate our society's negative view of prostitution. Thoughts like, "What would my mom think?" still go through my head.

When I arrive at a provider's location, I'm not sure if S.W.A.T. is waiting for me behind that door instead of the provider. That scares me more than disease, because I feel I can control disease through safe sex practices, but I can't control law enforcement unless I stopped seeing providers. At this point, I'm not willing to do that. Hobbyists tend not to think about the medical risks, as that tends to ruin the fun.

I'm totally over the societal view and have no issue at all with seeing prostitutes. I've met some great people (both men and women) and I'm mostly at ease with the concept of paying for sex, except for the part about how my mom would react if she knew about this.

I think the hobby is a good way for people to release sexual tension, explore their sexuality, as well as meet people they feel they can trust or confide in, since the legality of the arrangement introduces a mutual discretion by BOTH parties. Neither party wants to get arrested so they tend to keep their mouths shut. The hobby is also an avenue for some guys to find actual companions. The idea being they meet a provider and see her for a few sessions. They hit it off and at some point the hobbyist might develop feelings for the provider and want more out of their relationship. Sometimes the feelings are mutual and sometimes they are not. Things can start to get very complicated very quickly but I try to steer clear of the drama.

I like helping people and if I'm able to leave a good tip or give a lady some business when business is slow, I feel good about that.

I think I'm in control of things now but there was a time when I was NOT and you could say I was addicted. I let the finances get out of control and I ran up considerable credit card debt seeing providers. I used to see providers 3 - 6 times a week and sometimes I would see more than one a day. Now, I see a provider once every couple of weeks or once a month. Some months I don't see any providers at all. The ONLY time I consider seeing a provider is after all my bills are paid and ONLY if I have "extra" money to spend. If I have a lot of extra money I might see more providers or providers who charge higher rates. Recently, I started traveling specifically to see providers. I've made trips to Houston, Seattle, Las Vegas, and Los Angeles. Maybe this is more evidence of my addiction but I don't feel compelled to take these pleasure trips to see providers. Before the Internet, I can't imagine anyone traveling to a specific city to see a provider let alone some provider actually going on a tour of the country to see clients. If I have intense sexual urges and I don't have the funds I'll pop in an adult DVD and masturbate until I'm sore.

He was introduced to escorts through *Spectator Magazine,* which ran escorts ads.

I was too scared to see a street walker (still am) so I decided to check out a massage parlor specifically for the massage. I wouldn't seek sex since I didn't know I could. I had my first provider experience there. Then I called a 976 number which was a local escort listing, heard a voice that sounded cool, and called her up. That was my first in-call and it was great. Then I looked in the phone book and called an agency and arranged for my first out-call. That was cool but I was uncomfortable with the lady coming to MY place so I started seeing providers with in-call services who advertised in the Spectator. *I use the Internet adult sites extensively. I haven't spent much time on TER but I used to live on the Redbook message board and I met a handful of hobbyists through that board. http://www.sfredbook.com/). I haven't used BigDoggie much and I don't know why. I've made some friends with whom I discuss the hobby and providers, etc. They are good and decent people. We get together for dinner occasionally or correspond via e-mail or online chats, compare notes and see who's on our to-do lists, etc.*

I find the reviews to be very erotic at times and when I'm on the fence about seeing a provider, reading an erotic tale about an experience with her is sometimes all that's needed for me to contact her. I've had some EXCELLENT experiences and some not so great ones. The excellent ones involved the lady and I really connecting on a level that enabled us to enjoy each other to the fullest. Really passionate and intense experiences. As for the bad experiences, fortunately I've never been ripped off BUT I've been with ladies who were completely distracted or just waiting for me to "finish" so I could leave. They usually kept the TV on.

Except for my younger brother, no one else in my personal life knows I do this or they don't know the extent to which I do it. I've taken one lady out to dinner to help her out with some money. I couldn't afford a full "date" but she agreed to dinner for what I could afford. Afterward, we made out in the parking lot.

I've only smoked marijuana with a few providers. I've been offered other substances but kindly refused them.

I've met ladies who aren't full of themselves, and are down to Earth, good-natured people. I'm more into the quality of the session than the attractiveness of the provider. I've met some ladies who have enabled me to further explore my fetishes. I spent a fair amount of time with (a porn star) who enlightened me a LOT regarding sex and even my own sexuality.

Catluvr is a process server/court runner/legal messenger, earning twenty-five thousand a year. He was introduced to providers by a pimp on 42nd Street in Manhattan when he was twenty-one years old.

The hobby is a dream come true and a nightmare-in-waiting. A way of getting even with God, women and cultural dogma. I take great pleasure in spitting in the face of legislated morality. The fastest way to corrupt the law and breed contempt for it is to legislate morality.

He finds the hobby obsessive, addictive, and financial slavery. He is divorced and doesn't have a girlfriend.

I don't trust civilian women. They lie, are hypocritical mercenaries, and always have hidden agendas. When providers are not with a client they are people like you and I who have dreams, goals, fears, strengths and weaknesses.

The beauty of the Internet and TER is shopping from the comfort of my home for what I always dreamed of. I'm very regular with my ATF (all time favorite) and often see others repeatedly too. I used to be quite open about it but have learned that discretion is still important even among my male peers. If you legalize prostitution then the damn government will regulate it, tax it and homogenize it. Better to have it remain illegal but not prosecuted.

His advice to a woman who was thinking of it:

> *You can make GREAT money but your shelf life is limited and you MUST set up with an accountant for things like Social Security, health insurance, etc. etc.*

What he calls 'great money' is relative. Most of the hobbyists I interviewed earned five to ten times what he did.

Batman wrote,

> *I'm almost 40 years old, never been married, nor ever had a girlfriend or anything resembling an intimate relationship with a woman. I suffered a terrible childhood. Ridiculed because of my looks (glasses & bad overbite.) I had those things corrected, but went from being ridiculed to being ignored. I didn't get to develop socially as a teenager or a young adult. I was interested in girls I had no business being interested in, which devastated me emotionally and psychologically. I didn't have a date until I was 23. I have only had two women I met in everyday life go out with me on an actual date. I've had more dates through personal ads, but with basically no success. The most I've gotten together with the same woman on a social level has been four times. I have only had "free" sex once in my life, and that was back in 1989, with a nymphomaniac. It was a fluke encounter. Nothing I have said, tried or done to get women to like me or show interest in me has worked. I got fed up with women treating me the same way a baby treats a diaper. In the dating world, women would complain about how men treated them like dirt, but treat me the exact same way that men treated them. I basically gave up. I haven't had any kind of social get-together with a woman since the first Clinton Administration [almost 8 years.] I ended up suffering an emotional & psychological breakdown in 2000 because everything inside of me snowballed and just exploded.*

I consider paid companionship a "lifestyle" rather than a "hobby." Seeing escorts is the only way I can get sex and/or companionship with a woman. It has become my substitute for the girlfriend most other guys take for granted. If I had ever had (or ever do get) an actual girlfriend in everyday life, I would not be doing this.

My life has always been missing emotional fulfillment. I have begun to learn what to do sexually. I feel a lot more confident in my potential ability to please a woman now. I've had 3 or 4 sessions within a matter of a few days. I've also gone almost a year between encounters. I would say I average seeing someone once about every 2 or 3 months. I think escorts have regular lives, just like anyone else. They have bills to pay and other problems to deal with. I don't think about it much because I know I'm not a part of their regular lives and most likely won't ever be. We spend our time together for my personal pleasure and her financial benefit.

My introduction to paid companionship was in 1992. Previously, I had told myself, "If I have to pay for it, I don't want it." Being lonely, with no girlfriend, no prospects, and obviously no sex, I started thinking about perhaps paying for it. While looking through a couple of local alternative newspapers, I spotted a section of advertising for adult services, mostly escort services. I was very naive, and had no clue of how things worked. I didn't think "in-call" was available and assumed escorts would only come to hotel rooms. I got an inexpensive hotel room and chose one of the ads to call. I was petrified when I made the call. I told them I saw their ad in the paper and they told me someone would call me back. A few minutes later, a nice sounding woman named Josie called. She was very polite, asking me if I was looking for some company. She described herself, but the only thing I remembered she said was that her bust was size 40. That immediately got my attention, and I was very excited. I was very nervous during the wait, which seemed like forever. I didn't know if I was going to be busted by LE or not. If she turned out to be legit, I didn't know whether she was a "call girl" (sex) or a legitimate social escort (no sex.) I was a basket case. I finally got a knock on the door. I opened it, and an attractive woman stood before me, early to mid 20's, dressed in a nice top, jeans, and red high heels. She had pretty eyes and a warm smile. I was still incredibly nervous. We settled the finances, and she began to undress. She took off her top and all I could think was, "Holy shit."

She had on a black bra, and her boobs were as advertised, definitely 40's if not bigger, totally natural, and she had a dark tan. The jeans followed, and she stood before me in the bra & matching black panties. She looked fantastic and I was getting turned on fast.

Little did I know how inept I would turn out to be. I asked her permission before doing anything because I didn't want to do anything inappropriate. I asked about kissing, which we did lightly. I asked about touching her boobs, which she obliged."

I've edited the sexual details, which went on for several pages. I felt he was getting off by writing this.

This was only the second time I had intercourse with a woman, …………..(The first woman I had sex with was a nympho, and she was so loose and stretched out there was no friction. I was literally humping air.)………….

It lasted several minutes, and I finally experienced my first orgasm from sex. While we were getting dressed I told her I had never seen an escort before, so that's why I was so cautious.

She was understanding about this, then was surprised when I told her the reason I was seeing her. She told me I was a nice-looking guy, and didn't think I would have that much trouble. My first encounter with an escort went as well as I could've possibly hoped. The only drawbacks were that she wouldn't French kiss, and I could smell cigarette smoke on her breath during the brief kissing moments. (Part of the questionnaire on TER) *Otherwise, it was a positive experience, although it didn't give me any sort of good feelings because I had just paid for sex instead of getting it the normal way.*

I saw her again a couple of months later. It wasn't quite as good as the first time. She didn't seem to want to be there, and sort of rushed me. She did allow..........., but wasn't into it. She said 'I don't care' when I asked her if I could do that. It also took a lot longer for me to climax, basically the full hour, and she was watching the clock. Afterwards, she told me she was looking to get away from the agency. She gave me another number to contact her if I wanted to see her, so I could avoid the agency involvement. I didn't call her again, although I still have the actual scrap of paper she wrote that other number on 12 years ago.

The other thing about my first escort experience; the agency (and the girl) didn't pull the upsell on me. The price I was told over the phone ($150 the first time, $175 the second) was what I paid. With the general image of agencies today being awful (upselling, bait & switch, cash & dash, bad service), I look back now and consider myself lucky that my initial experience was legitimate, positive, and fulfilling.

I was a late bloomer when it comes to getting on the Internet (1999.) I was reading the **Playboy Advisor**. *Someone wrote in asking how to find* *escorts. The Advisor gave several suggestions, and then mentioned a website called "Big Doggie." I checked it out, and this one site led me to discovering other sites like TER, and many, many others. I use a multitude of these sites to find ladies, but my primary overall source is now TER. The info on TER does really make a difference in my selection process. I used to go about finding ladies in a hit or miss fashion, but TER really has simplified things.*

It's also nice to know what you're going to get. I try to see new ladies as well. This lifestyle isn't designed around monogamy; and as long as I continue I will try to experience as much variety as I possibly can, within the restraints of time & finances.

I have talked about it with three of my male friends. One of my friends has similar social difficulties, and he was thinking of doing it. I told him of my "secret life" and inspired him to delve full force into seeing ladies.

I visit strip clubs on rare occasions. I never have made them a regular habit. For a while, strip clubs were my only real source for physical contact with women. There were many instances where I would sit there for several hours and not have one dancer approach me, and many other times, not be approached by the ones that appealed to me. I realize the whole thing is just a show, but other guys are able to take it for that a lot better than I can. I have a difficult time getting into it, knowing they aren't really interested in me, and all the talk is mostly to get into my wallet.

My profession is in accounting and finance but I am currently unemployed.

Most of the women I've seen have been in the $200 to $250 per hour range. I have spent as little as $100 to as much as $700 (4 hr. session.)

Writing reviews usually does get me "worked up." In fact, it happened while answering your question about my first experience.

It was obvious, but it's better for me to let people talk, and ask probing questions later if I need to.

The ladies I've seen in this lifestyle have treated me more like a human being than any woman I've met through everyday life activities. I don't believe I will ever have that "significant other." I used to not be able to turn off my "emotional faucet." I would start liking someone and couldn't stop it, even though I was personally miserable because the feelings weren't reciprocated. Now, I can't turn my emotional faucet on. I haven't liked a woman on a remotely emotional level in over 11 years. The fact that I've never had a relationship weighs on me heavily both emotionally and psychologically. It also factors into my belief that I can't see myself being a good father, husband, or boyfriend to a woman.

Batman seems to view women as objects rather than people. He thought of his provider as a thing for his pleasure, and he was surprised that she was looking at the clock while he pumped away at her for an hour. I have a feeling he has other mental problems. I can hardly imagine what it was like for the provider, and yet she gave him her phone number. In searching for an identity he had taken on TER's 'Juicy Details' writing style as a way to communicate in general, even though it is pornographic. I imagine that's why he referred to seeing sex workers as a lifestyle rather than a hobby.

Nicolas wanted to be interviewed by phone. He is bi-sexual; though he has hardly ever acted on it. The urge is there. He had just ended a nine-year relationship with a woman. He was earning thirteen hundred a month on disability because he had an accident while driving a county vehicle for his job.

He lives in Orange County and used to pick up streetwalkers, but the city cracked down on them. He is not ready to date, because he lost his job, and when a woman meets someone forty years old, they want him to have a job. He had saved money and collects unemployment, so he started seeing escorts occasionally. Sessions with his regulars usually lasted all night, even though he only paid for one hour. The only exceptions were when they had other clients scheduled that night.

The hobby is a huge part of his life, but he can't afford it anymore, so he stopped paying for escorts. A couple of providers still see him without charge. He was lucky that they hit it off personally.

Nicolas has had sex with seven escorts and either developed relationships or gotten freebies from three of them. He once loaned money to an escort who disappeared, then popped back up and "made it even" by seeing him for free. He goes for a certain type of woman, which tends to offer more of a GFE. He feels the need to get a regular girlfriend and would be happy to drop the hobby if the right person came along.

He met a former escort online who had just broken up with a boyfriend. The boyfriend had been leeching off of her and she wasn't back in business yet. Nicolas had phone sex with her and she asked him to come over and take pictures. She was going to post the pictures on the Internet and become an escort again. He said,

> When I went to see her, I had no idea what she looked like and she looked a lot like my sister, who passed away last year. It felt strange. She's forty and has let herself go compared to most women in the hobby. If she and I had hit it off, I probably would have overlooked that.

After he took her pictures she invited him over another time to watch a video and hang out with her and her twelve-year-old daughter. She showed a Robin Williams concert, which Nicolas thought was "vulgar." He was uncomfortable watching it with a twelve-year-old girl. But Nicolas sent her flowers because he wanted to maintain a friendship. It turned out she was still seeing her ex-boyfriend from time to time, and he (the ex) got pissed off about the flowers.

> *I said I was cautious about getting involved, and it sunk in that there was no physical attraction. It got ugly and she stopped talking to me, saying she had to focus on her new provider identity.*

Nicolas said,

> *Most women in this arena say men need relationships more than they do. They like to be financially independent and meet a broad spectrum of men.*

Nicolas never had a bad experience when he screened through TER. He is not turned on by writing reviews but takes great care to explain his feelings and writes flattering, flamboyant reviews. Women have offered him freebies in exchange for a review. He's met with three other hobbyists numerous times and they had lengthy conversations about bad relationships or wives who don't want to have sex. He thinks the concept of a guy saving his marriage by getting sexual needs fulfilled elsewhere is perverse.

> *You need to be able to talk to your spouse. How would marriages be saved if their wives found out? If I were married but not having a positive relationship, I would leave my wife. I was the child of parents who stayed together for the children.*

He's dated a lot of women who had kids. He never wanted to be a biological father, but would like to adopt a child.

Regarding his bisexuality (which I didn't inquire about until late in the interview, though I suspected it from the beginning), he had not acted on it except that he was once in a house with people who were nudists.

> *There were things we did, but not penetration or oral activity. Personally, I could never be personal or affectionate with a guy other than sexually. The last time I did something like that*

> *was in 1990. I was playing with a guy at a party but we agreed we would not to go beyond that.*

He said he would have sex with a man tomorrow if it was the right guy and it was safe.

> *One ex-girlfriend said, 'Why not have a relationship with a guy?' Once he came I would lose my interest. My only focus on a guy is his cock. With a woman it's all of her, the whole woman. I'm very generous with them.*

He tells women upfront that he doesn't care if they get off or not, just don't fake it.

> *I hate fake. Hate fakes boobs or orgasms. Only half of them actually climax. I don't expect them to. Some women want the man to climax first, and then she can take care of herself. Others want to give the client a good experience, then get rid of him. Of the ones I've seen, one uses a vibrator, another can only climax if a guy goes down on her, another has to be on top. One couldn't climax during intercourse. I wasn't able to stay hard because she wouldn't let me go down on her, so we watched each other masturbate. She went on five minutes after I finished. Some women don't care. Most of the women I had relationships with didn't have orgasms the first time. Some never did.*

As for the woman he was involved with for nine years, she originally said, "Don't worry about me having a great time, I enjoy just giving to you."

Nicolas said,

> *My girlfriend was a giver, but that was not going to work with me. After a few months she could have an orgasm every time we had sex.*

It's interesting that Nicolas, whose voice sounded effeminate, is so attractive to escorts that they will see him for free. Perhaps the escorts he's seen are comfortable with a man who is sensitive rather than macho.

Rudolph hires porn stars as escorts to push his sexuality to the limits and he loves to show off. He loves the danger. He's never been good with the ladies, doesn't have a wife or girlfriend and this is his way of finding "relief." He apparently called me from a phone booth in a hotel lobby: he was whispering, had to stop the conversation when people were nearby, and was obviously having a great time. He gave me the name of a porn star he booked for fourteen hundred dollars per hour. He said, "She would be up for anything."

I'm sure he thought I was going to look her up, but I wasn't curious.

They went to a hotel room in the early afternoon and had some unusual sexual experiences, which he described in detail. It sounded like it was more about testing the limits than physical pleasure. With her consent, he videotaped their sessions.

Then they cleaned up, got dressed and went to dinner at a famous restaurant with a view of the city. At his request, she wore her sluttiest outfit, with no panties. He also wore no underwear. They dined sitting next to each other at a spot where virtually everyone could see them, hugging and kissing in a "public display of affection." He put his hand up her skirt and played with her. She did the same with him. They rubbed each other all over. He made it appear to the room that he was rubbing her breasts (appearances are everything.) He said,

> *She was a great French kisser.*

Then they went back to the hotel.

> *She had me fuck her in the ass. She really prefers that.*

He described various behaviors of questionable hygiene, followed by conventional (missionary) sex.

> *Then we adjourned to the bathroom.*

His voice quivered as he told me that they golden-showered (peed on) each other.

> *It was the first time I was able to come out with a fair amount. It's hard peeing in front of someone, but she made me so comfortable. Then we both*

> *shit on each other's bodies. It was just small turds.*

I guess it's the thought that counts.

He said, "I'm 45 and had come 3 times, which is unusual. Plus, we talked."

This sounds like one part pleasure, one part exhibitionism, and one part testing how far you can let yourself go.

A hobbyist called **Kinkigye** also uses the hobby to push the limits of his own sexuality. This affects the kind of providers he sees. He wrote,

> *Another aspect of the provider personality -- if there is one -- is what I would characterize as a "crisis-oriented personality." Many of the providers I know love crisis. They love living from moment to moment; the rollercoaster of ups and downs of the business; they love running out of money and being broke and having to wait anxiously for an appointment, then getting flush with cash and spending it all on shoes. They love the tension of new clients, the on-again-off-again romance with regulars. This may be an aspect of their "addiction."*

I suppose they take the individual outside of himself/herself.

Tbone feels that the Internet has given prostitutes and their clients a sense of community, and shown them there is nothing to feel guilty about.

> *It also lets us all see that we are not all criminals, but just people with desires. We are no more corrupt than corporations, government, or religions are proving to be. It is actually the socially accepted sexual practices of serial dating, monogamous marriage, followed by divorce, which is sordid, perverse and harmful. The dating scene now is brutal, and the marriage scene is little better. With the Internet, men and women will realize this more and more.*

The hobby has a wide potential for social change because it suggests a social shift in the way people are conducting sexual relations. It can be more significant than "The Summer of Love," and is quite possibly its logical conclusion. The negative, of course, is that the bad guys, law enforcement, can see all this, too, and if it does begin to be significant, I have to think the resistance against it might get heavy.

It's very therapeutic. But then I have some psychological problems that need therapy. I've had long periods of celibacy in my life, so I can make the comparison between how I feel physically and mentally, before and after intensely pleasurable sex. I've never had electro-convulsive therapy, but I suspect that it is just as effective. Maybe psychiatry in its treatments is ignoring the elephant in the ballroom. Maybe sex is the key. I was at a dead end before I joined the hobby. Marriage and monogamy held no satisfaction for me. Nothing I did felt significant. This has provided intellectual stimulation. I'm more ambitious. Suddenly my dead-end job I've had for seven years isn't good enough. Physically, I can exercise harder and more frequently, and work like never before to get fitter. I'm more creative. For the women I plan to meet, far from it being emotionally detached sex, it is more like having six crushes at a time, with an 80 percent chance of fulfillment, and the only thing getting in my way is the limit on my earnings. This no longer feels like a limit, because I feel that I have no alternative but to raise my earnings. And I think about the hobby, or the things I find on the discussion board all the time.

He wishes he could afford to see escorts more frequently.

I have no girlfriend and plan to have none from here on out. Unless there's a change in my psychology (perhaps brought about by the hobby) these sessions represent the only sexual encounters I will have this year. This is almost celibacy. It motivates me to want to demand more, to want to make more, and to have a better job.

It is a concession to the fact that I am never going to marry, and I'm never going to have a significant other. I started seeing providers after the fact was indelible. It may just, however, change me in a way that this is no longer indelible. In my short time in it I've had discussions and correspondences with providers that I never had with women on the outside.

I think most laws regarding consensual sex exist from false assumptions, misogyny, and bigotry. Men misinformed by their respective holy scriptures made these laws, and they've never been reconsidered since. I think the foolishness of keeping them in place and never debating them again is like giving the dead a vote over the living. Of course, the dead will always vote against sex and pleasure, the same goes for a legislature, not so coincidentally. So, I feel rather defiant about it. I consider the vice police who enforce these to be lower creatures than telemarketers, and to be honest, I see no reason to follow these laws just so the people enforcing them could feel like they're sane.

His general impression of providers is that they are so diverse that the hobby is the only thing they have in common.

However, the most successful independents have a great capacity to enjoy sex, regardless of the partner, that is absent in the general population. There are some nymphomaniacs among them whose sex lives would be a self-destructive addiction if they didn't get paid. I notice a few providers posting messages who are either suffering burnout, or are approaching retirement with anguish about the life they didn't have because the hobby was always so engrossing for them.

As to potentially marrying an escort, he said,

I have a large family, and there is a greater chance that some family member knows her from her "other" life and will "out" her, especially if her website doesn't obscure her face. All of the wives in the extended family will take an immediate hostility to her, and so will some of the more religious or priggish family members.

He felt that other men in the extended family would feel free to come on to her or even grope her.

My query letter asked the hobbyists about their professions and annual incomes. Tbone replied,

Rude question. I'm a writer and a telephone operator. My income is between $23k and 30k a year, too low for this hobby.

His sessions used to cost three hundred dollars, but he went through a complete makeover for his last session.

Haircut, manicure, new jacket, what have you.

That plus a two and a half hour session came up to nine hundred thirty dollars.

As for his reviews of sessions, he said,

I look closely and see what she did that was special, erotic or sensitive, and investigate exactly how the date and the sex, with all of its acts and positions, affected me and why. I also observe her responses. I go into much more detail than most reviewers do.

Then he rereads his reviews, gets 'thoroughly aroused', and wishes he could afford another session.

Tbone has only been a hobbyist a short time and most of his knowledge appears to be secondhand. It is too soon to see whether or not it becomes a positive influence on his life.

This supports the theory that men would still be living in caves and picking fleas out of their beards, were it not for their need to impress women. It is motivating him to do more in his career and improve his appearance, and he thinks about it all the time while performing a boring job. I don't know if the escorts he is communicating with are as sincere as he believes. He gave me a convoluted answer as to whether or not he found the hobby to be addictive.

Jasper, a hobbyist in Southern California commented on the Asian massage parlor girls.

> *So many of them are studying psychology in college it's scary. If I ever get put in the loony bin for sexual obsession, I'll probably find a couple of my doctors once gave me blowjobs.*

Another hobbyist heard that girls working at massage parlors were not there willingly, so he stopped going to them. I don't know if his fears are valid.

Faulkner is thirty-seven years old and went to see a nineteen-year-old escort. He felt that he would probably burn in hell for it. She was so young and innocent he was sorry that his lust for her overcame his better instincts. He usually lasts fifteen minutes but in this case he finished in about two minutes. He felt he was robbing her of her youth.

> *Just because a friend of yours has a cute daughter doesn't mean you have to fuck her. If you get turned on by reading this and see this girl I'll probably meet you in hell.*

Achilles is in his late fifties and started seeing escorts two years ago in New York. He has been married for thirty years but his wife lost interest in sex several years ago and is out of town a lot. She earns several million dollars a year and he is semi-retired. He had been successful in an intellectually rigorous and prestigious profession. He said his children have gone through college.

His life is more than half over, and he's always lived a staid existence. He is not a skydiver and doesn't buy jewelry or drive sports cars. He wouldn't see streetwalkers, but stumbled on escorts on the Internet. (Apparently, this is his way of dealing with a mid-life crisis, or a lack of feeling important and useful.) He said, "This is a pleasure I missed out on my entire life."

At first he saw very young girls, but there was not a lot to talk about. Their boyfriends were nineteen. Then he would see girls in their early twenties, then those closer to thirty, because they were more mature. The sex is better too, because they've learned how to provide a better experience.

There are a huge number of beautiful escorts in New York but he is only interested in high-end providers. He said the top ones don't advertise or have reviews. They use agencies and charge three thousand or four thousand an hour.

In Achilles' opinion the greatest beauties are not as much fun. If they are really beautiful and charming they get a rich husband or a sugar daddy. The escorts he prefers don't want to see a lot of people. They prefer married clients who won't pursue them or get out of line, and provide a mixture of sex and companionship. He looks for escorts who have other important interests. Ideally, she has another profession and sees only one or two clients, part-time. He never books for just one hour.

He recently moved from New York to Chicago, and finds it difficult to find the kind of escorts he wants. He only sees escorts when his wife is out of town He uses Viagra, but the sexual aspect is not the main determinate.

When he lived in New York, he used a furnished apartment and a phone registered in another name to see escorts. It was difficult getting his first appointment since he had no references from other escorts and they couldn't verify who he was. He finally got approved by an agency. He said, "In New York it's so easy once you have references you can get an escort in ten minutes."

Achilles began to see an independent escort on a regular basis. It wasn't just the sex; he felt it was a relationship. He would see her every other week for anywhere from three hours to overnight.

> *She only had two clients. I was falling in love.*
> *She had a boyfriend. I was in the middle of a*
> *triangle and it ended badly. She was pregnant*
> *and got an abortion. Even though I didn't think*

that I was the father, I paid for it, because I was very generous with her. We were close friends. She had mental problems – bipolar. Multiple personalities. When she was in a depressive state she couldn't remember what she had said or done in a manic state.

I told him I thought multiple personalities was schizophrenia but he insisted that she has three personalities, normal, manic (when she is fabulous), and depressed (when she is like death.)

She was seeing a therapist, who wasn't helping her. She was also an alcoholic, and had multiple abortions. Several marriages. It's a sad story.

He helped her start a business, not only financially but actually writing a business plan.

He said,

I would see her so much she didn't charge me unless we were naked, not for social things like lunches or walks in the park.

I asked, "How much did you see her?"

It was total blur, I can't really tell you. It started to morph between a friendship and business. She showed up one night with a bottle of wine and got drunk. I tried to take it away from her but she bit my hand. She bit me several times and I couldn't take it away from her. She was so drunk I had to carry her out, get her in a cab and take her to her apartment. I'd never been there before because she always came to my place. She wanted me to stay the night, but I said, 'Are you crazy? Your boy friend will probably kill me'. The next day she blamed me for getting her drunk. She said 'my boy friend says you are a bad influence'. I said, 'how am I a bad influence, because I give you money? Help you in your business? She reamed me for the next week for being a bad influence. She was a photographer and also took pictures of

*me. She could blackmail me with that. I am glad I
got out of New York.*

She had the abortion the day before he left. Then she told him
she had checked the calendar and he had been the father.

*You'd think that if I was the father she'd at least
ask me what I thought or talk to me about it.*

I asked him, "Would you have wanted her to have the child?"

He said, "No."

I asked, "How do you know she wasn't lying about you being
the father? It would be hard to know for sure and women have
been known to lie about those things."

*I don't really know. You can't separate fantasy
from reality with escorts. You never know when
she's telling the truth. They'll say what they
think you want to hear. Lying becomes so
natural, they can't tell truth from fiction. It
becomes a reflex. Sometimes they become quiet
when they don't want to lie.*

*Things fell apart for her when I left for Chicago. I
gave her several thousand dollars and told her to
stay in touch. I couldn't get her to call me and I
got pissed off. I would think that after everything
I did for her she'd at least call! She said she was
doing what she had to do, and 'I don't know why
you want to be friends'. It was one-sided. Left me
with millions of questions and pain. I was
building a friendship; she was tearing it down. It
went from 'I really love you' to 'Don't call me
again'. I probably spent $40,000 or $50,000 on
her alone. She may have had separation pains.
The night I took her to her home she offered to be
my exclusive client.*

I asked: "Wasn't she drunk that night?"

He replied, "Yes. And that's when she said she really loved
me."

I asked several times how old she was.

He finally said, "She's thirty-one, and is starting to look burned out from escorting, starting a business, going to school, and drinking."

"Do you think maybe she wants to marry someone her age?"

> *Yes. She's had offers from rich guys her age but she won't sign a prenuptial agreement. She doesn't even like her boyfriend, but he's rich. She wants to marry a rich man without a prenuptial agreement and still see other guys on the side. She said if I got divorced I'd be broke, because my wife earns it all. I told her I'd still be worth a couple of million bucks but she said, "That's not enough, I need five or ten million.*

I asked, "Would you have divorced your wife and married her?"

He said, "No."

After he moved to Chicago he sent her an email that was intended to be humorous. It made her angry. The problem was, he didn't know which of her personalities read the email.

> *It got worse and worse. I wrote her that she would never quit being an escort, and when she's older I'll see her at Hunts Point giving blowjobs for $20. That's where cheap streetwalkers work in New York. She blew up at me.*

She told him she didn't care about him, and he still is surprised that she doesn't want to be friends after all he's done for her. He got hurt by it all but she just moved on.

> *She has a good heart and is a good person. Her older sister brought her into the business. She trusts no one. I was trying to save her from herself. I felt bad for several months. I've started getting over it by seeing wonderful women in Chicago. The dilemma is that I have to like them, but can't see them too much or I'll become attached and get hurt again. I've seen someone twice who's fabulous, but what's true and what's not? So I find myself holding back. They are good*

at sensing what your needs are and delivering that.

He had a girl fly up from North Carolina for two days.

She was just doing it for the sex. She'd been a virgin up to a month before she became an escort. She comes from a wealthy family in a small town, and it would get around town if she screwed around there. The money is not important to her so she charged next to nothing. She thought it was wonderful that someone would pay for her to fly up and have sex with him. She pleased me mentally, emotionally, and physically. I never had so much affection!

I asked her age but he never answered. Later, she went on tour with other escorts and her attitude changed.

It's better I can't see her too often because I could get emotionally tied up with her.

He finds that most escorts are guarded about their personal lives. An escort he's currently seeing in Chicago gave him her real name. He bought her a Blackberry when she went out of state. She previously had a corporate job, but her boyfriend died in an accident and she decided to become an artist and do escorting on the side. This is a substitution for a relationship for her. She is the romantic type and likes the affection. It's like having a new boyfriend without the baggage. She has been commissioned for a large art project.

If an escort emails and calls me just to stay in touch I think there's something special. I want to go high-end, but I don't want to hire women who are so beautiful they think they are doing me a favor. I want someone who also has sexual needs. But how do you tell truth from fiction? Their personal and professional lives are so intermingled. Life becomes one big role-play. Women go into it for a few quick dollars and then get hooked on it. The money, the control, the sex, the excitement. Once they are past thirty or thirty-five they are not as desirable anymore.

> *They have to do things they wouldn't do before and it's hard for them to start in a new profession.*

> *In Chicago 90% of the escorts charge $300 an hour. It's almost like there's price fixing. There are only two escorts I will see and they charge at least $500 an hour. I don't want escorts who have published reviews. If they advertise a lot they want high volume, which I don't like. Most independents are in the creative arts; photography, jewelry, painting, and so on. The emotional stability is not quite there or they wouldn't be doing this. They would get a rich husband or sugar daddy. I have to talk with them on the phone first.*

One time he was going to fly an escort to Chicago from the South.

> *I called her agent and cancelled, because I had talked with the girl on the phone three times and all she talked about was business. She never asked who I was as a person.*

Personally, I think that's petty and vindictive. I told Achilles that I had heard that many escorts are bipolar. He said,

> *If they don't have bipolar when they enter this business, it could cause it, because of the dual role of setting yourself up for clients. You have to be two different people and it becomes ingrained.*

He was very eager to talk and wanted to know if other clients spend time with escorts without paying for it, or consider them friends. He was surprised, and possibly disappointed when I told him it was not unusual amongst the hobbyists I had interviewed.

It sounds to me like these young girls are playing mind games with Achilles. Despite his intelligence and maturity, he is driven by infatuation rather than logic. He took his New York escort's words at face value, even though she was drunk when she told him she loved him and has personality disorders. He expected her to show friendship to him after he left her and insulted her. Her statement that she didn't really like her boyfriend could well be a lie for his benefit. I pressed him on why he took everything she said at face value, and he said, "If she had been honest with me, she would have lost some money."

He said that seeing escorts doesn't affect his marriage because his wife lost interest several years ago. Achilles said he sees the escorts as real people and they are thankful for that. Hmm. He also admitted that he doesn't know when they are being genuine. His judgment could be clouded by a longing for his lost youth. I know how that feels.

I don't think my interviews with hobbyists reflect the high-achieving men the top providers referred to. Achilles is the exception, but I don't think he's typical of anything.

CHAPTER XXIV: MARY – THE FIRST CONTACT AND THE FINAL INTERVIEW

I kept trying to follow up with Mary, a smart, lovely sensual masseuse who wrote back to me before I had conducted any interviews. I identified with her reason for going into massage: flaunting society's taboos. Numerous attempts to get an interview with her were met with courteous delays.

She had studied journalism and was trying to write her memoirs. She lived in San Francisco, where providers face less harassment from police. Her reviews said she is good at teasing men and prolonging their pleasure.

I was about to wrap up my interviews and this would be the last time I would contact her. She called. Her comments contradicted everyone else's opinions, and were inconsistent within themselves, because she was in turmoil.

THE INTERVIEW

Mary always liked testing society's values. She has been on an emotional rollercoaster for a long time. She is doing very well financially and has more business than she could ever want but it isn't making her happy. She doesn't have a sustained feeling of joy. She describes herself as a very nurturing person and sees nothing wrong with touching a penis, but the problem is when people start getting attached. She sometimes gives too much, then becomes bitter and resentful.

Mary likes not having to work too many hours and having the freedom to come and go as she pleases. She does not like the office mentality and never wanted to work for someone else. Office work is not intellectually stimulating.

She has conflicting thoughts about this life. It is a needed service. There are certain people who hate the situation (this is clarified later.) She said she has no friends who do this. It is self-destructive to a degree but she believes that most providers aren't honest with themselves about that because they need a coping mechanism.

Mary was always intrigued with the underworld and got into it at age twenty. She danced, she was in domination, which was not for her, and she was an escort, each for a short time. She stopped working, moved from Boston, went to college, and earned a degree in creative arts and literature.

The whole topic of providers is fascinating to her. She is a mental chameleon and thinks about it in different ways. She said, "The higher the rates the scummier the types."

This is a direct contradiction to what everyone else said.

She was charging two hundred fifty an hour and finally asked the review boards to pull her reviews. She said she doesn't like the ratings and they are dehumanizing. It doesn't make her feel good to read about herself. It reminds her of an "old boys' club" mentality. Reviews also jeopardize the providers' safety and can be dishonest.

No one tells her what to do; Mary always does things on her own terms. When she was an escort, everyone did things safely. No one kissed or did unprotected oral. She was not so giving of herself. Now, if you charge a certain rate without GFE (girlfriend experience), you get a bad review. Girls will do things to get good reviews. When she was on review boards she could tell if a client had seen her on a review board before he made the appointment. She sees a certain mind set in those clients and some anger towards women. (Personally, I see it as lust or longing but not anger in most instances.)

She suggested I check out SF-REDBOOK.COM. I did, and found a lot of hostility back and forth between the sexes in the chat sections. She said that there is an "us against you" mentality on the review boards.

> It's discouraging and depressing. Comments are unbelievable. It's locker-room talk. Notches on ones belt. I became addicted to review boards.

I wanted to make sure I heard her correctly. After trashing a review board and getting herself removed from it, she was addicted to reading them?

Yes, and she still is. She has to read it every morning.

> Going to see a provider is healthy, but fulfills a loneliness. The hobbyist is pathetic.

She's frustrated and it angers her. In college, Mary minored in women's studies and said, "All this touches something that drives me crazy. The people I meet are not disrespectful, but when you read reviews online you don't know who they are. People who see massage girls would never see an escort."

She said, "People get very vulnerable. Many have not had a warm touch or warm word in a long time."

They respect her boundaries. Only those who see escorts would want more and she screens them out.

She has become a slave to the phone and has forty to sixty emails a day.

Mary has been unable to write because she can't face the words. Seeing it on paper is too depressing. She's hung on to this for so long. She spoke of herself in the third person:

> *I've been a master of sabotaging her lifestyle. Part of me is comfortable with it. I turn down thirty-eight callers a day. Anyone who is a sex worker wants to be in control. Ask most girls if they were abused and they will say 'yes'.*

So I asked her. Mary was raped at thirteen. Her parents did not stand by her for fear of ruining the family name. It was an upper middle-class family and they had their own businesses.

She said, "It's easy to fall prey to this, but it's not easy money. It's a very hard life."

After a session she is physically tired.

> *The sensual part is only ten or fifteen minutes, but the mindset behind it, wondering, for example, what does he want to hear? It's emotionally draining.*

Mary saves her money and doesn't wear flashy clothes or have a fancy lifestyle.

When she was an escort for a year she was repulsed with herself but felt high on the power. It was an adrenaline rush doing something she wasn't supposed to do. Excitement. Power. Control. But warped and twisted. She never saved a cent when she was an escort. She would get rid of it as fast as possible because it was dirty money. When she first started restricting herself to sensual massage she got offers to do more and more.

> *But in my head I remembered what it felt like to do those things. I don't want someone to control me for that money. I can look at myself in the mirror and not hate myself for what I do. My conflict is not shame, it's just that I've sold myself short. I'm not giving myself a chance. I've taken the easy way out.*

The memoir she is struggling to write is very bitter and full of anger. She said,

> *I feel an underlying anger at doing this. In one way, there's nothing wrong with this, but beyond wanting the connection, I think a lot of men who pay for sex were the people who did not get women when they were young, got turned down, and feel anger and bitterness. Lacking in good self-esteem. The men want a human connection, a kind word, a warm, loving hand. There's nothing wrong with that, but somehow it's twisted. Once they pay you – there's something wrong with that – they think they own you for the hour. Most men would do that if they had a chance, but the percentage of men who do is small. But now I don't trust men – half of my clients are married or have girlfriends. My head is biased now. You have an illusion that certain things are normal."* She asked me if many of the providers I had interviewed were married. I told her it was pretty rare. She revealed that she is married. (Her husband is probably the person she mentioned earlier who is troubled with her situation.) Financially, she has no reason to be doing this. Her husband knows what she does, but if she were an escort he would have left her. They've been together quite a few years. He has admiration and respect for her, but she could not handle the reverse. He's letting her do it until she needs to stop. She's too headstrong. No one could

order Mary around and she could never be tied down.

She said, "I have so many different opinions that don't go together on this."

Her ideas poured out in the following order:

Mary spends hours looking at sexy websites. It is addictive. She has blown off appointments for it.

I asked her, "Is reading a review a turn-on?"

She said, "No. It's exciting, to see what others are doing. It's an addiction – I can't tell you what it is."

Every morning she checks reviews of Internet providers.

I must go see what others are doing.

Even though she's part of this, she doesn't feel like she's part of it. She feels she's an outsider looking in and has a strong desire to talk and to hear people's stories.

Doing her website has been the best thing she's ever done. She can charge a lot more because it is so professional. Someone's text in their ads tells a lot about them. She said, "How you project yourself in your ads determines who you attract."

The more rules and boundaries you put up the more people respect you.

She always has been opinionated but comes across soft in sessions. She feels bitter today. Just today.

When she was an escort, she convinced herself she loved the sex. She had a much stronger sex drive during that time. Sometimes it was satisfying but she always wanted to leave. She has a hatred for the sex industry and sees it as an illusion you talk yourself into.

She never wanted a good-looking guy and now she can find beauty in anyone. "People sense that genuine feeling. They sense that you find something beautiful in them."

She is on a message board of the industry. The providers feel isolated so they read the same books and compare them. She will flip through the back of weekly magazines (which have a lot of ads for adult service providers.) In Boston most of them came from tough backgrounds. Now it seems like more come from a normal background.

She said, "I don't know if the stereotypes of the clients are true."

Her clients appear normal and are no particular type. She's had many arguments about these men with other providers. She thinks they are broken or missing something. Every man does it for some reason – emotion or sex. Usually not just sex. She has known a lot of them as good friends or confidantes. Mary chooses clients who are respectful and sweet.

Glamour girls on the Internet don't look as good in person and some reviewers are never satisfied. What's too personal for one provider is different for another. Mary can touch someone's penis but would never kiss a client. Even when she was an escort she never allowed men to get oral sex without a cover (condom,) In San Francisco, everything is covered. Otherwise, you can catch herpes.

But they want unprotected oral.

She would have never thought of it before she was involved in the sex world but having sex with a professional provider is probably safer than with others. She was concerned that review boards give more points for unprotected practices. She said, "Very few people read reviews."

(I didn't correct her.) When she had reviews, she got lots of mail from TER.

From my standard list of questions:

Q: How and why did you get started?

A: *I went with an 'agent', and was disgusted at his job.*

Q: How did your perceptions of it change over time?

A: *In the beginning it was fun. So much money for doing nothing. If you enjoy sex you say its no big deal and so much money. I was nineteen at the time, working at The Limited. I found being a provider so easy and fun I quit the agency and went independent, but it became more isolating. When you are at an agency you can talk about it with someone else, but when you are alone you can't lie to yourself. Many escorts have friends in the business, which makes it easier. Knowing a good person who is doing it, you can justify it.*

Q: How did this world change your life?

A: I've done it off and on during my adult life. I've become more cynical, have more resentment towards men. Don't trust men as much. If I wasn't married I'd be scared of finding someone faithful. Most professionals would never risk it.

Q: Do you plan to quit at some point?

A: Yes, but when, I can't answer.

Q: Do you have plans for what you will be doing in five years?

A: Owning businesses.

Q: Do you tell friends, family, girl or boyfriends about your profession?

A: No. Just my husband.

Q: Do you remember what you felt like just before your first date? A nervous 'first time' where you felt butterflies in your stomach before meeting a client?

A: I only remember the guy was in his late fifties, soft-spoken, not out of the ordinary. It did not feel foreign to me. Escorts are already people-pleasers. Givers.

Q: Ever back out of a date because you didn't like the person?

A: No. No one is rude or disrespectful.

Q: Do you know of other providers who have had quite different experiences, including bad reactions to this profession? Any thoughts on how they might answer the above questions?

A: Sara Anne [a friend of hers] gives off the impression she will be walked over. She has problems. Asks for high rates but never gets them.

Q: How does one avoid law enforcement? How much and in what way has LE harassed you or friends?

A: It is a different climate in San Francisco. Never had a problem. I look for keywords and end sessions immediately if anything seems suspicious.

That was the end of the interview, but then it was my turn to talk to her about her memoirs, about using her writing talents. I have had success as a writing teacher and mentor. I didn't keep notes but I remember telling her I did not want to put down the phone until I had talked her into a position where she could sit down and begin to write her story. Essentially, I said that writing it is the best way to confront her demons.

She said that her feelings kept changing and were in such great conflict. I told her THAT is what she has to put on paper, just what she told me. Start with an admission of the conflict and the story will grow. Finally, I felt that she could do it. Knowing how valuable a deadline is, I said, "Please have some pages before we speak again, and by next Friday."

End of interview. Later, she wrote,

> *Dear Jim,*
>
> *I have been sitting down thinking about our conversation and reflecting over some of the things I have said...It helped me clarify a few issues and provided me with some needed insight about my feelings towards men as well as myself. I have always had a problem accepting things at face value and was always the type of child that questioned everything. That inquisitive nature is still a part of me and I often feel that until I can truly understand my motives, I will never be free to say goodbye to Mandy, Mary, Kristina, Anna, or any other girl that lives inside me.*
>
> *I have spent many years of my life rebelling against society's imposed rules on what the perfect woman is supposed to be yet desperately trying to be her. That is the core of my conflict. On one hand, I resent being an object of desire, I long to be respected for my wit, intelligence and loving heart...but another side of me wants to be the woman that every man lusts after, the power of that feels too seductive to ignore. I sometimes think being a man would be easier...a man has permission to be all that he wants to be and still command respect. A strong-*

willed woman is always a threat or a bitch and a beautiful woman is usually considered dimwitted or manipulative. Neither choice is that alluring...

Do I hate men? (I realize that I expressed that emotion quite often throughout our discussion.) Not all of them...but I have been exposed to so many negative sides of human nature that my views are now biased. I am a person of extremes, one is either a sinner or a saint, on a pedestal or lower then the dirt under my feet. Funny how hypocritical I can be when it comes to judging the very people I resent judging me. Perhaps it is the characteristics of certain men I dislike; those who have an underlying hostility for having to pay for the company of a woman, those who look at me with pity and wonder what "a nice girl" like me is doing this for when they fail to look at themselves.

Sharing with you has been therapeutic for me, I appreciate that and will now take the time to explore my thoughts on paper rather then let them consume me in a negative way. Thank you and have a great weekend.

Mary

A week or so later, I wrote,

Dear Mary:

I'm doing well on the book and thought I'd drop you a line. You are the first person I wrote about. I really hope you are doing some writing, or anything that gives you clarity and fulfillment. Love your websites and advertising.

Jim

Hi Jim,

Hope this email finds you in good spirits...I am doing very well, just got back from visiting my mom and sister in Boston. It was nice to get away and take a break from my daily activities and spending time with family always makes me feel grounded.

I have been spending a lot of time working on writing in my journal; I cannot pinpoint what allowed my thoughts to flow again but whatever it is - I am thankful for it! I feel like part of me has been unblocked and I can freely express myself once again. I am taking it slowly, and I look forward to discovering what has been "hidden" inside me :)

I have also been working a lot less on massage and spending more time on other projects with my husband. One is a business that will be launching in September. The link to it is [a website url.] I am also starting a line of [products] for dogs - I have always been an animal lover so it is a fun project to work on. I have to admit that I am feeling a lot happier and excited about life overall! I am still a "work-in-progress" but for the first time in a long time, I am living in the present instead of worrying about the past or trying to predict the future!

So enough about me... how is your writing project been coming along? Are you almost finished? Did you accomplish what you set out to voice? I would sincerely be interested in reading it when you are done.

Have a relaxing evening!

Take care,

Mary

I felt that I had accomplished my purpose, which implies a lot about what my purpose really was. Is it connection? Nurturing?

I spoke with Mary months later. She had been through therapy. She no longer visited the websites or was fascinated with this world. Mary read a draft of her chapter in this book and wrote:

> *I am no longer that angry person. Being "Mary" and "Kristina" allowed me to vent the anger and shame I personally was not allowed to express* [for the rape.] *Acting out served a purpose in getting me to where I am today – on the brink of saying goodbye to this chapter of my life.*

> *But seeing your own secret thoughts on paper can be a scary thing. They stare you right in the face and dare you to deny the truth, but there is no escape when you know your old coping mechanisms can no longer protect you. It makes me sad to think that I wasted so much time living in the past, worrying about the future and overlooking the present, but I am finally allowing myself to FEEL sadness instead of stuffing it down. I have finally gained the clarity I had been so desperate to find. Some fear still remains but I have accepted the fact that fear is a normal part of life as long as I don't let it immobilize me. I feel excited about my growth and have many things to accomplish in this lifetime. This dreamer is finally ready to take action:)*

THE END OF THE INTERVIEWS

CHAPTER XXV: DR. PETERSON'S PSYCHOLOGICAL THEORY

Dr. Peterson wrote: Selling sex and paying for sex has been deemed as criminal, as psychopathological, as immoral, and as sexual perversion, but the longing for relationship rests on our human need to connect, to attach, to "be" with another in an intimate and vulnerable way.

I have often pondered how the role of the escort is similar to that of the psychotherapist in many ways. I am profoundly aware of my role as a provider of a relationship (albeit a healing one) with my patients. Holding them with words, and containing their intense feelings so that they can learn to eventually hold these themselves is the most powerful dynamic in a psychotherapy relationship.

I think it is important for a therapist to be loving. It is the un-teachable and fundamental quality to which people are attracted if they want to heal themselves in the presence of another. But it is not only the loving, which they are paying for − −it is rather a specific form of theoretically-informed intervention. This expertise is a second − and crucial− reason for payment being appropriate. People resolve their personal problems not because complex theories are applied to them, but because of a loving atmosphere, because of a respectful "I-Thou" stance from another, because of simple things like feeling heard and seen in one's dark moments.

While the escort will kiss, hug, and have sex with her client, the therapist doesn't − mustn't − literally kiss the client. But I for one find the 'metaphorical kiss' which the therapist gives his/her client in return for 'love-money' perhaps more challenging to understand than the paid attentions − the literal sex − that a prostitute gives her client.

People seek help because they feel lost or unloved or damaged, or they wish to grow. The actual exchange of money is not the fundamental issue. The more fundamental issues are ones of power and projection, which money may symbolize. Perhaps we could say that the paying of money is useful and even essential for highlighting and representing issues of power and authenticity and trust between therapist and client.

Perhaps intimate serious physical sexuality cannot involve a mutual meeting and 'equal respect' if it is paid for. I propose that therapy is to genuine loving friendship as prostitution is to erotic love. What you have in prostitution is sex, love, friendship and support, for sale. Subtract the sex, and then what is the difference from psychotherapy?

It would be interesting to interview psychologists in a serious fashion about the feeling they have toward themselves and their clients. Objectification is a common experience for both a prostitute and a therapist. When a client sees or treats you as his lover or mother, or as some God-like fount of knowledge, when 'in fact' you are just another adult, he is objectifying you. Sex-work and therapy have this in common. But a prostitute depends on being objectified, whereas a therapist works towards its dissolution.

Many of the reasons women enter the "selling sex" escort world are identified in this book. One author, (Bromberg, 1998) actually delineates nine profiles of women who engage in the sex-for-sale occupation. She identifies variables of poverty, desire to live outside social norms, coercion or outright violence, educational level, intellectual and psychological functioning, family system norms, and social skill as the factors which underlie prostitution. I would add that women who are physically attractive and/or large-breasted often enter it as the men are generally attracted to them and it seems an easy way to make money. Others like the drama and high living.

I think it would be a good idea to look at the relevance of childhood experience to adult sexuality in order to put my comments in perspective. Mutual interaction between mother and infant has often been identified as a precursor of the adult erotic experience. Mann (1997) in discussing transference and sexuality suggests that the patient relates to the therapist as she relates to her sexual partners and that these are related to the patient's image of the "primal scene" (for non psychologists, that is mom and dad having sex.) Extending this to the escort, it seems that the escort relates to the hobbyist in a way that is related to her image of the primal scene.

Sensual experience is essential to the infant for its survival and well-being and the early sensual experience is the precursor of the later adult sexual experience. The sexual aspect of mother-baby units is often ignored. While having sex, the escort (in coitus) is likely experiencing a repetition of her own experience of personal intimacy as it was experienced first with the mother and then later with the development of intimate relationships.

Perhaps women who turn to prostitution are attempting to over-control their own or another's sexuality through imposing parameters of time, money, and role on sexual behavior. Bullough & Bullough (1998) would not necessarily agree with this assessment. They aptly point out the varieties of interpretations of the role of money in the prostitution interchange. These include a belief that the exchange of money is a sign of mutual contempt (Choisy, 1961), a sign of the search for security (Greenwald, 1958), and an indication of misdirected anal desires of the child (Ferenczi, 1916.) It seems possible that each of these may be true, or may be found in one individual and not another. The relationship between money and control is ambiguous, but seems worthy of further investigation.

Limited research exists regarding hypo-sexuality and hyper-sexuality in women engaged in prostitution. One might assume superficially that prostitution would be an expression of hyper-sexuality on the part of the prostitute. However, given the fact that prostitutes often report dissociation, asexuality, and homosexual orientation, hyper-sexuality does not appear to be an important factor in the sex-for-money interchange for these women.

It appears that sexuality may be more impacted by the forces of over-control and emotional distancing from others for these women, in that sexual behavior has become a commodity. Aspects of sexuality such as personal sexual desire, vulnerability, and behavioral preferences of the seller are inconsequential.

In regard to prostitution, one may consider the elements of the money-for-sex interchange such as time limits, fee rates, and behavioral rules as structures, which alleviate the anxiety of the sexual interchange through the creation of narrow boundaries. All the same, this establishment of clear and unwavering structures could compensate for the anxiety-creating loss of control in the original abusive encounter. The disparity between the rigidity of the boundaries in the prostitute's interaction with customers and the lack of boundaries seen in her emotionally intimate relationships is interesting to consider. This is evident in the turning over of the sex-worker's earnings to her boyfriend, or when there is actual physical assault by these men. One way to account for this discrepancy is through the anxiety dimension of attachment. Possibly, prostitutes attempt to manage anxiety with emotional non-intimates through over-control, while utilizing self-compromise to manage anxiety with emotional intimates.

SUMMARY

Rewriting this book in late 2016, I find that Dr. Peterson's theory has even more relevance than I had realized, and applies to other matters in life.

I found a great diversity amongst the providers, as expected. Early on, I was probably whitewashing the profession, but that didn't last long and I believe the book is balanced, if not more negative than the providers intended. The providers who agreed to interviews are not a perfect sample, just as those who seek psychological help may represent a sub-set. Here are some recurring themes:

- Their mothers were unloving. None of the providers I interviewed was raped by her natural father.

- They started escorting during a financial crisis. Many had expensive divorces and became sex workers to hire lawyers and gain custody of their children.

- They were writers, or hoped to be.

- They were raised in ultra-strict, conservative religions, as were many of their clients.

- Some weak women were manipulated into becoming providers by boyfriend, pimps or madams, whom they treated like parental figures. They are so lacking in self-esteem they think it's the only way they can survive. These women did not provide interviews, but stronger providers asked me to pass on warnings.

- Other providers demanded control over their lives and their work, and they achieved it. If they had boyfriends many of the providers played the dominant role.

- The providers who gave interviews had above-average educations. They could set aside time and money they needed for further education or personal needs. They knew they couldn't continue being providers later in life, so they got higher educations, bought properties, or built businesses to sustain themselves when escorting no longer paid off.

- Higher-than-average communication skills. Even if they used to be shy, they learned to communicate in order to function as providers. These skills might have been enhanced by time spent with very successful, widely travelled, educated men with broad experiences. They communicated with a wide variety of men.

- Many wanted to raise the public's perception of their profession, which is one of its biggest drawbacks.

- Most independent providers describe the kind of clients they want to see, and the types they won't see. They generally end up being treated according to the way they present themselves, which is equally true in life outside the sex business.

- Hobbyists tend to lack satisfying sexual relationships with their wives, or are alone. Those who want to be debased are usually very high up in their professions. They might not make their desire for abuse known at the first meeting.

- Quite a few providers make clear in their advertisements that they are happy to be dominant or submissive. Quite a few will only see other girls. The letter 'T' next to their name indicates a transvestite. There are quite a lot of transvestites on escort websites, and you can't tell by the photographs. I've read that they often have the strong sex drives that straight men do.

- Many providers work with animals, which also involves sensory and nurturing interaction.

- Several said they had been betrayed by their parents or another woman who they thought was their best friend.

- Law enforcement had caused major damage to several of them. Fear of arrest forces a great deal of the work pre-clearing hobbyists and providers, and was a continual worry. Even a hobbyist a provider had seen before, and knew was not a policeman, presented a danger, because if he was later arrested for solicitation law enforcement would sometimes make him give them a list of providers he had seen.

- Fear of prison or loss of child custody forced several providers to quit selling sex. From the point of view of moralists who believe that sex workers are doing something evil or harmful, the police and courts can be seen as performing a positive role.

- Providers I interviewed were giving people, which I consider moral, though their morals may be different than much of our society, at least in their public statements. Many expressed a desire to treat the hobbyists fairly and not hurt their feelings. Some will manipulate hobbyists to spend more on them and feel its part of their job. There are ROBS, (Rip-Off Bitches,) but they are a small minority.

- Many of them had large breasts. Quite a few are very attractive, but some use photographic magic such as Photoshop to make themselves look more so online.

- Most are good listeners. They are attuned to what the other person wants, and can manipulate men into wanting what the provider wants to provide.

- Women tend to be very close to each other, but many providers kept a distance from women outside the profession, because they feared they would be looked down on if the truth were known. This is not true in Australia, where it is both legal, and not considered a shameful job.

- Most are feminists.

- Providers know how to handle men. Playing the weak victim is rare and not helpful.

- It's interesting that so many providers were former nurses, or practice both professions at the same time. A Gallup Poll surveyed what professions people admired most for honesty and ethics. Nurses came out on top, providers near the bottom, yet they are often the same people.

- Most providers find it difficult to have a strong relationship with a man while working, and many are not married.

- Quite a few of them started doing exotic dancing or sensual massage, then moved to 'full service'. Some moved in the opposite direction.

- While I originally underestimated the negative consequences of this profession, I was also surprised by some of the emotional benefits many of them reported.

- The two biggest negatives independent providers face are law enforcement and the perception of others. If they were "outed" they would be unwanted at PTA meetings or community groups.

- Most providers shared horror stories about unscrupulous and manipulative agencies, pimps or madams. The only attempt at morally justifying their work was that their workers sometimes made a lot of money. A few providers felt their pimps or madams were considerate.

Because prostitution is usually illegal and underground, there are no reliable statistics about it.

Most of the women I interviewed did not report a history of abuse, but those who had been abused seem to be helped by therapists. Some providers had been abused in a non-sexual way.

The more I thought about Dr. Peterson's theory, the more I learned about myself. Her theory connects two topics that run through this book: sex workers, their clients, and analyses; and my own fascination with them. The fact that Mary was so pleased with her new life was a resolution for me. I had changed her life, and it went both ways. I instantly knew the book's story was complete.

My strongest lifelong passion is touching an audience with something I wrote and directed, and seeing the audience laugh, hold their breath, stand up on cue, cry or moan with feeling. I'm fortunate to have achieved it a couple of times.

When I've tried to sell a screenplay it's often been annoying when an executive asks why a character did something, as if there is one simple answer. In reality, a character's actions reflect a lot of different motives. Women might get into the sex trade for many reasons. Perhaps they are desperate for money and thought they couldn't earn it any other way, want to flaunt society's mores, are materialistic, lazy, or are led to believe they are going to make a lot of money. They might be so beautiful that men are at their mercy. They might enjoy sex with numerous partners, or be easily bored, or crave excitement. A factor might be a desire to take advantage of men, like the provider who suddenly said it was revenge, then didn't know why she'd said that. Most of them agree it has something to do with power over men. Dr. Peterson's theory that it includes a near universal human need to touch or be touched seems to be another valid motive.

I think we should listen to the women who say that there is some denial and self-loathing, but we should also listen to the providers who say they really don't have a problem with the work itself, except for the prejudice against it, and the law, which not only threatens their safety, but allows some police to get away with abusing them. Police and military officers have been caught doing this and given very light punishments, but recently police have lost their jobs over it. Some providers are smart enough to avoid problems with the police, and don't care about society's opinions.

After I conducted the interviews, I spent over a year writing and collaborating with Dr. Peterson. I then checked out the websites of the providers. Most of them were no longer on the Internet.

WHAT'S NEXT?

What will the next sexual revolution look like?

The government is afraid to teach much sex education in the schools, but children are getting plenty of it elsewhere. Popular culture and the Internet are sexualizing young people. National polls report that in America, ninety percent of children have viewed pornography on the Internet by the age of eleven.

On June 15, 2016, BBC in the U.S. said that online pornography is 'desensitizing young people'. Young teenagers who are not ready for sex feel pressured to do it, and in the unrealistic and sometimes sado-masochistic manner they see in porn. Boys watching porn assume they are watching 'normal' sex, and are unable to perform what they see on their smartphones.

Young girls are subjected to painful acts, which comes across as negative. The BBC said that some English girls wear shorts under their skirts to protect themselves in case they are suddenly grabbed in public. More education was recommended.

On the other hand, on August 23, 2016, N.P.R. did a piece on the scientifically measured effects of pornography vs. the commonly held narratives. Scientific studies showed that the bad effects of pornography are not there statistically, contradicting claims that it causes rape, addiction, or sexual dysfunction for males. Men who have viewed pornography are LESS likely to commit rape or other sex crimes.

Laypersons refused to accept it, but they had no evidence to back up their opinions. Psychologists say that those that perceive pornography as a terrible thing are actually expressing their own sense of shame over it. Pornography seems to be watched more frequently by people with conservative religious backgrounds.

Dr. Peterson feels that when parents watch pornography while small children are there, the main problem lies with their inability to consider the effects of their actions on their children, indicating poor parenting skills.

Sexuality is obviously becoming more common in popular entertainment. Teen pop stars act like strippers. Sex is omnipresent on television and the Internet. Most television and movie-makers still depict escorts or exotic dancers as faceless sex objects with no expressions, not real people.

Will this create a more sexual society? I asked that around 2003, and the answer seems to be "yes", along with a strong backlash. Will we become more tolerant, like in Amsterdam, where pretty much anything goes, but the people are not fixated on it. I believe there is more tolerance towards sex from adolescence on. As to the Internet, I have an impression that young people get bored with pornography after awhile, and their exposure to sex might make us more like Europeans, less obsessed with it.

Dr. Peterson wrote me: "Many close and warm friendships have been developed with some of the providers as a result of your interviews. They have been given an opportunity to share their stories, ideas, hopes and fears. What kind of a future can we envision for these women? This book could assist in helping to create a new world or paradigm for providers and hobbyists."

Response: I am not sure what will happen to them. Several of them were already moving on to something else. I hope and believe the interviews played a positive role in some of their lives. Some of the providers had invested their money in properties, which could support them later in life, or they had earned advanced degrees and met industry leaders, giving them advantages. Because of the secretive nature of this business, I don't know their real names. A couple of providers were happy to share their stories with me, but later asked me not to use their interviews. They couldn't tell me why. Perhaps they wanted to discover their inner feelings, but seeing them in print removed a layer of fantasy or protection.

Many of the women who seemed most likely to quit this business were still advertising on websites a year or two later. Others were not, or might be, but have changed their online names. Several young providers who were working while in college seem to have retired after completing their educations.

I erased cross-references to their working names and changed most locations. As Taylor said, their lives start over every few days when they meet new clients. That would make our interviews a distant memory.

I hope that this book improves the lives of providers and hobbyists generally, and that it alerts readers to the pitfalls and benefits of this profession, to the humanity of providers and hobbyists, and promotes tolerance.

A PERSONAL REFLECTION

Dr. Peterson asked me: "Through the writing of this book it was necessary to become a part of this world, forming friendships and on-line relationships with providers and hobbyists. How did this research change the opinions and behavior of the researcher"?

Response: That's personal! I'll try. I learned about the diverse motivations that can lead a woman to becoming a provider, demonstrating an old Chinese saying, "Every human being is a completely different thing." I learned a lot about humanity.

Creating a worthwhile piece of writing is often an obsession, and I admit that researching this book seemed like an addiction, until I received the final letters from Mary and knew the interviews were over and I no longer felt the need to explore this world. It was an "I-Thou" experience, as Dr. Peterson described. It led me to a better understanding of what formed me and drives me. Now I can move on to new obsessions.

I realize how fortunate I've been to have so many warm friends, a loving family, and such a wonderful wife, who not only puts up with me but also seems to enjoy my 'impish nature'.

I think I evaded that pretty well. I have learned a lot about myself from it, and more from re-examining it. I don't think I should burden or bless the readers with all of it here.

FINAL NOTE FROM DR. PETERSON

Dear Jim,

It has been an education working with you on this – I did not know what impact this work would have on me as a woman and/or as a psychologist. I have gained an appreciation for the complexity and depth of the human psyche and its struggle to survive when the odds are not necessarily in its favor.

With warm regards,

Chris

RESOURCES

The author is not required to provide copyright or authorship information of the resources. The lists of websites are incomplete and some sites may be out of date. The author and publishers are not responsible for any errors or omissions. The majority of these websites should only be viewed by people over eighteen years of age, and pursuant to the laws in their locality. The sites listed and similar sites should only be viewed with anti-malware software installed and active, but viewing these sites might still expose the user to receive malware, which is any kind of computer code, spam spyware, etc. that may do harm to your privacy or your computer. If you choose to explore these sites anyway, you do so at your own risk.

Indiana University's Kinsey Institute for Research in Sex, Gender, and Reproduction.

PENNET is a sex workers' rights organization based in San Francisco.

A Vindication of The Rights of Whores, an anthology edited by Gail Peterson in 1989, including the First World Charter for Prostitutes, Amsterdam.

The Art of Sexual Ecstasy, by Margo Anand, Published by Tarcher/Putnam, 1989.

Women of the Light…The New Sexual Healers, edited by Kenneth Ray Stubbs, Ph.D. published by Secret Garden, 1994.

Amazing Grace, a Vocabulary of Faith, by Kathleen Norris, published by Riverhead Books, 1998.

Vanity Fair, August 6, 2015: "Tinder and the Dawn of the Dating Apocalypse" by Nancy Jo Sales.

N.Y Times Magazine, May 22, 2016: "Legalizing Sex in Rhode Island" by Manisha Shah, an Associate Professor at U.C.L.A., and Scott Cunningham, Associate Professor, Baylor University.

The Business Side of Escorting, by J.D.Roberts, CPA, published by IUniverse, 2004.

BELLE DE JOUR, movie distributed by Valoria, France, 1967, based on the 1928 novel *Belle de Jour* by Joseph Kessel.

The Happy Hooker….My Own Story by Xaviera Hollander with Robin Moore & Yvonne Dunleavy, published by Dell Publishing Group, 1972.

Mayflower Madame by Sheila Devin, published by Arbor House, 1987.

FREE WILLY, original screenplay by Keith Walker, movie distributed by Warner Bros, 1982.

Star Search, created by Alfred Masini, T.P.E. Rysher Entertainment, 1983.

American Idol, Fox Television, 2002.

INTERNET RESOURCES

Websites advertising providers are almost easier to find than avoid. In addition to their usefulness, viewing them has become addictive for millions of people. Treatments for addiction are listed under "sexual addictions" on Google. Leading web browsers often warn viewers before entering these sites that they may contain graphic material some might find offensive, plus warnings for people under eighteen to stay out. It is recommended that viewers use caution in revealing personal information.

The Erotic Review (TER), founded in 1999 by David Elms. Bought by Treehouse Park, SA in 2004. Website: theeroticreview.com

Preferred411.com/(P411)

SWOP – various chapters in cities in the U.S., Canada, and the UK.

SeekingArrangement.com™ © 2016 in conjunction with W8 Tech Limited and its related companies. Available as an app on iTunes or Android.

AdultFriendFinder.com, © 1996-2016. Founder: Andrew Cornu became part of FriendFinder Networks Inc. It was owned by Various Inc. and bought by Penthouse and Broadstream in 2006.

Zbone.com © 1995-2016.

TheBigDoggie.net, an expired review and discussion board.

Cityvibe.com, an escort directory.

City-source.com/pamper.htm, an adult directory.

Rubmaps.com, Asian Massage Parlor U.S. Directory, © Rubmaps.com 2016 -

Eros.com, an adult directory.

LAadultdirectory.com, a Los Angeles escort directory.

Escort-locator.com, An adult mall, (Canadian content.)

Thatmall.com, an adult directory.

Artemisguide.com, list of women's studies programs.

familysafemedia.com/pornography_statistics.html#anchor 1 – Family Safe Media promotes family values, protection from pornography, and a large amount of statistics by country and activity.

sfgov.org/dosw/mayors-task-force-anti-human-trafficking-0

The San Francisco Mayor's Office, Department On The Status of Women

ABOUT THE AUTHOR

James Tugend has had scores of articles published by magazines as diverse as the *Writers' Guild of America West's Newsletter and Journal, Writers Digest* and martial arts magazines. His original screenplays and teleplays have been optioned for purchase numerous times. His teleplay THE FOUR-SIDED TRIANGLE was produced on the *Tales From The Crypt* HBO series. He taught writing for the Writers' Guild Of America, West's Open Door Program, founded to teach screen and television writing to minorities and get them into the Guild; and for East/West Players, an Asian-American theater group in Los Angeles. He wrote and directed the short films SOUL MATES and THE CARETAKER, which were released professionally. Both won Gold Special Jury Awards at Filmfest Houston. SOUL MATES won awards in five film festivals, was licensed to a distributor and aired on Showtime and internationally. THE CARETAKER was used by social service departments, police departments and banks to prevent elder abuse. It supported a non-profit charity for a decade. Tugend has co-produced or associate produced twenty TV films, and directed for theater, including *An Evening of Pantomime,* which was reviewed in *Newsweek*. He worked as a technical writer for several companies, including IBM and FINAL DRAFT. Tugend received a B.A. from Pomona College, attended Boston University's Graduate School for Directing. He is a member of the Writers Guild of America West and a former member of PEN.

ABOUT DR. PETERSON

At the time of her contributions to this book:

Chris Peterson, Ph.D., has been a practicing psychologist since 1981, with a certificate in Psychoanalytic Psychotherapy, specializing in Substance Abuse Psychology. She was the Chairperson of the Ph.D. Clinical Psychology Program at Pacifica Graduate Institute, and Director of the Training and Core Faculty Clinical Psychology program. She has taught Legal, Ethical and Professional Issues, Group Process, Depth Approaches to the Family, Alcoholism, Addiction and Chemical Dependency, and Clinical Practicum and Supervision. She is affiliated with five psychology and psychoanalytic groups, including the American College of Forensic Examiners. Her paper, "Ruthless Compassion", on treatment of an alcoholic, was published by Sage Productions, July, Vol 3, pgs. 234-249. She has written an article in 2014, partly based on her theory in this book: http://www.psychotherapy.net/article/therapist-love-hate.

ACKNOWLEDGEMENTS

Foremost, I thank my wife, Jennie Lew Tugend, for her encouragement, ideas, feedback and editing. Also, many thanks to Laurie Lamson, for editorial advice, and preparing the manuscript for printing. Christopher Keane and Diane Cummings for editorial advice, and the input from all the providers and hobbyists, who generously gave their time and shared their feelings, whether they are in the book or not, Skipp Press for his advice on the realities of publishing. Thanks to Jeff Cohen, Cohen Gardner LLP, and Carissa Knol Esq. for legal advice, and my friend and lawyer, Ted Baer, for his legal and moral assistance. (Yes, they can go together.) I was especially fortunate to have found Dr. Peterson, who brought so much to this book and to me personally.

Book Website: TugendMedia.com

Comments & reviews welcome.